Dawkins' Dilemmas

Deluded or not deluded?
That is the question!

Michael Austin

Copyright © 2008 by Michael Austin

Dawkins' Dilemmas
Deluded or not deluded? That is the question!
by Michael Austin

Printed in the United States of America

ISBN 978-1-60477-666-9

All rights reserved solely by the author. The author guarantees all contents are original and do not infringe upon the legal rights of any other person or work. No part of this book may be reproduced in any form without the permission of the author. The views expressed in this book are not necessarily those of the publisher.

Unless otherwise indicated, Bible quotations are taken from *The Holy Bible, English Standard Version*. Copyright © 2001 by Crossway Bibles, a publishing ministry of Good News Publishers. Used by permission.

Persons referred to in a fictional manner, as in chapter 8, are entirely imaginary. They have no basis in actual persons, who at any time, or in any way, may have been associated with the SETI Project. Any similarity of fictitious persons herein, with actual persons, past or present, is completely co-incidental.

www.xulonpress.com

Acknowledgements

Sincere thanks are extended to the following copyright owners for their permissions:

All quotations from *The God Delusion* by Richard Dawkins, published by Bantam Press. Reprinted by permission of The Random House Group Ltd.

Excerpts from THE GOD DELUSION by Richard Dawkins. Copyright © 2006 by Richard Dawkins. Reprinted by permission of Houghton Mifflin Company. All rights reserved.

MERE CHRISTIANITY by C. S. Lewis copyright © C. S. Lewis Pte. Ltd. 1942, 1943, 1944, 1952.

MIRACLES by C. S. Lewis copyright © C. S. Lewis Pte. Ltd. 1947, 1960. Extracts reprinted by permission.

Preface

Richard Dawkins' book, *The God Delusion* is stirring a lot of reaction!

Will his hard-hitting atheism grip millions — quickly fade, or cause doubts to linger for generations? — The issues are huge, and the debate continues.

In this book I look at the foundations of our thinking, and offer a reply based on biblical Christian belief in the living God revealed in Jesus Christ.

By using this approach I explore some of the assumptions made about *reason* itself.

This will help you to see some of the deep dilemmas in Richard Dawkins' thinking.

This also gives *you* the interesting opportunity to think about the assumptions and beliefs *you* use to weigh up Richard Dawkins' beliefs.

I hope you enjoy thinking through these issues with me, and that you find this approach stimulating and helpful.

Michael Austin

PS. I am not always consistent in using gender inclusive words, and I hope you will overlook this.

Contents

Preface vii
Introduction   Why Argue? xi
Chapter 1   Dawkins and Atheism 17
Chapter 2   Christian Theism 29
Chapter 3   The dilemma of a flawed world 43
Chapter 4   The dilemma of humanity 53
Chapter 5   Almost certainly 61
Chapter 6   The dilemma of which 'god' to deny 81
Chapter 7   The ultimate paradox 87
Chapter 8   SETI — the search for meaning
             and significance 93
Chapter 9   Light in the darkness 103
Chapter 10   Christ and meaning 113
Chapter 11   Reality and redemption 125
Chapter 12   Let's face it 137

Introduction

Why argue?

Despite my dislike of gladiatorial contests, I seem somehow to have acquired a reputation for pugnacity towards religion.

Richard Dawkins, *The God Delusion*, p 281

Most of us prefer to avoid arguments. But then, there are different types, from reasoned debates to quarrels, to sustained rows, or worse. In this discussion I shall try hard to keep it on the level of a reasoned debate. Not everyone will accept that I succeed, and some may even be inclined to the view that reason has all but vanished from my arguments. Be that as it may, those decisions will be yours!

In his tearaway bestseller, *The God Delusion*, Richard Dawkins, who is the Professor for the Public Understanding of Science at Oxford University, has informed us that religious people, who persist in their beliefs, are not only, 'dyed-in-the-wool faith-heads'[1]: the diagnosis gets worse — they are deluded.

Is this merely a jibe to embarrass his opponents, or make them smile? Does he mean it? Of course, in a qualified sense, because he can't think they are *that* deluded, or he wouldn't be wasting his time writing a book to sort them out! Anyway, who needs an insipid book title? But beyond that, perhaps there's more than a hint of hard-hitting annoyance at how religion is spoiling, even ruining the prospects for a better world.

Dawkins suggests that his own position on atheism, as the final truth about reality, is urbane and compelling, and only the worst cases of bigotry will not see it. Indeed, he hopes that through reading his book large numbers of people will become atheists.

As the sort of delusion that he refers to is not insanity, but a religious type, commonly suffered by many, Dawkins is optimistic that there will be 'plenty of open-minded people out there'[2] who, after reading his book, quickly throw off their folly.

Someone or no one?

Just what is the issue between theism and atheism? What, if anything, is at stake? Put at its simplest, is this nothing more than two groups of organised chaos, squabbling over a difference of opinion about whether all of the organised chaos, including themselves, was brought into existence and organised by either a supreme Someone, *or* no-one!

How come this either/or sort of thinking? And how would these two groups possibly be able to know? That we might be able to know — really *know* that we are a part of a created, real vast *something* made by Someone, or that it was not made by Someone, might seem a tall order for homespun logic on either side of the argument! From where does so much confidence come — from cerebral chemistry? Interestingly, he defines delusion in terms of either the cause or the result of what most disturbs him about theistic beliefs.

From where does Dawkins gather so much conviction that his reasoning against theism is not merely a pluralistic perspective, but a valid insight into a 'true' reality? Looks interesting — indeed, if logic were only homespun I doubt whether we would be able to have this discussion at all.

Why does each group wish to influence the other — is anything to be gained? A classic case of the sociology of dominance and control, or is more at stake? How do you grade the scale of disputes? Just a good old row, or something that will affect how you live for the rest of your life. Very large numbers of people believe that God's existence is an ultimate issue.

Reporting on a serious strike threat, an industry affairs correspondent observed, 'All disputes are resolved eventually, by both sides talking.' Yes, indeed, but for a start this isn't an industrial dispute so the same rules don't necessarily apply. Industrial disputes, like interpersonal ones, rely on finding a conflict resolution strategy that first gets to grips with the core issue, then aims to find areas of mutual interest, and which then tries to foster various exchanges that lead to new insights. The goal of the process is then reached with a brokered agreement or a compromise.

Proceed with care

How much this sort of approach applies to different worldviews will depend on the particular participants, their views, and the extent of any common ground between them.

An ecumenical merger between theism and atheism? I doubt it. But it does emphasise the usefulness of talking to sharpen our insights and understandings of each other's position, whatever the nature of the dispute.

At the outset, I will propose that this supreme issue is not open to conclusions based on research gained from empirical evidence sufficiently cogent to be called 'proof.' We are not talking about measurable quantities or examining the properties of matter in the physical universe, as subjects capable of being quantified by our close scrutiny and scientific research.

But, I will submit that any discussion about 'proofs' or the balance of 'probabilities' that apply to evidence-based research, or empirical science, ultimately derive their validity from biblical theism.

Certainly, this depends on our main assumptions. Richard Dawkins has made his position abundantly plain, so we shall need to see his basis for it. You will quickly notice that I assume the validity of my own thinking. 'Just as well!' you may say. This is vital for my side of the argument, because I need to develop a basis for it that is consistent with my assumptions. The basis for this validity, if sustainable, will then help us to assess our different viewpoints or presuppositions, especially as Dawkins is using *words* in an effort to convince people about an ultimate delusion. Can finite human thinking bear such weighty considerations? How would you know if logic and reason were only homespun — the products of your mental chemistry?

Some debates are emotive and liable to raise steam. A written response is a time-honoured way that gives a wider audience a share in an atmosphere of reflection.

Strategy

Part of our strategy will be to dig deeper to see how our own thinking is working, and how we might trust its validity. It appears, if reading Dawkins' book is anything to go by that atheists believe in the validity of their own thinking just as much as theists. Of course, there is a well-known conundrum lurking in this: if we want to check the validity of our thinking, we have to assume its validity in the first place, and around we go, spinning in circles!

Which brings us to the basis of our knowledge — just how do we know we know? The technical name for this is *epistemology*, an area of study that deals with the theory of knowledge, its basis and validity.

Why argue? Because it may help to show that Dawkins' atheism is based on the assumption of the validity of his thinking, (the whole edifice of his scientific work and his atheism is built upon this): a validity whose basis, I will aim to show he is unable to justify on any rational basis *gained from atheism*, but upon which he, crucially needs to rely.

While I shall try to clarify the main issue later in the discussion, it doesn't take the reader of *The God Delusion* too long to see that Dawkins' really big protest is that theists, and particularly biblical monotheists — people who believe in the objective existence of the *one* supreme, living God, are the main subjects of a religious delusion that has caused much of the world's ills. And as he believes these can be traced directly, or indirectly, to the door of the God of biblical theism, he gets rather judgemental towards those who claim to espouse this God as their own, and considers they have a large case to answer. Hopefully, we shall see.

For the moment, Dawkins has gone on the attack, as his best form of defence. In an effort to respond, part of my case will aim to show that using logic or reason in an attempt to deny the existence of the fount of all being, reason and reality; the infinite, personal God of biblical revelation, is a use for which reason and logic are singularly unsuited. Here, world-views collide!

At the same time I offer a meaningful basis for personal confidence in the living God. This confidence in God does not abandon reason by an irrational leap, but rather requires the fullest exercise of that reason. But, hold on, this is not a journey into a world of dry intellectualism — far from it! Later, you will see why I say that, when in some of the final chapters, I support my case from one of the most well-known of all Christian writings: John's Gospel.

Meanwhile, Dawkins has entered the fray, but before we look at his dilemmas, we need to hang on to our heads, and clear the ground.

Chapter 1

Dawkins and atheism

Either he exists or he doesn't. It is a scientific question

Richard Dawkins, *The God Delusion*, p 48

As far as Dawkins is concerned, the law of the excluded middle — either, or — applies to the question of God's existence. Either he does, or he does not, and there is no middle position. Dawkins is not a fence sitter and *The God Delusion* is infused with strong anti-religious fervour that in places gets quite angry. As he does, he moves away from the more typical areas of scientific research into discussions of personal values and religious beliefs.

Many of these beliefs he dislikes with an intensity, but using the law of the excluded middle, you can't have it both ways — either this is science, or it's not. And what Dawkins says 'is a scientific question' you are free to call by some other name. However, I accept, that from his point of view this is his sort of science, and we shall need to try to understand why he gets so intense. In doing so, I aim to focus on the core issues of Dawkins' direct challenge to theism.

What do you mean?
In any discussion, we need to be clear about the critical terms. The two most central to my case are *God* and *delusion*. I accept both of Dawkins' definitions, which follow respectively: 'there exists a super-human, supernatural intelligence who deliberately designed and created the universe and everything in it, including us,'[1] and 'a persistent false belief held in the face of strong contradictory evidence, especially as a symptom of psychiatric disorder.'[2]

Arising from the definition of *God*, it follows that a *theist* is some one who broadly accepts that same definition. Dawkins also gives a working definition of theism: 'A theist believes in a supernatural intelligence who, in addition to his main work of creating the universe in the first place, is still around to oversee and influence the subsequent fate of his initial creation.'[3]

What about *atheism*? The Greek letter alpha of *a*-theism is a common prefix used to denote an opposite meaning or a denial of the root meaning that follows. Atheism thus means that God, defined as the supernatural, personal Creator, does not exist. With these basic definitions, an atheist is not a person who merely doubts God's existence or who has finished with all forms of religious belief or practice. Classical atheism is a resolute denial of God's *existence*. Dawkins confirms that belief in a supreme, supernatural Person as, 'God, in the sense defined, is a delusion; and as later chapters will show, a pernicious delusion.'[4]

Often, the way a word is used in a particular society may change dramatically over a long period of time. Back in the second century, the Imperial Roman authorities were accusing Christians themselves of being 'Atheists,' and sent many to their deaths for denying the highly vaunted gods of the Roman pantheon who were closely tied to the prestige and power of the ruling Caesar. However, I am using the word with the modern, conventional sense.

Dawkins muddies the waters a little here, as he proposes to discuss God's existence using estimates of probability, and says it doesn't matter if God is not 'disprovable (he isn't),'[5] but aims to show that his existence is highly improbable. I shall discuss in a later chapter whether or not this approach represents a modified form of atheism. As Dawkins makes a lot of the word 'delusion' referring to a closed, religious state of mind, it would appear that he believes atheistic belief is a mark of openness to the truth. We shall see later upon what basis he thinks that his belief corresponds with objective reality.

As Dawkins develops his arguments, some are peripheral to his main case. I shall not deal with his exposure of the traditional arguments or 'proofs' for God's existence. These old arguments take for granted a theistic way of thinking in which the conclusions are already implicit in the basic assumptions. As such they are *a priori* arguments and, while of historical interest, are not strictly relevant to the way I advance the discussion. As it is, none of the old 'proofs' give irresistible conclusions, which is no surprise — at best they assume what they set out to show: the reasonableness of theistic belief.

Any general defence of religion, as such, is also outside my scope. For a Christian, much that passes for religion in a fallen world shares too much in the fallenness for me to labour for its defence. Subjects such as the roots of morality and why atheists have reasons to uphold ethical values, while important in their own right, are likewise not vital to the answer I shall develop.

Overall, Dawkins' book is more than an attempt to demolish theism and promote atheism in isolation. Rather, he wishes to offer atheists, or would-be atheists, a cultural manual to nourish a meaningful life that will, he hopes, lead to a new mainstream consensus.

In addition, sections of his book are occupied with denigrating a variety of religious attitudes and beliefs that are promoted, as he views them, by a range of religious extremists: for example, their views on education, science and personal morality. Here, Dawkins stigmatises what he takes to be some of the consequences of religious belief, rather than any direct attempt to demolish theism. A strategy he finds irresistible.

If he thinks religious belief produces such mindless thought and retarded behaviour, including, how it undermines modern science, then theism itself must be the root cause. However appealing he finds this line, it is secondary to his main argument.

Reasons and assumptions

My main interest is to examine how Dawkins advances his atheism, and the reasons he relies on to win, he hopes, its wide acceptance in favour of Christian theism. He mentions other religions, of course: diverse and wide-ranging from the past and present, mainly polytheism, Judaism, and Islam, which are distinguished from the philosophical ideas of pantheism. But as he keeps most of his verbal lashes for the God of Judeo-Christian Scripture, I will focus my reply framed within a biblical Christian theism.

Why Dawkins reserves his most fluent and vitriolic streams of invective for the God of Old and New Testament Scripture will become clearer, as we proceed. For the moment, this permits what I hope will be a focused response.

What sort of framework does Dawkins erect for his belief system? This is important as his beliefs do form a recognisable system, even if some of the fault-lines lie hidden below the surface. (We shall examine some of his dilemmas later). For a start, Dawkins tells us that he is 'a dyed-in-the-wool monist,'[6] and confirms this negatively by saying he is 'not a dualist.'[7]

Monism: the philosophical base for his belief system refers to the view that there is *one* tangible, material reality. For Dawkins, monism overlaps with naturalistic and evolutionary atheism. The natural, physical reality embraces everything. Quoting Julian Baggini, Dawkins confirms, 'What most atheists do believe is that although there is only one kind of stuff in the universe and it is physical, out of this stuff come minds, beauty, emotions, moral values — in short the full gamut of phenomena that gives richness to human life.'[8]

Dawkins' rejection of dualism denies that minds exist, or thoughts, as non-material entities. Everything is grounded in a material reality and is open to the probing of scientific research. His position on monism and naturalism is clear when he says of the existence of God, that, 'Either he exists or he doesn't. It is a scientific question.'[9] Underscoring this, he adds, 'The presence or absence of a creative super-intelligence is unequivocally a scientific question, even if it is not in practice — or not yet — a decided one.'[10]

With these commitments, Dawkins clarifies his atheism, 'An atheist in this sense of philosophical naturalist is somebody who believes there is nothing beyond the natural, physical world, no *super*natural creative intelligence lurking behind the observable universe, no soul that outlasts the body and no miracles — except in the sense of natural phenomena that we don't yet understand.'[11] Naturalistic philosophy is a belief system that includes an ideological view of science, as Dawkins advises, 'Contrary to Huxley, I shall suggest that the existence of God is a scientific hypothesis like any other.'[12]

Monism, as embraced by Dawkins, excludes theism of any kind, although monism may technically be used to describe pantheistic belief, that the All is one impersonal being. As described by Dawkins, both naturalistic philosophy and monism are essentially atheistic. Turn it around:

an atheist like Dawkins is a committed materialist and a monist.

Dawkins' atheism fits well into his Darwinian position. As a younger teenager, he may not have been a resolute atheist, but once he started to embrace the assumptions of Darwin and had his 'consciousness raised'[13] by naturalistic, evolutionary thinking, and had his doubts reinforced about the nature of religious belief, it was not a large step to become 'a dyed-in-the-wool monist.' At that point — whenever, supernatural theism was necessarily excluded from his beliefs.

Atheists look to several sources for explanations of reality, including their own deeply intriguing complexity. Most believe that intelligence, creativity, and meaning have all arisen late in the history of the universe. This concept is key to Darwinian evolution, which sees simpler mechanisms gradually being built, step-by-step into the most complex intelligence of the human brain. And how reality is seen and interpreted depends on the conceptual models each person builds.

No one can fail to miss how Dawkins' atheism quickly becomes a forceful protest. A quietly, cloistered atheist? No way — his is the body and soul type stuff of a true reactionary, driven by a passion to attack 'Religion,' the poisonous fruit of an awful delusion. So he gathers his forces: 'I am not attacking any particular version of God or gods. I am attacking God, all gods, anything and everything supernatural, wherever and whenever they have been or will be invented.'[14]

Absolutely

A vigorous atheist, Dawkins is an absolutist in the sense that he is totally committed to his principles. He believes he is dealing with final reality, and because he is unable to negate a proposition without the logic of antithesis, he also needs an absolute commitment to the validity of his reason. So he hangs on to the logic and all the apparent reasons for his atheism with a high intensity. Without a basis for the validity of his reason, he knows he has no reasons. Here is the nub of the whole argument: totally committed — yes, but is the basis for the validity of his reason as secure as he thinks it is?

Dawkins' naturalistic philosophy holds that a person's reason cannot know the unknowable, which sounds fair enough, but refers to any type of knowledge excluded by naturalism. Not a big surprise. Any thought of a transcendental subject or supernatural category is beyond the scope of rational thought, and impossible to know. For Dawkins, a monistic reality is *all* there is. Everything knowable is within *one* circle. And *if* there is a God or gods he, or they, are by definition, part of this *one* circle of spacetime, matter and energy.

If, as a prior assumption, you reject that there are fairies at the bottom of your garden, they are already excluded, and whatever reasons you later give to show your denial of their existence follow from your initial assumption. Naturalism forbids fairies — fair enough, and in one fell swoop, deities or a supreme deity, all fall into the same category. Anything outside the circle defined by naturalism is not permitted to possess objective being.

Naturalism functions as a supreme licensing authority: come within its terms of reference and you are permitted to exist, otherwise objective existence will be denied you. The non-material is so much excluded, barred, or banned by its atheistic reference frame, as a sheer fantasy, that Dawkins calls it, a 'delusion.' On this basis, to say he is an absolutist seems reasonably apt.

As Dawkins' confident atheism takes on every type of religious belief and particularly the theisms of Judaism, Christianity, and Islam, it is difficult to see it as anything other than a sort of anti-religious fundamentalism. But, could atheism be religious? Any system of belief that denies theism, which Dawkins admits is 'disprovable,' and offers instead the antithesis is a faith system that offers rival or substitute concepts, such as an explanation of the origin of the universe, the ideals of humanity, the key to moral values, and universal meaning. However, in Dawkins' monism everything is open to the scrutiny of science, while religion is unscientific, and deluded.

What do you see?

With this approach, conventional distinctions between science as the study of the natural world and, say, the philosophy of religion become blurred. For Dawkins there is one species of knowledge that he discovers using his naturalistic science. He has one key to interpret reality. That science 'works' and power stations produce electricity, electronic calculators function, aeroplanes fly, and so much more, all point to the general validity of science. But, then to extend that legitimate confidence to all fields of human interest and behaviour, including a monistic view of reality, is a big step beyond verification.

Dawkins' approach is rationalistic,[15] that is, one that aims to rely solely on the powers of reason to deliver a negative verdict on the ultimate question of God's existence. With man at the centre, he decides how to live, assign values to his own significance, and choose which key to interpret the meaning of everything. Now, the creature assigns supreme value and status to himself as the apex of creation in a way that is little different from self-worship. Is this really science?

When he interprets the Christian Faith through the lens of his atheism, the result is no big surprise. Vast caricatures, deformed (for Christians) beyond recognition, tower above the skyline of Dawkins' home city. A Bible full of fraudulent prophecy, blood lust, violence, deranged rituals, guilt-demented, superstition-ridden 'faith-heads,' and a 'Jesus' whose death to make atonement for sin is one of the worst fictions of immoral propaganda ever to haunt the tranquil homes of atheists. Dawkins' atheism is antagonistically anti-Christian. Filter the central message of Scripture through the grid of atheism and the distortions that follow to blight Dawkins' world loom large. He detests the religious features of the twenty first century, and is disgusted by the weird vitality of the primitive fungi of religious fundamentalisms. To Dawkins they seem to be all of a species. Just when evolution with its powerful ally of natural selection, 'a solution of stunning elegance and power'[16] was set to climb to new heights sufficient to excite Dawkins' approval (he's not a neutral observer after all), multitudes veer off to scar mankind with the delusions of Religion.

Off course

Toward these erring rebels far outside the benign influences of Darwinian natural selection, Dawkins turns his acerbic pen with a moral outrage that is palpable. As the perversion of religious influence is so widespread, he finds a number of reasons to account for this vast aberration: if only there had been a more Darwinian enlightened outcome for the human race! But Dawkins hasn't yet given up hope. Is he promoting evolutionary atheism to shape his ideal society? Absolutely — and perhaps he sees himself among the peaks of what natural selection has produced, and must beckon others upwards.

A variety of unusual behavioural patterns are examined as possible links and analogies with how religion could have appeared in a Darwinian universe, which generally minimises wasteful activities of every kind. Dawkins refers to one of these; the strange habit of some birds called 'anting'[17] which he suggests is analogous to how religion is used for reasons that are peripheral to the main activities of living.

What he doesn't refer to is the equally strange custom that atheists have like himself of writing elaborate books against theism, using reason and logic to discuss ultimate realities as if this served some wonderful Darwinian purpose of promoting the goals of natural selection, by assisting 'it' as an arch-promoter in order to further reduce the wasteful, 'anting' activities of religious rituals and beliefs.

After all, if Dawkins didn't believe he was in a position to discuss final realities with a high degree of objectivity, presumably he wouldn't bother. No postmodern relativism for the atheism of Richard Dawkins. There is no way that he wants his atheism to be understood within the context of our current toleration of pluralistic perspectives. Not on your life! Dawkins' atheism is deadly serious, avowedly anti-pluralistic and just about as absolutist as it is possible for a monist to be.

What is interesting is how repeatedly he assumes that his convictions gained from science-based certainty are capable of being extrapolated into final goals and causes and imbued with the same certainty of conviction, as if it was all a done deal. Now the methods that secure the assured findings of science have percolated and pervaded his philosophical opinions and suggestions to such an extent that he is now able to advise us on final goals and causes — that these are *not* related to the God of Christian theism. And, as a consistent naturalist, he assumes that his empirical research, applicable within the physics-based reality, applies to everything.

Advocates of the naturalistic worldview gain their belief that there is nothing except the material, physics-based view of reality, not on the proven necessity of the case, but from their belief in naturalistic philosophy. An argument in a circle for which a commitment is required — if I believe there is nothing beyond this spacetime reality, then whatever causes have given rise to what I think is 'there,' have no basis in a final cause or purpose.

I am nothing more than a gigantic fluke, and my sense of personal significance is only a useful ploy to assist natural selection. Of course, how I know this is going to be circular thinking, so no useful object is served by my research apart from quenching the meaningless curiosity that the atoms, energy and natural selection, have given me.

So, Dawkins takes a leap and thinks he is processing real information that has some degree of correlation with a meaningful final reality. A belief system that accepts its own validity on trust? Certainly, and one that he believes he is able to advance with sublime cogency using *language*!

Yes, Dawkins believes in the validity of his propositional thinking as an authentic process, in which his words carry an inherent dynamic, intended to evince positive chemical responses from his readers' brains — interesting — we shall need to stir our chemical responses carefully!

Complex chemistry

Armed with such convictions, the 'God' or 'gods' Dawkins denies, appear to belong to the genus of fairies or goblins, or the gods of ancient mythological belief. So the degree of reality with which he credits his arch opponent is no more, and probably even less, than the contents of a bad dream. Not surprising that Dawkins thinks he has done a good job in demolishing such ethereal nonentities. They were excluded by his philosophy in the first place!

What is intriguing is to see how his mental chemistry gets superheated when he comes to deny the God of the Bible. No trivial one — this is a mega-delusion. For Dawkins, it is a supreme tragedy that so many people should be *so* deluded. He dismisses a general belief in one or many deities as a 'figment of the imagination.'[18] But then, as he vents his streams of invective on a 'figment of the imagination,' Dawkins shows that something deeper than chemistry is going on about which he never gives a convincing explanation.

He relies on the validity of the fundamental logic of either/or — true or false, and knows without any shadow of a doubt on which side of the forward slash he happens to be. In a fundamental way I would contend that stating the problem in this way, in the present case, is an inappropriate use of logic. That is because I have no final validity for the conclusions of my reasoning apart from its basis in biblical theism. I know this is circular reasoning, and I will come back to the problem and explain it in more detail.

For the moment, if God does not exist, you or I have no basis upon which to rest the validity of our thinking. If *nothing* has any ultimate meaning — then that assumption is also included, and how would you have ever found out? And if you never found out, but believed that there was either no ultimate meaning out there, or that there was, would you also be deluded? C. S. Lewis has written in similar vein and I believe his appeal to the validity of logic, as I have represented it, is compelling.

To extend this, I need to develop a theistic basis for the validity of reason. You will not, of course, accept what I offer as 'proofs' (they are not) any more than you will accept Dawkins' atheistic denials of God's existence as 'proofs.' Does that mean we're on an evenly balanced seesaw with arguments of just about equal strength on each side? The answer you give to that question will depend on whether or not you accept the conclusion I reach about the validity of reason. But, without it you may not be able to come to a conclusion!

Chapter 2

Christian theism

I shall have Christianity mostly in mind

Richard Dawkins, *The God Delusion*, p 37

When Dawkins looks at Christianity through the lens of his atheism, no one should be surprised that what he sees is not biblical Christianity.

In an effort to clear the air, here is a summary of biblical Christian belief against which I aim to evaluate Dawkins' atheism, and later discuss his deep dilemmas. This is all the more necessary as many people are not familiar with the Judeo-Christian Scriptures and may be inclined to accept Dawkins' descriptions of Christian belief at face value.

Two negatives to begin with: the Christian Faith has *not* arisen spontaneously or accidentally without a meaningful ultimate origin or cause. In consequence, neither has the Christian Faith originated as a creative response to the mystery of our humanity solely from within that humanity. On the contrary, a structured belief system has arisen out of the central theme of the Jewish Old Testament Scriptures: the self-revelation of the infinite, personal Creator God, who *himself* has originated all objective reality, visible and invisible, and who, in the Scriptures he inspired, progressively discloses promises that focus on one person — Jesus Christ.

Christian belief forms an organic, consistent unity with the earlier exalted monotheism and redemptive history of the Old Testament, which from the outset defines its own goal and moves towards one final consummation. Thus the whole cosmos, visible and invisible is under the sovereign control of the living God, for whose praise and glory alone it all exists. There is no doubt that these are large claims.

Historic

The historic Christian Faith is precisely that — rooted and grounded in the historic events of the life, death and resurrection of Jesus Christ. As such, and this is of key importance, Christian foundations are open to, and invite, rigorous investigation. We have ample eyewitness testimony corroborated by a cluster of historical evidences to advance that these events occurred in human history. Anchored in the past, they are relevant today. The case for Christ stands or falls on the basis of the truthfulness of the central claims made by him and for him on the pages of Scripture.

Biblical Christian theism focuses on Christ-centred, revealed truth that is able to stand on its own, and offer the key to its own meaning. Jesus of Nazareth is the long-awaited Jewish Messiah, the anointed King and Saviour, who comes to reassert, and inaugurate the royal reign of God. God has spoken and acted supremely in Jesus Christ, the Son of God, through whom he created all things, and in whom he comes into the world at the climax of the ages, to give his life for others. As he responds to deal with the terrible fall into moral anarchy, he initiates his own self-giving into death upon the cross. R. C. Sproul underscores this when he confirms:

> The heart of the Gospel is that our holy, loving Creator, confronted with human hostility and rebel-

lion, has chosen in his own freedom and faithfulness to become our holy, loving Redeemer and Restorer. The Father has sent the Son to be the Saviour of the world (I John 4:14): it is through his one and only Son that God's one and only plan of salvation is implemented.[1]

Christ alone is qualified and authorised to give himself into the condemnation of moral lawbreakers and take on their liabilities. He died in the place of others to reconcile them to God. Christ is the centre: his incarnation, his morally flawless life, his divine and human natures, his substitutionary death on the cross, and his bodily resurrection in space-time history that culminates in his ascended glory as Lord of all. This same Christ, who originates all things, will come again as Judge and Saviour to restore and consummate all things in the new perfected cosmos.

Meanwhile, God continues to uphold and sustain all things, including what we mean by 'nature' or the physical reality. So, there is a sense in which all of the material cosmos is both supernaturally created and sustained. With all the uniformity of the natural world, there is a biblical acceptance that it is perfectly legitimate for God in Christ to suspend or intrude that uniformity, and in even more apparently direct ways, act in the world to further his own purpose.

The Christian proclamation of good news is addressed to all, who without exception now share a profoundly abnormal condition in a flawed world. Such is the nature of this good news in relation to its hearers that they often only hear a message of supreme folly: that is, *before* the relevance of the good news is grasped, and people are transformed and brought to faith in Christ.

Christianity is not just another religion, not merely a scheme of belief and practice; it is a vital relationship with Christ. And so, Christians are neither shocked nor dismayed that there are atheists like Richard Dawkins. Many Christians were also once atheists and understand something of the reasons for the antagonism that often controlled their thinking.

What do you think?
How do you 'see' your own particular vision of reality? What beliefs do you use to help you make sense of it all? In this complex arena, we are exposed to conflicting world-views or meta-narratives. To sharpen our insight, Ronald Nash offers a summary: 'A world-view is a conceptual scheme by which we consciously or unconsciously place or fit everything we believe and by which we interpret and judge reality.'[2] The biblical position is a complete world-view that focuses on the glory of Christ's person and work, as the power of God for salvation, which is able to restore man's total relationship to God, including his *thinking*. As James Packer reminds us, 'Christian revelation is a complete world-view, supernatural from last to first.'[3]

The way we think and come to our beliefs and conclusions is of profound importance. My main aim is to develop the validity of reason based on biblical theism in order to examine Dawkins' atheism, and as there are several ways we might do this, we must restrict ourselves to one main approach. While biblical apologetics offers a range of tools, our entire case will depend on one central argument. One is sufficient. That we are confronted with one meaningful objective reality, and one revealed personal Creator God.

That Christians are afraid to think and ask questions, or must dispense with their reason are caricatures. The Bible makes many appeals to carefully considered responses. To facilitate a thoughtful response, biblical apologetics focuses on the reasoned, strategic defence of Christianity. This defence does not shield something inherently fragile or weak, but it takes the form of an open declaration of biblical

Christian belief, giving reasons for its claim to be God's revealed truth.

In making these claims, we examine subjects such as biblical and secular history, the historicity of Jesus, his crucifixion and evidences for his resurrection, the textual support for the Old and New Testament, the conversion of Saul of Tarsus, the growth of the early Church, or assess Christian theistic evidences, to mention a few. But we shall not be taking an in-depth look at any of these. An extensive literature already deals with these, and a lot more.

The view is commonplace that science continues to provide objectively true findings in comparison with Christian belief that is seen as a pathetic leap of faith into fantasy, rather than an acceptance of seriously credible, revealed truth, grounded in the historic Person, death and resurrection of Jesus Christ.

Scientific methodology, including a neo-Darwinian view of the natural world, is assumed to provide factual, incontrovertible evidences and data, in comparison with which Christian belief is narrow, bigoted, and leads to intellectual suicide. We aim to rebut this.

You will, no doubt, quickly see that I am trying to establish the validity of reason on the assumption that my own is already valid. Will my conclusions offer nothing more than what is already implicit in my assumptions, and be so obvious that nothing more need be said?

Circular?

Is not this the ultimate in circular reasoning? Yes, I do assume the objectivity of my own reason, because as a Christian, I not only accept its validity, I also understand how and why I possess it, based on an absolute reference — the living God himself. Ultimately, I aim to show how the validity of reason rests exclusively upon biblical theism. What I am *not* trying to show is that all of my thinking, in consequence, is flawless — well you hardly expected me to try!

With an objectively true basis for this validity, the main propositions I shall advance are that arguments used by atheists to support their position are finally invalidated by their own assumptions. There is nothing underhanded or subtle about this, it is entirely transparent. This will become particularly conspicuous in chapter five, which looks at atheism and probability, and in the chapters dealing with Dawkins' dilemmas.

The position that I advance aims to be internally self-consistent with Scripture. Colin Brown makes this point about self-consistency when he explains how, 'The Christian gospel must henceforth stand or fall — from the philosophical point of view — by itself. Christianity must be capable of vindicating itself by itself.'[4] Ultimately, Christian truth-claims must be self-validating, coherent and compelling if they are to succeed in exposing whatever fatal flaws there may be in atheism. David Gooding illumines a theistic basis:

> We should always remember that God is, so to speak, his own evidence. That is to say, since he is the Creator, he is the ultimate source of everything. There is no being in the universe who is altogether independent of God and is able on that account to give us an independent assessment of God's claims to be God! Neither is there anyone able to provide us with evidence that did not ultimately originate with God himself.[5]

This principle of dependence upon revelation is going to be crucial as we later look at Scripture for answers to some of our questions. But does that mean you will need to throw away your reason, take a deep breath and gulp hard? No, not all — hold on to your thinking cap for all your worth! A thinker, like Dawkins, generally draws from a bank of existing trends in world-views, as this thumbnail sketch illustrates.

Sketch

As a reaction against the biblical position, theological liberalism, in the late nineteenth century, had already become conspicuous by its denials of the supernatural in Scripture and was well fitted to embrace Darwin's evolutionary theory. This new theology that became quite dominant in the English-speaking world was the product of a European (mainly German), rationalistic philosophy, which from the eighteenth century had worked, in many complex ways, either to reject Christian belief or reshape it to fit the modern, critical outlook.

In outline, the emerging liberal movement became marked by a diluted theistic belief and its view of the progressive evolution of religion. Man was on an upward climb, an ascent in which his religious aspirations had advanced over millennia through primitive forms of animism and polytheism, ultimately reaching upwards to monotheism, to create a theistic evolutionary belief system.

Even where liberalism had not taken strong root, perceptions of rapid social and scientific progress combined with the erosion of Christian belief, facilitated the incompatible marriage of Christianity with Darwinism. A rejection of divine revelation inevitably relies on a cluster of new *beliefs* as it attempts to build a coherent system. Now Scripture was filtered through an anti-supernatural world-view, which blocked out a view of Christ as the eternal, divine Son of God and sinless man, who had endured the full penalty of sin (the consequence of a true historic Fall) in his substitutionary death. Instead, teaching proclaiming God's universal

Fatherhood and Jesus as the archetype ethical example became commonplace.

Against this setting, original Darwinian thought was more agnostic than atheistic, but with the subsequent rise of secular humanism a neo-Darwinism has become popular. And, certainly the way Dawkins effortlessly embraces the ready-made integration of Darwinism with his monistic atheism, indicates an easy compatibility.

This combination results in an ideology that offers exclusively natural means to account for biological origins in an atheistic matrix, rather than biblical supernaturalism that reveals the unique, special creation of mankind — pristine origins followed by the Genesis Fall into a flawed world. Uniquely, the biblical view reveals a framework for understanding the subsequent genetic, physical, and moral deterioration that have taken place in what is now, our deeply abnormal and flawed world — and the role of Christ to save, restore, and recreate a new humanity and a new cosmos.

Collision

Biblical theism is grounded in the essential revelatory character of Scripture. The historic Christian position holds that God has revealed himself through the verbally inspired Old and New Testament Scriptures. Verbal inspiration equates with propositional revelation: that is, divine truth has been communicated through words.

A huge collision between conflicting world-views is taking place before our eyes. And those who wish to deny verbal or propositional revelation on the basis of a theological or philosophical position will probably do so without accepting that their denial cuts off their only support for the final validity of their *own* thinking and of their reasoned arguments.

The earlier, secular linguistic philosophy, for example, of Wittgenstein held that anything of final importance lay beyond the limits of what mere words were able to express. (He later revised his ideas). In comparison, the Christian position provides a verbally revealed basis for the validity of our rationality and a sufficient basis for our confidence in it. Many people may still say that they hold an unshakeable belief in God, (that is, confidence in him) without necessarily accepting the verbal nature of inspiration. I will not deny their unshakeable belief, but I will say that the grounding of biblical Christian theism in verbal inspiration provides a more consistent position.

The biblical roots of authentic rationality are grounded in the living, personal God who has made himself known by the eternal Son, the Lord Jesus Christ, using propositional language. We have no warrant to abandon reason, but stretch it to its utmost. In the final analysis, the Creator God who speaks is himself the only absolute reference, the final and supreme authority.

Clearly, no position is able to present a coherent basis for the validity of its thinking without a prior commitment to such validity. What we are aiming to demonstrate is the absolute and final nature of the biblical basis of its own validity. A classical chicken and egg. That the argument for the final validity of biblical revelation is circular is inevitable (where a conclusion is already explicit in the original assumption). Indeed, ultimately it is essential in order to sustain a consistent treatment of the exclusive and autonomous authority of divine revelation. Any claim for an objectively true revelation necessarily involves circular reasoning: it is intrinsic to the nature of revealed truth.

Robert Horn is explicit that, 'God is and must be His own proof — a circular argument if you like, but if God be God no other option exists.'[6] This is the clear position of Scripture, which is corroborated by the work of the Holy Spirit and his own witness in the believer's heart and mind. Horn then develops this, 'It is quite false therefore to think that "proving the Bible by the Bible" discredits the whole procedure and its conclusions. If the Bible were merely a human book, this would be so; but if it is from God, we must go to God speaking there for the truth He reveals.'[7]

We are not merely using a prior attachment to the validity of reason, based on the laws of logic or our experience, in a ridiculous effort to discover what we already believe — the validity of our reason. Rather, Scripture clearly teaches the nature of its own divine inspiration (see 2 Tim. 3:16), and in the final analysis, God's infallible word certifies the validity of our reason.

While atheism and theism are essentially incompatible, perhaps we should ask, do we share *anything* in common? Certainly, in such areas as our deep interest in humanity, in language and logic, and things like the thirst for significance, love and meaning. Bound up with these we shall see that naturalistic thinkers, while rejecting biblical supernaturalism or 'revelation,' do accept as a natural part of life what Christians include in the *content* of general or natural revelation, and in fact, they are unable to live without these things.

Natural revelation is imbedded in our own psyches; it is inescapable: our sense of being a significant part of a valid reality in which we assume the validity of our rationality, the sense of human significance and value, our thirst for love and acceptance, and the insatiable interest we have in finding a key that will make sense of it all: a unified field of knowledge — that reality is a composite whole with meaning.

Roots of science

The transformation of Western culture that began to accelerate in the sixteenth century was, in part, due to the powerful recovery of biblical Christian Faith that placed man in the context of an understandable, created universe. This widespread, clear view of reality began to release the surging wave of scientific enquiry, and rational, evidence-based research, the heritage of which is still enjoyed today. Doubtless, the Renaissance and the spread of learning through the printed page, coupled with such things as improvements in metals technology, and lens grinding, brought a flow of further advances.

This new approach to reality was in sharp contrast to the superstitious beliefs that had dominated thinking for centuries and blocked rational pursuit of genuine scientific discovery, because it was not able to grasp the nature of man's relationship to a meaningful, objective reality. Inevitably, superstitious belief is capricious, irrational, and spawns confusion.

A new spirit of enquiry was revolutionising the Western world. Peter Hammond summarises how in order to carry out meaningful research: 'A proper, philosophical base for investigating the universe was needed, and only the Christian doctrine of Creation has provided that base. — Many ardent atheists dominate science today, but they are working off the foundations and presuppositions of Christianity.'[8] What we now take for granted was not won without serious intellectual debate and struggle. Francis Schaeffer explains how it began to be clearly grasped that:

> Christianity gives an explanation of what is objectively there. In contrast to Eastern thinking, the Hebrew-Christian tradition affirms that God has created a true universe outside of Himself. When I use this term 'outside of Himself,' I do not mean it in a spatial sense; I mean that the universe is not an extension of the essence of God. It is not just a dream of God. There is something *there* to think about, to deal with and to investigate which has objective reality.[9]

Christian theism claims to give a final basis for the understandability of objective reality. Now, we are able to investigate the physical world, knowing that it is really there, and that whatever measure of success we enjoy is due to the unchangeable character of God. There is true, consistent order inherent in the nature of reality, of which the serious search require an honest integrity, a humility to admit mistakes, and a passionate sense of adventure. Given the biblical view of creation, the Christian heritage continues to provide an absolute framework for making and sharing further rich discoveries for the benefit of mankind at large.

Christians have often been in the forefront of research. But the findings of science are always partial and relative, occurring in a stream that may lead to further developments and new insights. However exciting, such findings are never absolute, they are always provisional, and never immune from the ideological and interpretive framework of the researcher. And in more general terms, wherever people wish to think, and use verbal discussions aimed at discussing and evaluating the views of others, they inevitably assume the objective validity of their reason.

Certainly, Dawkins adopts some of this heritage, including the validity of reason, and later we shall see more clearly how he grounds this validity, inconsistently I shall maintain, in his evolutionary science. As a result, whenever Dawkins assumes the validity of his reason and a meaningful universe, he faces a dilemma — will he base his research on theistic assumptions, or on the ultimate meaninglessness of atheism?

We have surveyed the basis and key beliefs of biblical Christian theism in order to show that Dawkins' atheism occurs as a protest within a wider context of theistic belief. Later, we shall assess whether he is able to substantiate his protest.

The historic Christian position holds that the central truths of Scripture reveal the character and purpose of the living God: a purpose that following mankind's Fall, focuses on restoration through the saving work of Christ. These central truths continue to be as relevant to our world as ever: they are the word of the living God, the gracious God of Christian theism who, 'has spoken to us by his Son, whom he appointed the heir of all things, through whom also he created the world' (Hebrews 1: 2).

Chapter 3

The dilemma of a flawed world

*I decry supernaturalism in all its forms — I am attacking
God, all gods, anything and everything supernatural —*

Richard Dawkins, *The God Delusion*, p 36

Richard Dawkins' atheistic views are shot through with this dilemma. We meet it again and again. In view of all that Dawkins examines to support his atheism, he might have seen how impressive and eloquent is the witness for biblical theism. But he doesn't. Instead, he describes how he has sifted all the evidences for and against theism in a clinical and scientific manner.

As a result, Dawkins *thinks* that he is able to draw a valid conclusion and deny with high probability the existence of God. Indeed, how could anything so manifestly ridiculous as the idea of the supernatural ever have entered anyone's head?

But it has taken such a hold, that now he sees the world swarming with crazy religious fanaticisms, before which Darwin's natural selection stands, at least for the present, unable to direct the zealots into more peaceful pathways. Something seems to have gone awry, or worse — unhinged, to prevent Darwinism from yielding its mellowed fruits. His dilemma is the ultimate meaning of humanity within the cosmos: is it truly flawed, or just partially developed?

Subjective meaning

He has no final way of resolving the dilemma, and makes what is apparently an arbitrary decision. I simplify his procedure: first he draws up two sets of lists under two columns, headed 'theism' and 'atheism.' Under theism he places all the morally shocking outrages and beliefs he has collected from world history and different religious writings, but mainly the Judeo-Christian Scriptures — that he considers have given rise to many of the outrages.

Ultimately the choice is made for him by his identification of theistic belief with much, if not most, of the wicked madness and moral corruption that have plagued the world for thousands of years. So, to escape from all this and enjoy a more civilised sanity, Dawkins chooses atheism.

Under his heading of 'atheism' he focuses his natural optimisms for future generations, and lists things like natural selection, morality, evolutionary progress, the benefits of science, education, medicine, technology, consciousness raisers, culture, the arts, and civilisation itself. Is Dawkins' diagnosis as obvious as he makes out? We need to sketch the Christian explanation for our flawed world, and offer an appraisal of Dawkins' position.

Beneath the Christian worldview is a foundation: one living Creator God who has created one objective, meaningful universe, of which we are a unique, personal and complex part. Reality is not a cosmic dream. From the outset, Genesis shows that men and women possess both reason and responsibility in relation to the claims God makes upon them. We see this clearly when God addresses them as authentic moral agents.

The inferences are clear: Adam and Eve know they are persons, who recognise God as their Creator and ultimate reference. Significance, relationship, authority and meaning thus flow from *him*. They also have a cognitive grasp of the words God speaks to them, and know they have been made for an accountable and obedient response.

They also begin to grasp the meaning of symbols: how particular verbal shapes stand for units of communicable reality in God's mind that he wishes them to receive. There is a direct inference in Genesis that the first pair is on a direct wavelength with God and know 'the language' he uses to address them. Part of Satan's subtlety is that he usurps God's place with such brazen audacity and presents himself as an equally authoritative but alternative 'god,' also able to communicate through a transcendental dimension.

Perhaps Eve is caught on the horns of a dilemma, that when she listens to Satan subtly proposing that God's words aren't as credible as she had thought, that she and Adam are personally capable, if they so choose, of calling God's word into question. But instead of checking the credentials of this newly arrived 'authority,' it seems an intriguing alternative, full of promise. And so the first seed of doubt is planted.

Is there more than one true world-view? The answer, of course, is 'no' and Eve should not have been taken in by the usurper. Adam and Eve are not mere automatons, mechanically or chemically programmed for deterministic obedience, (or they wouldn't have been personally responsible for moral obedience, but only automatic conformity, where objective morality means nothing). In consequence, the pair must learn to discern and resist the wrong course and in true freedom gladly choose to obey their Creator.

Space-time Fall

Is the first pair, as reported in Genesis, merely a mythical projection of human wishful thinking: a primitive explanation of universal feelings of guilt and failure? No, to attribute a mythical status to our first parents is itself the projection of futile wishful thinking.

What is very significant is the observation that *they know they know* and hold true knowledge as an unquestioned presupposition. Within their own awareness is a true knowledge of the objective reality in which they find themselves. As such, this profound knowledge is an essential part of the revealed subject matter of Scripture.

An awareness of significance and objective reality flows from their authentic and special creation 'in the image of God' (Genesis 1:27). Without any question they accept the validity of their capacity to hear God and receive knowledge from him, because they know they live *in* the transcendental dimension of this ultimate Personal reality. This observation will form part of the biblical basis of revealed, propositional truth that we shall later develop.

Part of the terrible downfall occurs when Eve begins to accept the insinuation directed against God and the promise of gaining exalted god-like status, and the wisdom associated with it, which in no way was within Satan's remit to grant.

Being deceived they attempted to snatch what was not theirs to possess, lost their walk with God and the joy of pristine innocence and finished up with Satan's direct, malevolent hold upon them. They also finished up with a nature marked by perversity, blind folly, and malignancy towards God — and thought that this was wisdom. The goal of Satan's wicked subtlety is laid bare. Suddenly, instead of ascending to dizzy heights, they fall to unimaginable depths. Greg Bahnsen develops this:

> The epistemological situation was thrown into upheaval when Eve began thinking that she could have a meaningful and proper understanding of reality apart from God's revelation. In that case she

was free to examine what God had to say and autonomously determine its truth over against the conflicting hypothesis of Satan. — she abandoned loyalty to her Creator so as to make herself His equal (Gen. 3:5), determining good and evil for herself. She took her stand as a "neutral" judge over God's hypothesis, thereby exalting her "autonomous" reason over God's epistemologically necessary word.[1]

As we proceed, we will look more closely at the validity of reason, including the content of some of our knowledge. For the moment we note that fallen man, as the spoiled, self-focused image of God, universally continues to possess valid, substantive knowledge of final truths about God, such as his sovereign glory and eternal majesty. A creaturely, personal knowledge that is knowingly suppressed through sinful rebellion and translated into vehement denials.

In spite of his atheism, Dawkins, along with all of us, possesses significant, personal knowledge of objective reality that to be consistent with his position, he must deny. Inevitably, this denial leads to various dilemmas.

As he denies any revealed reference frame for his understanding of what he is, or of what the universe is, or of why it exists at all, he is left in a serious quandary about evil and cruelty. Francis Schaeffer explains how that, 'man, whether somehow created by a curious thing called god or kicked up out of the slime by chance, has always been in this dilemma, the dilemma is part of what being "man" is.'[2] Dawkins doesn't like the idea of personal cruelty more than any one else.

So he expresses his sense of moral outrage at numerous despicable things that religious people have done in the name of their god, an outrage that Dawkins appears to hold as more than just an arbitrary response, but one that is related to an absolute frame of right and wrong — no, he definitely wouldn't accept that, even if his moral rage fits well into an absolutist frame. He is caught in a dilemma: are things really bad and wrong, or just trivial little frustrations that he's exaggerated (who knows?), but which, over time, natural selection will weed out? Dawkins has lost an objective frame of reference and is unaware that he is himself also part of the *result* of the original rebellion.

Enigma and chaos

He sees reality through the eyes of a man who is the image of God, and also with terrible tension and uncertainty. So, he believes that it is high time social and educational forces ought to be overcoming, what he presumably sees as, the vestigial remnants of evolutionary developments that continue to hang around, and which annoy and frustrate him. And when he doesn't see this happening in a powerful and progressive manner, but instead sees outrageous backward movements to whatever religious 'fundamentalisms' he chooses to stigmatise, he wants to hit out, attack and uproot them, and replace them with his own vision of reality.

Yes, religion does have a huge impact in the confused, fallen world, because so much of it is mans' desperate and futile attempt to sort out the muddle and make sense of the mystery. Just like Dawkins is trying to do. He is angry at what the Fall has produced without knowing why he is angry. And, of course, because he is a sophisticated intellectual, he knows that the greatest influence he can have is upon people's thinking is to reason with them. But, Dawkins makes a serious error of judgement in the strategy he adopts to diagnose the cause of the world's ills, because he rejects the God-given diagnosis.

We have already noted his blurred distinction between science and philosophy. Is his atheistic approach that aims to show that theism is invalid a religious philosophy? It's certainly not the physical sciences that he's using to advance his case, because his goal is to deny the personal final Reality. Empirical science *per se* has no terms of reference for such an enterprise. But he is trapped in this dilemma that Schaeffer saw so clearly:

> the French art historian and poet, Baudelaire, is right when he says, "If there is a God, he is the devil." This statement was simply the logical deduction from the premise that man, with all his cruelty and suffering, is now as he always has been. At this point Baudelaire was consistent and refused to give any kind of romantic alternatives as an explanation. But the Bible says that this is not the situation.[3]

Without the revealed account of the Fall, all Dawkins can do is speculate, dream and vent his anger. His confusion of cause with effect is a serious one, but unavoidable all the time he continues to accept his evolutionary atheism.

Flawed world

Dawkins rejects the true, God-given Genesis account of a spacetime Fall into sinful rebellion and human catastrophe, and instead, finds numerous examples of fallen, perverted religious belief, and posits them as the *cause* of much of the world's present ills, instead of their being part of the continuing stream of *effects* and consequences. Certainly, this is complex and we need to distinguish between primary and secondary causes, because all of the world's ills are the result of the ongoing sinful rebellion, some of which is expressed in perverted religious practice. But because Dawkins is unable to distinguish between real and fictitious causes of the world's ills, his own confused view of Christian theism inevitably becomes *part* of his diagnosis of a flawed world.

In response, he cannot escape from sitting as judge, projecting his sense of moral outrage onto a 'cause and effect' universe, some of which has got so bad with corrupt and deluded religious concepts that he must lash out with all the creative ingenuity at his disposal to explain how such noble processes as evolution and natural selection could produce such perverse fruits. He will write a blockbuster of a book to assist the course of natural selection. His 'independent' assessment of why the world has become so perversely religious leads to his response that it's time to act decisively to rescue the world from pernicious theism before it's too late.

In this crusade Dawkins is caught on the horns of a dilemma: that the validity of his reason and knowledge that he uses to interpret final issues and diagnose the world's ills, is a validity and knowledge which, strictly on the basis of his presuppositions, includes dimensions he is supposed not to possess. He is, after all, supposed to be a partly developed collection of matter, with a materialistic basis for his reasoning capacity.

With this belief system, Dawkins is only ever able to engage in self-expression. He has no finally true explanation for his deep and profound tensions. And when he stands, self-critically outside of himself, flailing around at so much that's wrong, he's never sure whether he's just projecting his own thoughts onto his self-constructed model of reality, or looking at a *real* flawed world, of which he is a part.

He's never sure if his explosive rage is only in his head, because he's not supposed to be a man made in the image of God, expressing real moral rage at what is truly wrong.

But it seems like he's angry at a world that is really flawed — he believes it, but then suppresses the thought that it's true moral rage, related to an absolute reference. And, make no mistake, that is a terrible dilemma for anyone to be in.

Part of the terrible tragedy is that as a serious observer in a seriously flawed world, Dawkins' diagnosis is deeply flawed. His Darwinism is a key that cannot unlock the awful reality of a flawed world because it closes its eyes to the awful seriousness of the historic Fall and, instead, attempts to interpret human history as the forward march of an ideological development without a final goal.

No wonder Dawkins' evolutionary atheism is on the horns of a dilemma: will it become the great panacea of the human race, a meaningful key to a meaningless humanity that will usher in universal peace, or will it look on with horror as the crazy supernaturalisms veer out of control. Which will it be? Will atheism become the religion of hope or despair? Is humanity flawed, undeveloped, or plain crazy? Will Dawkins make a sociological gamble in a cosmos without any ultimate meaning?

Ultimately, Dawkins' denial of the truly flawed world revealed by biblical theism leaves him with disturbing dilemmas.

Chapter 4

The dilemma of humanity

Human thoughts and emotions *emerge* from exceedingly complex interconnections of physical entities within the brain.

Richard Dawkins, *The God Delusion*, p 14

If we could gain an insight into the nature of our humanity we might be able to form a clearer view about the basis of our discussion. Are we only arguing about symbols flowing from our cerebral chemistry, or are we talking about objective reality? If our thoughts are models of physical entities in the brain, are we in a position to know the difference?

Is mankind endowed with an objective intuition about the existence of God or not? A selfish gene — a delusion? Whatever our answer, it will depend on our belief in the validity of our thinking, and our own view of humanity. So, who knows? Maybe you believe in the objective validity of that intuition about God, or that humanity has no objective value or significance.

Reasonable reason

We have already laid out our stall in the two previous chapters, and noted the basis of Christian theism, and of mankind's Fall into moral catastrophe, and how that event continues to reverberate in our thinking and living today. Part of the reason why a Christian has confidence in God as the foundation of all truth and meaning is because we accept the revealed basis for the validity of our rationality.

In a recent discussion on the fundamental validity of reason, McDowell and Williams explain how:

> When we try to prove absolutely the validity of reason, we find ourselves facing a strange dilemma. As C. S. Lewis pointed out, it is impossible to prove that human reason is dependable because we must use human reason to prove it. If you question reason, you can't trust your own reasoning process to affirm its validity. —
>
> If we are to trust the dependability of reason, we must be sure that it has the undergirding support of a solid absolute. —
>
> Unless we can find this absolute, we are left to face the dilemma that Lewis posed in which reason has no validating authority but itself.[1]

These observations bring us to the nub of the paradox. Reason is unable to confer validity upon itself without falling into the logical fallacy of a circular argument. We have already discussed this in relation to the Christian view of Scripture. Assuming the validity of your reason, without a sufficient reference point, is like the person who believes his belief. In a review of the so-called 'proofs' of God's existence, Bruce Milne notes how the 'mental proof' is presented:

This argues that pure materialism is unable to explain the capacity of the mind to move logically from premises to conclusions; only the existence of a transcendent Mind explains the effective operation of our human intelligence, or indeed of other non-material qualities of the mind and imagination. If there is no divine intelligence, it asks, how can we trust our thinking to be true, and hence, what grounds can there be for trusting any argument advanced in support of atheism?[2]

This 'proof' is not intended to be rigidly conclusive but proposes a reasonable line of thinking. C. S. Lewis came to a similar conclusion, when he underscores how the validity of reason requires an absolute reference point to support it:

> All possible knowledge, then depends on the validity of reasoning. If the feeling of certainty which we express by words like *must be* and *therefore* and *since* is a real perception of how things outside of our minds really "must" be, well and good. But if this certainty is merely a feeling *in* our minds and not a genuine insight into realities beyond them — if it merely represents the way our minds happen to work — then we can have no knowledge. Unless human reasoning is valid no science can be true.
> It follows that no account of the universe can be true unless that account leaves it possible for our thinking to be a real insight. A theory which explained everything else in the whole universe but which made it impossible to believe that our thinking was valid, would be utterly out of court. For that theory would itself have been reached by thinking, and if thinking is not valid that theory would, of course, be itself demolished. I would have destroyed its own creden-

tials. It would be an argument which proved that no argument was sound — a proof that there are no such things as proofs — which is nonsense.[3]

According to Lewis, the very act or process of reasoning is self-validating, but not on the principles of naturalistic atheism. For Lewis, reasoning that was the product of a blind evolutionary process would be a contradiction, it ought not to exist, but if it did, would never be able to support its own validity. Without a valid rationality based upon a revealed reference point we are left always trying to build a bridge out over the abyss of meaninglessness to reach a fixed point from which to derive our significance. But without revelation we never reach that datum. With it, we are able to secure the validity of thinking on an adequate support in biblical theism. However, referring to this as a 'mental proof' is traditional usage and not meant to attribute unwarranted force to the argument.

Image of God

With these clues to the validity of human rationality, we may now view it in the context of mankind's creation in the image of God. Alex McDonald gives a brief summary of the biblical position:

> Man is not the end product of the purely blind and random combination of atoms. He has been created by God as the only personal creature that inhabits the material universe. He is described as being in the image of God (Genesis 1:26,27; 9:6; 1 Corinthians 11:7; James 3:9), a description that does not cease to be true after the Fall, as three of the above references are to man in his post-Fall condition.[4]

Mankind — specially created and uniquely personal in the material universe, confers a noble rank with a high calling. After reviewing the context of the Genesis passage in which God's 'image and likeness' occur, McDonald suggests that the expression refers to 'man's rule,' his 'dominion' over lesser creatures, and how 'the worth of man is linked to his superiority over animals.'[5] He is then goes further by saying:

> It is better to say, therefore, that the image of God is *expressed* in man's God-like abilities, rather than it *consists* of these abilities. — The Creator has endued man with the God-like qualities of rational thought, creativity and speech, he has crowned him with glory and honour, and he is pleased to declare that man is made in his image.[6]

This explanation shows how rational thought in man corresponds, on a finite level, with the same characteristic in God. The biblical position thus makes the connection between the validity of man's reason and its source in the divine rationality. Although spoiled by sin, man's rationality is a finite paradigm and mirror of the divine rationality.

A correspondence between divine and human rationality follows from verbal revelation and our own rationality. Man's unique rank by creation as the 'image and likeness' of God, introduced in Eden personal communication and relationship.

Herman Bavinck was at pains to show how man's spiritual, moral and rational constitution is, 'a perfect and totally corresponding image of God. Such as man is in miniature, such is God in the large, the infinitely large outline —. Man stands infinitely far beneath God and is nevertheless related to him.'[7] Granting that he allows for the ruinous effects of the Fall, the point that he makes is very important. Only in light of the biblical revelation of the supremely rational, infinite self-conscious God could we account for a corresponding but finite, valid, rationality in man.

In a discussion on the validity of reason, and the Scriptural support for the law of noncontradiction and the law of causality, Robert Reymond affirms, 'that every person, because he is the image of God, innately possesses the laws of reason as the bestowment of the divine Logos himself (John 1:3, 9).'[8] We understand cause and effect, both in the realms of science and in moral choice because, as the image of God, our personal being *transcends* nature.

Unique

Here, reason is grounded in the divine rationality of the *Logos*, from the Greek for 'Word,' a special title for Christ that is given in the opening section of John's Gospel. Humanity is profoundly unique. On this view, our minds possess a transcendent dimension that cannot be explained merely in terms of physical processes within the brain. We possess personal and moral dimensions, for which cerebral chemistry alone cannot account. As a result, viewing ourselves as molecular machines or automatons isn't half the story.

We are a personal part of an objective reality imbued with a real or 'true' significance. Our perception of reality is like a mirror, which although imperfect, is illumined by Christ the *Logos*, 'The true light, which enlightens everyone' (John 1:9). Douglas Vickers extends this and concludes: 'We are the finite analogue of God both as to our being and our knowledge. In short, the fact that absolute being, absolute personhood, and absolute meaning and knowledge exist in God establishes meaning and the discoverability of meaning in the external reality that God has spoken into existence.'[9] We are a significant part of the total picture, and able to make discoveries of what is truly there. A biblical doctrine of natural revelation assumes the God-given validity of reason, but *never* the supremacy of reason.

Dawkins enjoys believing some of these truths, especially our significance and perception of our being part of a valued and meaningful, objective reality, but such insights don't come from atheistic presuppositions; they slip over quietly unseen from the theism that atheism denies. This exposes his thinking to a deep tension and dilemma. Does he believe in a significant and meaningful, objective reality or not? If he says 'yes,' he has jumped optimistically outside of the circle of his monistic universe and become inconsistent (because atheistic monism has no final meaning): but if he says, 'no,' he knows he cannot use his reason to deny supernatural theism. Dawkins needs to deny what he needs to retain.

Complex denial

Ultimately, that is what we shall see, increasingly, that while Dawkins intends to use reason to deny the existence of God (for which project reason is not equipped), instead he uses the *illusion* of reason. It's a serious charge that we shall need to substantiate. Only if we are in a position to justify the ultimate validity of reason — for which we need biblical revelation, will we be able to discuss the ultimate issues of theism and atheism.

Naturalistic thinking is an unfinished bridge reaching out into the abyss, never able to reach the other side. This is Dawkins' dilemma — he must deny any transcendental dimension in his awareness of reality, but at the same time, he needs to hold on to the ultimate validity of his reason (grounded in theism) so he can argue against theism — he is on the horns of a dilemma — he must deny what he needs to retain. He cannot resolve the dilemma and decides to hold on to just enough of what he thinks will help him to deny theism. He needs truth from God to make his attempt to deny God.

In comparison, with the biblical view of our humanity as the supernatural creation of the divine *Logos*, we have a basis for man being the creative, personal 'word spinner.' We are a part of the objective reality that God has called into being. And we are all alike dependent upon revelation from God, both natural and supernatural. Logic is a wonderful gift but we must use it carefully to draw true inferences and make valid deductions based on revealed truth. If you feed misinformation into your personal logic processor the result will mislead you.

Don't look for a meaningful, atheistic reality; it doesn't exist — all truth ultimately comes from God, who in Christ has come from the other side, and bridged the abyss.

Chapter 5

Almost certainly

> What matters is not whether God is disprovable (he isn't) but whether his existence is *probable*.
>
> Richard Dawkins, *The God Delusion*, p 54

Our ideas of certainty and probability are intertwined. The centrepiece of Dawkins' book is his assessment of the improbability of theism. He makes no bones about this: 'The argument from improbability is the big one.'[1] His chapter four is entitled, 'Why there almost certainly is no God.' This is where Dawkins aims to hit hard and repeatedly, and where he intends to focus his formidable logic with deadly effect. By this argument he intends to demonstrate that belief in God's existence is so absurdly improbable that you may rest assured in its denial. It is one of the most intriguing arguments Dawkins uses, and one I shall discuss in terms of a serious dilemma. In an earlier introduction to the subject in chapter two he gives a concise summary:

> That you cannot prove God's non-existence is accepted and trivial, if only in the sense that we can never absolutely prove the non-existence of anything. What matters is not whether God is disprovable (he

isn't) but whether his existence is *probable*. That is another matter. Some undisprovable things are sensibly judged far less probable than other undisprovable things. There is no reason to regard God as immune from consideration along the spectrum of probabilities.[2]

Dawkins then draws up a spectrum of probabilities to illustrate how he assigns probability parameters to the existence of God. A convenient seven-point scale ranges from an extreme '1 - Strong theist' to a '7 - Strong atheist,' at the other end. Based on his self-assessment he places himself at point 6 — 'Very low probability, but short of zero. *De facto* atheist.'[3] But admits that he is leaning towards 7: a strong conviction that God does not exist. The numbers 6 and 7 represent Dawkins' philosophical convictions. Of course, you may use numeric ranking to indicate your personal convictions, if you wish. But this spectrum is designed to be illustrative, and prepares for his more extended argument in chapter four.

Before we go too far we may be struck by the apparent simplicity of Dawkins' overall case. Because, what is very interesting is the idea by which he aims to show that an answer to the ultimate question of God's existence is within our grasp, if only we are prepared to consider the relative likelihood evaluated as a balance of probabilities. Reason and information that is already to hand are sufficient to extract and deliver an answer to the ultimate question. It nearly sounds too simple. We shall need to follow his logic carefully. And you will need to decide whether or not to call this 'science,' in the way that Dawkins does.

Outline

Dawkins fleshes out this argument, and develops it along several lines, central to which is a probability analysis. An outline of how he presents his argument goes something like this: the existence of the universe and all life forms on our planet give the appearance of being designed by an intelligence. While, on the surface, this is one of the strongest arguments in the theist's armoury — the argument from design, in fact, functions as the opposite. So that, contrary to the theist's intention, Dawkins wishes to show that the appearance of design is perilously flawed and so improbable that in fact, 'The argument from improbability, properly deployed, comes close to proving that God almost certainly does *not* exist.'[4]

Any appearance of intelligent design is thus an illusion and a trap, because chance is purely statistical — blind, not causative and must not be invested with causal agency. Mere chance is insufficient to account for the vast array of complex things that exist: 'Chance is not a solution —. Design is not a real solution either—.'[5] We need something more impressive and potent than chance to account for the appearance of design, because, 'Intelligent design suffers from exactly the same objection as chance. It is simply not a plausible solution to the riddle of statistical improbability.'[6] This is because of infinite regress, the fatal flaw in intelligent design, 'Indeed, design is not a real alternative at all because it raises an even bigger problem than it solves: who designed the designer?'[7]

At this point, Dawkins begins to introduce us to his alternative to both chance and design and leaves his debt to Darwin in no doubt: 'Natural selection — is the only workable alternative to chance that has ever been suggested.'[8] So impressed is he by the principle of natural selection, Dawkins describes it as a, 'solution of stunning elegance and power.'[9]

Dawkins accepts that Darwin's ideas were intended to apply to biological improbability and observes that, 'although Darwinism may not be directly relevant to the inanimate world — cosmology, for example — it raises our consciousness in areas outside its original territory of biology.'[10] It is important, however, for Dawkins' case that the principle of natural selection is admitted to be of universal application: to origins, to cosmology — to everything. He does not justify this large step from biology to universal cosmology, beyond saying that it's a consciousness-raiser, which, as I view it, bears hallmarks of a leap of optimistic 'faith,' especially as it now brings us into an attempt to explain why there is something rather than nothing.

But to help us see how the energetic universal process operates, right from the origin of the cosmos, Dawkins explains: 'Natural selection works because it is a cumulative one-way street to improvement. It needs some luck to get it started, and the "billions of planets" anthropic principle grants it that luck.'[11] If the anthropic principle is in a position 'to grant luck' to natural selection, we had better delve, briefly into how he proposes this propitious co-operation occurs. But, notice this strange linguistic transition. To be consistent with his hypothesis, Dawkins needs to evade theism, almost literally like the plague, and must instead, transform an impersonal 'principle' into a benignly positive causal agency.

He warns about, 'the psychological bias that we all have towards personifying inanimate objects as agents,'[12] but has few qualms about applying the helpful agency of 'luck' (even if veiled as impersonal), allowing the anthropic principle to kick-start natural selection as an alternative explanation to design.

In fairness, we generally concede that 'nothing' is an insufficiently plausible, casual agency to account for 'something,' but Dawkins is fairly hard pressed and needs to call on 'luck' to help him out. Does this really confer, or increase, the plausibility of an explanation that is intended to prove fatal to theism, especially when Dawkins wishes to avoid investing the impersonal first cause with the ability of benign agency?

'Solution'

He says quite a lot about both natural selection and the anthropic principle, which are his key explanations of how we are here — that there is something rather than nothing. Natural selection, this 'solution' of how things develop with increasing complexity is thus married to his account of how things got moving in cosmological origins with the aid of the anthropic principle, the fine-tuning of the universe with remarkable mathematical constants, which permit order, rhythm, and ultimately, life.

With this proposed solution, Dawkins shuns anything complex early in evolutionary history, because the 'simplest' cells, replicators and organisms must come early to give natural selection sufficient time to climb the ramps gradually to attain the evolved complexity that is so apparent to him. Classical Darwinian theory: but what Dawkins doesn't give is an account of how or why these two features, one a process, the other a principle, somehow come to be intrinsic to the structure of reality — this is just the way things are or must be.

In fact, at a fundamental level, the traits attributed to them are a descriptive analysis, based on observation, of the way various types of causes and events already operate in a complex universe, with natural selection conveniently moved from biology to cosmology, and the anthropic principle placed in the grand scheme of things, right from the start.

On a biological level, Darwinians don't have the monopoly here, and biblical Christians accept that adaptation and natural selection are terms that may be used, outside of a Darwinian context, to summarise the way *existing* genetic information, in given populations, form slightly different combinations down through the generations (so-called 'micro-evolution'). But these new combinations do *not* produce new kinds, or drive towards superior information. Inevitably there is a gradual loss and degradation of pristine information, which runs completely counter to the ideological, Darwinian progressive climb of primeval microbes up to man, or of microbes to anything else for that matter! Full-scale Darwinian macro-evolutionary theory interprets all its 'findings' through its humanistic idealism, a philosophical view that includes the progressive development from one simple-celled origin to our present diversity and complexity to explain why we are all here.

Dawkins offers no explanation, on his own terms, of how natural selection and the anthropic principle might have evolved from simpler, less elegant processes or principles — either the thought genuinely doesn't occur to the Darwinian mind, or else it is too reminiscent of the infinite regress type of logic that he needs to reserve exclusively for what he takes to be the foolish reasoning that favours an Intelligent Designer.

The empty, absolute nothingness before the beginning of beginnings is not an attractive postulate for Dawkins to consider, because it asks for too little (or too much!). Absolutely nothing, no time, no protons, quarks, or space, anywhere. And no potential pre-existing possibilities (no inherent probability) of what might happen — no, that would be investing the possibility with an impersonal, benign casual agency in order to spark a start! But this kind of utter nothingness doesn't possess enough of the seeds of optimistic potential to account for all that has subsequently happened.

Notice, in passing, how atheists cannot get too far without masquerading the revealed attributes of God (which Romans 1:19-20 reveals are universally known), such as his power and wisdom shown in the structured operation of the material cosmos, and pressing them into Darwinian service as if impersonal, inanimate processes and principles, possessed similar wonderful powers and causative agency to account for the world and universe. They then delight to extol the suitably depersonalised power and sublime simplicity of these stunningly elegant principles that are so conveniently present and perfectly active right from the start!

Dawkins, however, is still optimistic that given such a vast set of astronomical possibilities something eventually happens and one thing leads to another that, given Darwinian man as a highly intelligent observer, natural selection rather than the illusory appearance of design is the sensible, atheistic explanation of its origin.

So, we must not think that our intelligence is derived from a higher One. This reaps disaster. Following Darwin, intelligence is a late arrival in the universe, and should not be looked at to account for origins, which need to be kept as simple as possible for the theory to fit. Dawkins thus explains that the cosmos does not owe its origin to a supernatural Creator. A supernatural Creator is a complex solution, and therefore disqualified from being a serious candidate. But the anthropic principle, natural selection, and luck — why, of course these are such *simple* things, sufficient to get it started! Wait a second — to get *what* started? — What was already there?

Check rational basis

The main argument of Dawkins' atheism, that the vast amounts of time, and the immense numbers of events, with all their locked-in potential, are sufficient to account for reality, amounts to suggested 'maybes' stretched beyond reason. I suggest this is rather an illusion of reason. And there is no intrinsic necessity built into the naturalistic structure of reality, for *nothing* to begin to be something, and why an immense number of meaningless events possess the inherent necessity of progressively moving towards a goal of increasing meaning and order. That the universe and rational observers must, necessarily, have no rational origin is a tenet of atheistic faith.

So Dawkins bids us eschew all reasoning in the direction of a Creator — that only leads to the greatest absurdities, the highest improbabilities, and to the worst of delusions.

Just look, there is already such awesome and astronomical complexity ranging from the structure of the simple cell, to galaxies, nebulae, black holes, quasars, to human brains that to accept such complexity has arrived by chance is already unbelievable. We need something more plausible to convince our mental chemistry, because it has a need to know.

Be careful how you take the next step: intelligent design is a non-starter, and neither is chance the solution to the riddle of awesome complexity, but natural selection solves the riddle. Dawkins credits Darwin for having 'raised his consciousness,' and he frequently mentions this to reinforce his intellectual enlightenment and conversion to Darwinian science.

Dawkins elaborates, 'A deep understanding of Darwinism teaches us to be wary of the easy assumption that design is the only alternative to chance, and teaches us to seek out graded ramps of slowly increasing complexity.'[13] In consequence of all Darwin has taught us, to posit a *super*natural intelligence as an explanation of the apparent design of the cosmos is ridiculously weak. All it does it set up a chain of infinite regress by asking, 'Who designed the Designer?' That this line of reasoning would ever arrive at the first cause is impossible.

Then, in order to illustrate the strength of his probability argument, Dawkins applies his spectrum of probabilities ranging from the highly likely to the highly improbable and proposes that theism scores the highest of statistical improbabilities. Accordingly, the God hypothesis represents the least likely of all plausible explanations to account for the creation of reality, because, 'Far from terminating the vicious regress, God aggravates it with a vengeance.'[14]

According to this argument Dawkins believes he has virtually delivered a deathblow to the idiocy of biblical theism. So, which way will we go? Will we all be swept along by an appearance of irresistible logic, or is there just the slightest chance that his reasoning merely rests on his cerebral chemistry and his philosophical assumptions?

How do we respond to this argument, which for Dawkins is overwhelming and compelling in its strength and simplicity? As well as pointing out the apparent absurdity of the infinite regress argument, Dawkins baulks at the God of theism on the basis of his assumed complexity. If the complexity of such a God is so unnecessary for what Dawkins thinks was required at creation, he concludes that this is so unlikely, forget it — such an entity is much too early in the evolutionary scheme of things. And so, the vast complexity at so early a point in the time-line entails a vast improbability. The supernatural, living God is subjected to the constraints of Dawkins' monism, and Darwin's theory, and rendered an astronomically high evolutionary improbability.

Nothing is new here — for millennia men and women have thought they could dispense with God, and manage the universe without him. Darwin's theory is symptomatic of the original rebellion — a late arrival of an age-old movement to reject mankind's special creation, the biblical Fall, and the living God, and place man centre-stage.

On this basis Dawkins thinks the infinite God of Christian theism most probably doesn't exist. He is outside the range of Dawkins' conception of naturalistic possibilities, as dictated by his evolutionary reference frame. And don't forget Dawkins says he is a scientist. Now I know he would probably qualify that, and say he is a Darwinian scientist, and therein is the rub.

Weigh it up

How do you usually evaluate probability? You weigh up the likelihood of an event occurring, or of a state of affairs happening, or perhaps the occurrence of an alleged event being true or false, as a judicial process may determine. A lot of probability is based on observation of comparisons with other similar or comparable events that happen in an already orderly cosmos. Something is probable, compared with other similar, or related events with which you already have some familiarity.

We may apply probability loosely to the unlikely occurrence of an event, say for example, what chance have you of becoming the President of the USA, or the King or Queen of England, and, after some serious reflection, (forget the equations!) you may conclude that there is virtually no chance of the event occurring. Or say, on a less grandiose level, in an industrial context, you may consider what are the chances of defects occurring in a population of a thousand products manufactured in succession.

Some probabilities, like the old coin flipping or dice throwing exercises, are much simpler to work out, but to make a serious shot at probability you really need firm convictions about the uniformity of natural causes, and some data. In your statistical quality control situation, you may follow sampling plans, and based on a history of measured defects in given product populations, and given similar manufacturing conditions, you may, with some degree of repeatable success, inspect just enough parts to assure yourself that the vast bulk of them are within an acceptable level of quality.

One of the key assumptions that Dawkins relies upon to give his result is that recourse to probability theory has the capability of offering a uniquely convincing tool to support his case. He believes that tools useful for empirical, evidence-based research are equally applicable to the question of God's existence. But when Dawkins applies probability estimates to the existence of God he is back into the circular argument, intending to assign high improbability to a state of ultimate ontology — the *existence* of God, rather than a particular event occurring, or not occurring — that he has already decided to deny on the basis of his atheistic belief.

In other words, his atheistic belief dictates that he scores the result of high improbability he wants to achieve. Dawkins' denial of theism has already predetermined the outcome of his analysis, and not given us a reason for his atheism, but the illusion of an increased plausibility for it.

Don't forget probability analysis, like any mathematical process, won't show you anything until you assign values to key parameters. Clearly, he believes that the data you feed into mathematical equations depends on that data being admissible corollaries of physical realities. If the data is admissible the results correlate with the arena of research. The values you use in the equations control the answers they supply. You need empirical data before you are able to estimate or calculate probabilities. Has Dawkins processed empirical data as he evaluated the probability of God's existence? No — he has used elements drawn from his ideological belief system.

Is probability analysis applicable to God? A little condescending perhaps? We have already seen how Dawkins has made his position plain, 'Contrary to Huxley, I shall suggest that the existence of God is a scientific hypothesis like any other.'[15] He needs this sort of hypothesis to sustain the credibility of an empirical probability analysis, but he has already offered a working definition of 'God' that includes the term 'supernatural.'

Can Dawkins have it both ways? Has he suddenly let himself off the hook? If God is supernatural, he is not amenable to scrutiny by empirical research, but Dawkins' system excludes that, and says the question is a scientific one. He allows a definition of 'God' that includes a category (supernatural) for which his naturalistic probability argument is not fitted.

Now, of course he is consistent with his monist position, (that, by definition, a 'God' cannot possess objective supernatural existence). He has no plausible arguments to support his denial of supernatural theism, because his monism already (*a priori*) excludes it. But now, he believes that natural selection has conferred him with sufficient correlation with objective reality that atheism is a final truth about reality. A tall order? Yes, he has already admitted at the outset that God is disprovable and that human thought is only a product of physical reactions in the brain.

Assumptions are *a priori*

If you are a monist, you have *already* excluded a supernatural Creator from your universe. And all this recourse to probability does is to show, by a rather elaborate means, what you *already* believe — it is your credal, faith system. So, why does Dawkins believe so strenuously in the high *improbability* of God's existence? Perhaps, because he doesn't wish to appear to be absolutist and be seen to rely on expressing his atheism in terms of the theism that it denies. Doubtless, it will seem more scientific to subject the hypothesis to a probability analysis rather than make an absolute denial.

All the time he says that belief in God's existence is a delusion he avoids the dilemma of attributing final truth to his own position and final falsehood to theism. The final truth of atheism sounds a bit too fundamentalist for Dawkins. No, he is aware of this dilemma and prefers to say that there is a very good chance that atheism is right and theists are not only plain wrong, but deluded!

His opponents haven't just misread the scientific data and come to the wrong conclusion. No, they're deluded, presumably because they have a Christian-theistic view of science and believe in a *super*natural God, and don't espouse atheism! Yes, that's it, if you reject his monism and believe there is a transcendent, personal Creator you're deluded! Is this empirical science or philosophical bias? Dawkins appears to have a difficulty accepting that his monism is a philosophical position, because that would drive a wedge between philosophy and the superior, final objectivity of science. But, Dawkins has one scheme — his 'science' *is* his philosophy. His monism is a philosophical view from which he derives his naturalistic assumption that everything is explicable in terms of his naturalistic science — even other philosophical views and religion! Now his monism is completely unable to disprove theism, and so he resorts to an attempt to rubbish the argument from intelligent design by stigmatising it with the absurdity of infinite regress, and then transposing it into candidate for probability analysis! Is this pseudo-science or what? — Does it show anything more than paradigms of Dawkins' paradoxical, atheistic assumptions?

Do facts as carriers of information just fall out of a meaningless universe, or is Dawkins borrowing a theistic assumption, that scientists are able to draw valid conclusions, because the universe has been created by the Personal source of all true meaning? Edgar Powell reminds us that, 'Modern atheistic science is schizophrenic! Why is that? Because it operates on the basis of two mutually exclusive paradigms.'[16] The first assumes a meaning*ful* created order in which authentic research may occur, the second assumes a meaning*less* final reality, 'where facts come out of a chance universe.'[17] Within this deep conflict dilemmas abound.

Which way?

Is this either science, or quasi-religious philosophy, or a mixture of incompatible categories? As if God's existence were open to probability analysis, Dawkins uses mathematics to lend credence to his case. Is assigning probability estimates to philosophical convictions a valid category of rational activity? If you so wish to present your personal convictions, but Dawkins' probability analysis is unable to deliver an analogue of final reality. After all, the process assumes it has the answer at the *start* of the calculation! So, what did it demonstrate? That Dawkins is an evolutionary atheist — that's all. Suddenly, the party balloon bursts.

If Dawkins chooses to trust the key of his atheistic monism to interpret reality it will deliver 'information' filtered through his belief system. It will not deliver final truth, or even approximate final truth, but merely ensure that his findings appear consistent with his ideological viewpoint.

The biggest problem with the infinite regress that Dawkins uses several times as he tries to expose the case for biblical theism, is that it assumes *created* 'gods.' Each one needs another to account for the existence of the previous one, and on we go, *ad infinitum*! Yes, it stands to reason, but is inescapable, because Dawkins is locked into his monistic universe. And reasoning from his philosophical beliefs, Dawkins thinks he has made biblical theism look ridiculous.

His argument, however, doesn't go anywhere near the target. We are talking about the Uncreated, who is independent of time and matter, who is underived, and who has neither beginning nor end. The logic of infinite regress applies within the created order, but not to the self-existing, living God. At the end of the day the 'luck' that Dawkins' scheme needs to get it started is his code word for 'God.' Only *he* is sufficient to account for the expanse of created reality.

Dawkins' monism lets him down and leaves him confined inside the created circle. He is trapped inside his dilemma of infinite regress as if it was an argument that conferred its own final authority, when all it shows is that atheists will try to rubbish theism using paradoxical arguments and call its advocates, 'deluded.'

Dawkins' naturalistic science relies on a logic that is ultimately self-refuting because subjective thinking lacks an absolute reference and is unable to confer upon itself a transcendental correlation with a meaningful objective reality. Neither is a naturalistic thought process able to extract or interpret the ultimate significance of that reality which, without a rational basis, he optimistically believes is concealed within it. Dawkins' scheme rests on naturalistic philosophy that confers upon 'science' the mantle that *all* potential knowledge is discoverable by empirical research.

Don't forget, biblical theism proclaims the revelation of intelligent design — the starry heavens, a little wild flower, and a bird's feather — *not* as a philosophical argument for God's existence, but to show that we are all personally culpable, that we have already received enough evidence, and are without excuse — we *already know* he is there!

Modified atheism

Earlier we said we would discuss whether Dawkins' procedure to weigh up the probability of God's existence rather than make a classical atheistic denial, makes him a modified atheist. Certainly, *if* all is matter then empirical science 'rules' and our beliefs are generated by complex chemical reactions in our brains. But if all that goes on in peoples' heads — following Dawkins' monism — are complex reactions, it's not surprising that, at the end of the day, Dawkins picks the route of trying to reason, using an inherently meaningless argument that God's existence is highly improbable, because he's got nothing more to do it with than cerebral molecules. Call it enterprising if you wish, audacious, or perhaps unduly optimistic. But it does point to his dilemma.

Will he advance his belief to make an outright denial of supernatural theism, and be a real atheist, or just a modified, high probability atheist? His ambivalence is quite clear: a modified atheist? Yes, as far as his empirical science is concerned, or a classical dyed-in-the-wool atheist? Yes, when it comes to his antagonism towards Christian theism and general theistic belief, his atheism is dogmatic. His empirical approach won't let him get beyond the self-expression of molecules, while his *personal* bombast, ridicule, rhetoric and evolutionary belief rally to support his dogmatic atheism.

When we make observations and interpret our findings we do so within the framework of our beliefs. Our worldviews are not impartial or neutral, just as Dawkins appears to have become attached to his Darwinian and monistic philosophical convictions, which now lead him to a degree of certainty, because he has come to believe his philosophical convictions and assume the validity of his thinking: a full circle.

Two subjects, at least, are stirred into the same pot — philosophical beliefs and the validity of thinking, and the first assumes the second. If our philosophical beliefs confer authority to the validity of our thinking, we are reasoning in circles, and going nowhere, because we also need a prior confidence in the validity of our thinking to confer credibility upon the basis of our philosophical beliefs.

This conundrum was well put long ago by J. B. S. Haldane, and quoted by Lewis as an example of how strict materialism is (absolutely) self-refuting: 'If my mental processes are determined solely by the motions of atoms in my brain, I have no reason to suppose that my beliefs are true — hence I have no reason to suppose my brain to be composed of atoms.'[18] Materialism asserts the exclusive empirical validity of materialism, but is unable to rest *that* assertion on an empirical base, and refutes itself. In spite of which, Dawkins continues to *think* that his reasons for believing atheism relate to objective realities, when all the time his naturalistic thinking is based on pinning his hopes on his tentative suggestions.

In comparison, Christian-theistic presuppositions continue to be widely assumed as a basis for meaningful research that leads to objective discoveries, whether the scientists are theists, atheists or pantheists, or whatever else. Edgar Powell confirms that, 'Scientists do come to valid conclusions in their research, largely because the metaphysical assumptions that underpin their observations are legitimate: God has created the universe and reality in such a way as to make them legitimate.'[19] This powerful impulse has diffused widely into society and largely continues to be enjoyed by Christian and non-Christian alike.

Our thinking needs a framework that supports its validity and leads to conclusions that correlate with what is objectively there. Theists and atheists working in the sciences invariably use many of the same assumptions, except when atheists try to argue against theism, which on theistic presuppositions is not evidence-based science! This is when atheists become most at sea, vulnerable, and illogical. That science 'works' in no way supports or proves the atheism advanced by Dawkins.

Is atheism on its own terms of the final meaninglessness of everything, (including atheism) able to deliver meaningful, scientific reasons for the falsehood of theism? No, because Dawkins likes the idea of an understandable universe, and a rational humanity within it, which he has inherited from theistic presuppositions. His probability analysis masks his *a priori* dependence upon atheism and is self-refuting.

Then he comes to consider origins. Granted, this is challenging, so the special help of an entity called 'luck' is enlisted. Twice he says luck is needed to get natural selection started when it is applied to cosmological origins. He has already poured derision on people who use God to account for any phenomena beyond their grasp: the 'God of the gaps.' It is weak, and we don't follow it.

Biggest gap

What is interesting, however, is that when faced with the biggest gap of all — origins, Dawkins falls back on 'luck'! He knows chance has nothing to offer. Monism outlaws the living God of biblical theism, so that leaves 'luck.' Does he explain what he means by 'luck'? Does he ask if luck has a rational, scientific basis? Or if luck is really a sufficient cause? Or does he ask about the probable validity of his logic, and whether 'luck' refers to a model in his head, or an entity in objective reality? Does he conduct a probability analysis of how prior existing principles might facilitate the appearance of luck, or what conditions might have been propitious for luck to emerge? No, it is beginning to look much too like infinite regress, which he has debunked. If you believe in Dawkins' 'luck,' you will probably be just as willing to accept other myths or make-believe.

He assured us that when 'properly deployed' the argument from improbability 'comes close to proving that God almost certainly does *not* exist.'[20] How close do you need to get to be close enough? Of course, he has properly deployed the argument, because this was his 'really big one' that was going to doom delusory theism for ever.

Does a high reliance on such a helpful, non-entity as *luck* become part of a 'scientific' explanation that will prove fatal to theism? Presumably Dawkins thinks so, which tells us a lot about how far he is willing to trust make-believe to deny the God of biblical theism. On atheistic grounds there is no objective, rational reason for the origin of anything. There is no final reason for the appearance of order, and beauty, or meaning as a *true* insight into the structure of reality to emerge out of nothingness.

It is important to see this next step, because you will need real logic, (more than mental chemistry and models in your head) capable of processing *final* issues to be able to follow my thinking — *if*, as atheism teaches, there are no reasons for final truth to exist objectively in the structure of reality, or inside our heads, then either the final validity of reason does not exist, or it lacks an adequate basis, which, *if* that were so, denies that *reason* is able to process final issues. In which case, you wouldn't even know whether you were deluded or not, because it wouldn't mean anything, or relate to a final reference frame! Besides, how was the discovery made of the final truth that *final truth* in an objective reality does *not* exist?

Dilemmas begin to multiply, but one you are left with in this argument is that, on an atheistic premise, you have used the validity of reason to deny the validity of reason. Atheists live with the tension of using their knowledge of a transcendental dimension to deny it! As we noted in the previous chapter, reasoning like this must deny what it needs to retain. Which is fallacious. Another dilemma you are left with is that your rational mind cannot believe nothing. On its own terms, atheism is unable to deliver a meaningful universe with a rational structure.

Dawkins' argument from improbability was the 'big one.' I am left wondering just what sort of science this is: monistic 'science' perhaps? He might, at least, have offered to show us how useful this sort of analysis had been to show the virtual non-existence of other classes of beings that researchers believed were figments of the imagination. I mean — if you already believed *that*, what did we expect your probability analysis to say about their existence! Does it *discover* anything you didn't already believe? Of course not.

The very idea of probability assumes an orderly cosmos in which the flow of rational, repeatable events is given by the theism that guarantees, in the first place, the high probability that the theory works! From the way Dawkins handles the subject, he wants to accept the orderly cosmos, which gives him the theory, (useful when applied to the right sort of empirical problems), but use it to deny theism. Is this the presentation of findings based on the patient application of passionate probing into the nature of final reality? I'm sorry, but I don't think so.

In all fairness, the argument from improbability is an elaborate use of smoke and mirrors that creates the impression of dealing with valid categories of empirical 'science' in an effort to yield a rational conclusion. Dawkins' goal is to accomplish a lot more than creating impressions, but his hands are tied. Exclude the God of biblical theism and there is *no* rational answer, because rational answers don't exist without God, the source of true, final rationality, who provides meaning, probability theory, and valid reasoning in the first place.

This is of great importance — Dawkins has shown us conclusively that atheism is unable to locate a rational basis for the validity of the thinking intended to support it, because it is inherently anti-rational. Remember, he advised us at the outset that the main part of his definition of 'delusion' was, 'a persistent false belief held in the face of strong contradictory evidence.' Well — was it science, or something else?

This leaves him with a large dilemma: if his case for atheism lacks a rational basis, will he continue to believe the unbelievable? And if his reason and rational correlation with objective reality come from the reason and mind of the living God, why does he use them to deny the undeniable? But if they don't, why does he work so hard using them as if they did?

Chapter 6

The dilemma of which 'god' to deny

> *My definition of the God Hypothesis included the words 'superhuman' and 'supernatural'.*
>
> Richard Dawkins, *The God Delusion*, p 71

As we have seen, an atheist like Richard Dawkins, who is a professional scientist and communicator, tends to have a flair for presenting his vision of reality in a way that scientific views and personal philosophy *appear* as a coherent system. So, perhaps we don't immediately see how the strength of his personal conviction in philosophical matters is a personal belief. Or, perhaps we are pleased to accept his beliefs based on his distinguished intellectual standing and professional prestige.

What usually happens is that individual pieces of scientific evidence are presented and woven so thoroughly into the warp and the woof of a philosophical world-view that the result appears to be an integrated system. However, as I have begun to show, whenever an insufficient base for the validity of reason and attachments to ideological views are assumed, dilemmas begin to float up to the surface to make their uneasy presence known.

Fault lines

Dilemmas like this indicate fault-lies, or inherent contradictions. They show that such arguments ought not to be taken at face value. Now, we need to continue to look at the basis upon which some of Dawkins' arguments are advanced.

After reviewing a number of sciences, and their 'consciousness-raising' capabilities in his chapter four, Dawkins concludes, 'If the argument of this chapter is accepted, the factual premise of religion — the God Hypothesis — is untenable. God almost certainly does not exist.'[1] However, Dawkins knows that once he assumes his monistic view of reality that, by definition, the supernatural, living God of Christian theism is excluded. So, what sort of arguments will Dawkins use to deny the God that his scheme won't accept in the first place, but whose definition, for the sake of argument, he has accepted? He is on the horns of a dilemma. We looked briefly at this point in the previous chapter. Here we examine it in a little more detail.

Instead of calmly marshalling conclusive arguments to demonstrate the final validity of monism or naturalistic philosophy — which, if logic is logic, must necessarily demonstrate the final invalidity of supernatural theism — he assumes his case is *already* the new orthodoxy. He has no way of being able, on naturalistic presuppositions, to disprove or invalidate a position posited on supernatural presuppositions: he just doesn't believe them.

Neither can he demonstrate the final validity of naturalism, because it is not open to final proof or disproof. All he can ultimately do is admit his personal attachment to an atheistic, philosophical belief system. Dawkins accepts that the current state of scientific research is unable to furnish absolute proof of the non-existence of the supernatural God.

He also makes it clear that the definition he gives refers to 'the God Hypothesis,' which he intends to negate with a high probability.

But when it comes to preparing the ground for his argument, which 'God' will he deny? The supernatural God of his definition, or one stripped of supernaturalism and confined to a monistic universe? Or are *all* 'gods' of equally dubious existence? Here, as elsewhere, Dawkins knows his own mind, 'Life is too short to bother with the distinction between one figment of the imagination and many.'[2] With this all-embracing sweep all distinctions disappear. In the context, he was denying distinctions between any and every 'god' from the polytheisms of Greek, Roman and Viking beliefs, but from his overall discussion, it is clear that the God of Christian theism is included. As far as Dawkins is concerned, any 'God' associated with supernaturalism, is as much a figment of the imagination as any other.

Clearly, his intention is to make sure that we don't find any types of deities that are outside his definitions. Now his strategy begins to emerge as a case of foregone conclusion.

For how will, even, Dawkins demonstrate in any plausible sort of way that what he *already believes* is a figment of the imagination, doesn't exist as an objective entity? He is in a dilemma.

He knows he must assume the hypothetical existence of the supernatural God, for the sake of argument. But then, when it comes to his actual arguments, he must be consistent with his naturalistic and atheistic assumptions and deny the supernatural God Hypothesis and say it's only a figment of the imagination. So he dispenses with any serious discussion of the God of Christian theism. *He* must be excluded from the outset, because, as Dawkins has told us, this was an issue for 'science.' Science, carefully applied and interpreted, would supply the answer.

I need to clarify something here. Sometimes Dawkins refers to genuine evidence-based science: for example, that the human brain includes an exceedingly complex network of neural connections, but he often refers to his own ideologically-grounded beliefs as if they were also derived from evidence-based science: for example, that the human brain may be used to deny Christian theism.

Christians are by no means against science, but we just don't accept the ideological and philosophical basis of evolutionary atheism as a finally true basis for scientific research! At least we are now aware that as far as Dawkins is concerned, there is one uniform, naturalistic reality — it is his main ideological presupposition on which his arguments are based. (I outlined my own basis in a sub-section near the end of chapter two).

Question the procedure

As he develops his procedure, Dawkins argues against a 'god' whose existence he defines in terms amenable to the denial he wishes to make — one with a naturalistic frame of reference. And the supernatural dimension is set aside, and described as if it was absurd, because it is excluded by his monism in the first place. By this simple strategy Dawkins sets up a target near enough for him to think he is making a direct hit.

Most of Dawkins' dilemmas that we are looking at arise from tensions within his belief system, but the dilemma in this chapter is related more to what I suggest is his inconsistent procedure. Or, if you wish, look at it another way: that his ambivalent procedure may have equally arisen out of his dilemma — which 'god' — supernatural or created? As a monist, Dawkins' philosophy of logic is grounded in empirical pragmatism and chemistry. Is this a sufficient basis to derive the final truth, or even the most probable truth, of atheism? Are chemicals, even by the slowest gradient on 'mount improbable' able to arrive at self-consciousness in an objective reality, and able to make pronouncements about the absence of the personal Creator?

Here, the main grounds for his atheism — the presupposition that naturalism is virtually certain to be a true philosophy of reality, is an optimistic leap. And if you are going to attribute this sort of virtual certainty to your propositions to make that leap to deny the existence of the supernatural God, your denial is invalid, because, if you are an atheist like Dawkins, you have no rational basis for an absolute upon which to rest your logic in the first place.

This leaves Dawkins in a deep dilemma: that if nothing has any final meaning, then neither does his atheism. Dawkins knows he needs to hang on to the validity of his reason for all he's worth, or he won't be able to assume that his denial of theism has any validity. And that is the nub of his dilemma. Again, he is caught in a monistic circle into which he needs to bring some of the central assumptions of biblical monotheism in order to give an appearance of validity to his efforts to undermine it.

So which God will Dawkins deny, the supernatural God or a figment of the imagination? If he merely says that the definition he gave of the supernatural God also refers to a figment of the imagination, we are perfectly entitled to ask, 'Whose imagination?' If he says 'The theist's,' I will say that his empirical science has no way of disproving that my personal belief in the supernatural, living God, does not refer to final objective truth. The content of his assertion that my belief is only a 'figment of the imagination' merely tells us what he believes as an atheist, and is not evidence-based science.

While he says that he is attacking all gods and everything supernatural, his approach of foregone conclusion that denies the supernatural and sets it on one side, merely shows what he already believes, but does nothing to invalidate

Christian theism. And, which, in the attempt, only shows that his attack misses the target.

Chapter 7

The ultimate paradox

Each of us builds, inside our head, a model of the world in which we find ourselves.

Richard Dawkins, *The God Delusion*, p 361

At the root of Richard Dawkins' atheistic position is a logical paradox — if we hold that there is no final meaning, what we have just asserted is also included. And as soon as we think like that, we have contradicted ourselves. In other words, if there is *no* finally true meaning in the universe, I would never have been able to find out such a paradoxically meaningful piece of information in the first place!

Dawkins dislikes leaps of faith, but he still leaves me wondering, how his mental chemistry appears able to construct a system of logic and thought that believes in the final authority of his world-view, and the validity of his atheism — and deny that it's a leap of faith. Does Dawkins believe something is true even though he is unable to prove it?

A model of reality

In many ways this is the ultimate paradox for some one like Dawkins, who rejects the revealed validity of reason, because the result is always the same: without the revelation of an infinite, rational God, the creator of a meaningful cosmos, and of our possession of a valid rationality, we have no way of knowing whether our beliefs about ultimate issues are merely the paradoxical projections of the internal models we have constructed, or not.

After all, reality on atheistic presuppositions means nothing more than an, 'in my head' chemical response; a perceived model *reality* that I have constructed within myself. What I think is *out there* is only what is going on inside me. An *expression* of what I am thinking, but not necessarily of what correlates with what is truly there, (on atheistic premises, no one knows that — final truth doesn't exist). For research into, and discovery of, a finally meaningful reality, we need the Christian position of man as 'the image of God' that we discussed in chapter four.

C. S. Lewis makes an astute observation, the kernel of which I have already used above: 'If the whole universe has no meaning, we should never have found out it has no meaning.'[1] In the face of the enigma of human rationality posited on an atheistic worldview, that must rank high as a contender for the ultimate paradox.

This is indeed a deadly serious dilemma for a theory of perception built upon naturalistic assumptions, which denies that the universe has a final significance or ultimate meaning beyond my arbitrary thoughts about it. But Dawkins does not wish to live with this kind of dead-end tension and its maddening frustration. While he wants his atheism, and does not wish to look into the face of God, he also knows that he does not want *all* of the conclusions of his atheism.

Instead, he must continue to operate using *some* of the assumptions of theism that his words are imbued with true meaning that correlates with a final objective reality, because if they didn't he wouldn't be able to engage in his scientific pursuits *and* write books trying to deny theism.

In an age of philosophical pluralism, when absolutist positions are out of fashion are atheists and Christians trapped in their opposite camps, playing a game of out of step with all the other walkers? By no means — from the ground that I have already covered, the Christian has an absolutely secure basis for the validity of both his position and his reason.

Van Til sums up the position well, 'The best, the only, the absolutely certain proof of the truth of Christianity is that unless its truth be presupposed there is no proof of anything. Christianity is proved as being the very foundation of the idea of proof itself.'[2]

Is this merely a blatant, partisan way of ensuring that Christians win the argument? No, what Van Til is driving at is that ultimately the Christian position is the only valid basis for a meaningful cosmos, and of our being able to draw true conclusions from what is *there* beyond our mere sense impressions. With the Christian position, we have a final basis for an objectively meaningful cosmos and of a valid rationality that allows us to analyse arguments, draw inferences, make deductions, and draw authentic conclusions, without which you probably wouldn't have even reached this page!

All Christian truth coheres together as one consistent system, able to explain the Personal transcendent Creator, the origin of the cosmos, the final meaning of man in the context of his terrible, flawed abnormality, and the profound solution, all within one unified field of knowledge. Christianity provides the foundation for the processes that lead to rational proof.

Without revealed biblical truth and its apex in Christ, other belief systems, including atheism, are unable to provide a basis for the intelligibility of logic, an observable objective reality, a moral integrity to discern self-deception and to reject it, and uphold final truth. A rejection of revealed truth always leaves belief systems beset with internal contradictions, never fully able to account for what *is*.

One thing is *reasonably* certain; Christians stake their claims in such a way that we court the most rigorous enquiry into the claims of meaning, and of how we are able to secure the validity of our rationality upon the basis of a revealed reference point.

It's a serious dilemma

Dawkins must somehow transcend his naturalism in order to give an independent evaluation of it as the only final reality there is! But, lacking an absolute reference, ultimately he is unable to move beyond finite self-expression. And his belief in monism is his opinion. But he doesn't seem to be aware that he is transcending naturalism in order to *appear* to give an objective and independent assessment of it, because on naturalistic premises his thinking is only a complex reaction in his brain, unable to transcend its own nature to make such finally true and independent assessments!

How is he able to make this massive jump to transcend his naturalism, while still believing he hasn't transcended it? There is only one final answer — ultimately Dawkins, along with all of us, derives this sense of authentic correlation with objective reality from his humanity made in the image of God. Dawkins' personal *being* already transcends his naturalism, and makes a huge optimistic leap, because he enjoys his true correlation with an objective reality, but he must deny the God who gives it. This inevitably leads to strange tensions and uncertainties.

He believes his naturalism, and perhaps an updated version of empiricism — originally popularised in the eighteenth century, that we have no real experience or knowledge of the external world, except the impressions or sense data that objects leave on our senses. Certainly, Dawkins' view that we build models of the external world fits quite well with empiricism, but it doesn't explain how he enjoys a personal awareness of being part of an objective reality. His belief system is able, in part, to account for his mental sense data, but not his much larger correlation with an objective reality.

So he freely admits that he cannot think how to disprove the suggestion of several science-fiction authors that 'we live in a computer simulation, set up by some vastly superior civilisation.'[3] With this sort of fantasy we are now more like three-dimensional hologram images, trapped in a vast computer-simulated virtual reality game. Do you see why Dawkins' isn't sure about reality? When he denies revealed absolutes, the foundation disappears and his objective reality begins to disintegrate. Now, in Dawkins' view, we're like the toys beginning to talk to one another on Christmas Eve! Denial of final truth always leads to profound uncertainty. And if Dawkins is unsure whether he's in a *real* reality, or a complex, computer-simulated one, what chance has he got of showing us that his atheism is a *real* explanation of the ultimate reality?

As he continues to deny the personal living God, the source of all significance and reality he's left with uncertainty, in which nothing has any final value or meaning. Too bad that millions were wiped out in those wars, or that aeroplane crashed, or you lost your job — it was just a part of the computer simulation. One day the super intelligences operating it will tell us why: meanwhile don't worry about simulated human responsibility — it's just a ridiculous conundrum. If you deny revealed truth, you also deny reality, and begin to lose it, with the result that almost any idea you think of sounds as convincing as the next.

What this also shows is how much atheistic beliefs foster a climate in which people are not sure anymore of what is real.

Abandon the biblical revelation of an absolutely authentic reality, including a historic Fall, accountable human responsibility, and the personal living God, and we are well on the way to becoming amorphous ciphers, flotsam drifting on the mysterious tides of a dream world.

Dawkins' ambivalent thinking leads him into serious confusion and dilemmas for which his atheism has no resolution. The Christian position shows that the natural thinking of mankind is subject to futility and false beliefs. We see this in the appearance of the reasoning that Dawkins offers to support his denials of supernatural theism.

If our model of the world is only inside our heads, as Dawkins bids us to believe, his understanding of the meaning of atheism is inside his head and he has, on his own terms, no way of knowing whether it relates to an objective reality or not: it simply agrees with his monistic philosophy, which is his preferred model of reality.

Yes, indeed, if the whole universe has no final meaning — just like the computer-simulated sub-reality — we would never have found out. But, if on the other hand, the universe does possess final meaning, is the model inside Dawkins' head sufficiently developed to present atheism as that final meaning, (how would he ever know?).

Or, are we prepared to consider the truth claims of revealed Christian theism that the only consistent answer to the ultimate paradox is that our own personal rationality is a very special part of a meaningful cosmos created by the supremely rational, living God? The ultimate paradox helps us to see that the very idea of final meaning — which if there was none, we would never have found out — only makes sense if there *is* final meaning: a final meaning paradoxically denied by atheism, but secured by the rational, living God revealed in Christian theism.

Chapter 8

SETI — The search for meaning and significance

I think it is definitely worth spending money on [duplicating the origin of life] — and — by the same token, on SETI because I think it is likely that there is intelligent life elsewhere.

Richard Dawkins, *The God Delusion*, p 138

Suddenly, out of the blue, the main receiver at the SETI Headquarters' complex began to oscillate with an eerie flutter. Bruce, who was first into the Tower that morning, noticed that the universal semantic processor (USP for short) had already translated a strangely cryptic message into flawless English. He quickly noticed the signal distance, and that all the instruments confirmed authentic data. Millions had lived for this moment.

As Bruce reached for his mobile to tell the Director, his eyes began to scan the printout: he was euphoric — until he read further:

'To whomever this memorandum applies: We trust this note finds you well, committed and maintaining control.

We now wish to take this opportunity to convey our most recent findings, which confirm much of our earlier work. After recent deliberations, we believe the time is right to advise you that our research, covering things right back to the primordial event, showed conclusively that nothing was ever going to have any final meaning; we repeat, absolutely nothing.

So we have not wasted any more time, and, in fact, faced quite a dilemma about whether or not to notify you, in view of the sort of impact this might have on you.

However, after several sessions in committee we finally decided that we would bare our souls, so to speak.

There is no need to reply, especially as we would probably never receive it and that whatever you communicated would mean nothing to us.

In spite of which, we remain,

Yours faithfully,
Subsidiary branch authority.
(We prefer not to disclose personal names).
PS. Unfortunately, our research data is strictly confidential, and not available on any terms and conditions, outside of our own regional authority.' Sba.

What audacity! In the past, people have been hung, drawn and quartered for less treason than this. How dare they! But now it comes from some far away corner of the big picture, so how would we ever know? Our petty little existence, rubbished! But, hold on — on second thoughts, maybe we should think about this message as communication received in our own context. We need to interpret this contextually. Some kind of intelligence has communicated this information, that based on our semantic and logical conventions involves a paradox of the highest degree — that meaning isn't what you thought, and actually means nothing! So how do we find out what it means? Even if it were in such measured English, how would we ever know the basis of the intelligence that sent it?

Quickly, the Director called a meeting to decide whether or not to issue an international press release, including the SETI communication. Nearly as quickly the consensus held that quiet secrecy should be maintained for the time being. They might, after all, be able to comment on it more favourably, after further reflection and a round table discussion.

A week later, just when everyone had drained every conceivable milligram of semantic possibility from whatever meaning 'The message' might or might not have, especially if it didn't mean anything, came a second:

> 'To all of you who were waiting, we thought we ought to keep you as fully informed as possible, and must let you know that our ex colleagues, senders of the earlier transmission for which you waited with such admirable patience, decided to overlook that it lacked an objective basis against which to report that "nothing has any meaning," and was, accordingly, you will be reassured to learn, beset with an inherent logical fallacy.
>
> In light of this, we need to confirm what you already know, that everything, that is, absolutely everything, has some meaning and significance, and that ultimate questions point to final meaning.

However, many in some regions are highly resistant to this. Interestingly, what we have discovered, based on careful observations, is that when final truth is denied, the denial becomes — we might almost say, a new 'species' possessing an apparently final, but false and opposite meaning.

Many have fallen into this dark hole of self-deception. We had not originally intended to be quite so forthright, but as supremely important outcomes are at issue here, it is better that you be armed to deal with the subtle new species of information. We are, however, not at liberty to disclose to you how we know what you do, or do not know.

But we remain,
Yours cordially,
Parallel network Authority.'

With this, it was time to set up a New Hermeneutic Committee, because unbiased specialists with psychological and linguistic skills were urgently needed. It was also vital that they filter out all religious bias from their interpretations. Employing specialists with only the highest Darwinian credentials would ensure that all traces of bias were eliminated.

This time a special budget had been granted at almost breakneck speed. One of the key appointments was an Editorial Director, because naturally they wanted to begin to collate all the new revelations, (as there would almost certainly be many more), into a single source, and publish them widely with explanatory comment and personal application. The new star-spangled book would give such value and solace to their followers, some of whom were beginning to wonder.

After only three sittings of the Committee, the eerie flutter began again. Yes, there was definitely going to be a spate of this correspondence. This was a lot more than they had originally foreseen, even in their wildest dreams. And once again, the same flawless, bureaucratic English began to appear. This time, eyes began to glaze:

'Further to earlier communications, (Kindly note that their actual antecedence may or may not be successive) we would like you to be fully cognizant of the implications of raising your consciousness. As you are becoming more aware of the utter strangeness of some of the dimensions of reality proposed by quantum theory and other advanced conceptual constructions, it is only fair to inform you that the source of this apparently intelligent communication does not exist, anywhere. You might say that it comes from nothing.

The very concept of existence is so completely unnecessary for intelligent reason to embrace that we must ask you to establish worldwide seminars to re-educate as many as possible of the professional classes to accept that in the final analysis, nothing exists — we mean absolutely nothing — it is an idea simply bursting with life, and fortunately one that happily just happened to fall out of the mystery of nowhere.

As for any apparent correlation with what appears to exist, it is an illusory inversion, a mirror image, if you like, of the idea you had in the first place. We regret that this new way of using your intelligence may be challenging, but we are optimistic that you will be able to adapt within a reasonably short period.

However, to avoid either further unnecessary research or, on the other hand, excessive disappointment, you will appreciate that it is preferable to accept that there *really* is nothing, as we have discovered from eminent intelligences such as Marx, Nietzsche and Dawkins, rather than the old, illusory images. That our interpretation is open to more than one meaning is so highly improbable, we advise your immediate acceptance.

We realize that you may have some residual doubt causing you to question our professional competence, but since you are already very adept at accepting the views of advanced thinkers, such as the aforementioned, you should have no problem in accepting ours.

Accordingly, we urge you to let your good sense prevail, as we have been so heartened by many conspicuous displays of it in recent times.

Yours cordially,
Subordinate branch Authority.'

Searching spacetime

SETI has a strong fascination for atheists, because our humanity cries out for that word from outside. We want to understand, and to be understood, on our own terms, as if we were the final datum.

This creates a strong appeal to atheists, who denying biblical revealed truth, prefer to turn their attention to outer space, (Mystics prefer inner space). Outer space, atheists urge, offers huge potential to be a fruitful source of intelligent information. In response, NASA, the American Space Agency has, for many years, pumped millions of dollars into their SETI programme, the Search for Extra-Terrestrial

Intelligence that hopes to receive signals from other rational beings in the depths of space.

One of the goals of SETI is as clear as crystal: to prove evolutionary atheism. Carl Sagan, the influential atheist, was one of the early promoters. SETI is a response to a need: one that hopes that science will confirm the theoretical basis of evolutionary atheism. After all, *if* intelligent life has occurred spontaneously once, (an atheistic assumption that hopes you will be impressed by the intelligence of its hindsight), then at least one other occurrence would provide powerful, confirming evidence for evolutionary atheism — or so the thinking goes — as if a safe verdict for the first instance had already been secured.

If you view all the evidence in creation through an atheistic lens, what did you expect to get but the result you wanted? Is such a goal within the reach of empirical verification? No, and so far, there are huge amounts of slightly desperate optimism and no evidence. Ultimately, nothing proves atheism, so how would you expect meaningful science to verify the ultimate meaninglessness? Is atheistic information conveniently going to drop out of the abyss? Hardly — atheistic beliefs are propagated by *minds*.

How extraordinary! What a pile of assumptions is stacked up in this talking game! A complete theory of information is the main assumption: that there might be a similar order of being with our own rationality, and even epistemology: one that uses a concept code capable of being cracked by our intelligence. That we are projecting our wishful thinking 'out there' because we feel so alone in this vast, empty cosmos, and long to make connection with beings who might tell us about themselves and what it all means.

With a large leap of optimism, we think we have reasons for believing in some kind of objective meaning, something more significant than what our pet canary or cat thinks of us, and that we are made for meaningful communication — to be a part of the final explanation of everything. (But what if 'they' were to tell us it all means *nothing*, except that morsel of information, would we believe them?).

If only — but maybe

We assume that the categories of significance, value and meaning, truth and falsehood, beauty, order, wonder and delight are all somehow going to correspond with other personal beings in the same objective reality of which we are a part. And then we assume that our signal receiving equipment has a technical and semantic correspondence with the signals that might be transmitted.

It's difficult enough translating ancient Babylonian or Sumerian cuneiform, let alone language code from other intelligent, personal beings with sufficiently close mental correspondence with our own. In an irrational universe in which nothing has any ultimate meaning, what hope is there of minds evolving from cosmic broth that might make sense of my mind? In that context there is no such thing as 'making sense.'

Even irrationality only has meaning relative to its antithesis; some kind of objective, rational significance, otherwise one guess is as good as the next, and there's no point in arguing. We can guess what squabbling chickens are 'saying' to each other, but the point of this exercise was to find something beyond guesswork.

A key assumption of SETI is the uniformity of natural law in a spacetime continuum, and a unified field of knowledge. When it suits us, we like pluralism, but when it doesn't, we have an unquenchable attachment to *one* meaningful reality that speaks with one universal voice. Atheistic romanticism? Why, yes, of course, because atheists still long for objective, meaningful communication that will satisfy their yearning for true significance, value and love beyond the molecular biochemistry of models in their heads.

Will all these assumptions dovetail together like the solution to an immense puzzle in a meaningless universe? And as they already believe that their own reason comes from molecular interactions, without any reference to an ultimate reason, it has no way of knowing whether it is true or false, even on an arbitrary or relative basis. But this is most unsatisfying, and SETI advocates prefer quietly to assume an optimistic attachment to the universal validity of reason — that atheism, on its own terms, is unable to offer.

With all our enigma and wonder we suppress the true knowledge that we are created persons and what we know about the eternal being and power of our Creator God. We would rather not have anything to do with *him*, and so we try to blot out the signals that we have *already* received from within our humanity, but which we do not wish to confront.

In doing so, we unavoidably replace both special revelation and the inner light of natural revelation, (that we introduced in chapter two) with something more appealing: the light of our own self-made, autonomous spirituality, that *we* create, that lets us feel *we* are wise and in control of our own universe, rather than the supernatural God himself.

That's one of the reasons why the Bible calls us fools. 'Although they claimed to be wise, they became fools and exchanged the glory of the immortal God for images made to look like mortal man and birds and animals and reptiles' (Romans 1:22-23). Of course, revealed information isn't politically correct, and damages our self-interest because it tells us what we don't want to be reminded about.

On naturalistic assumptions words are the human tools of culture, a pragmatic code, a flowing stream of semantic symbols that rise at the source of our cerebral biochemistry and interactive experience. And if, there has never been a propositional word from 'outside,' then end of story, and drop any thought of correspondence with a meaningful objective reality. That is the ultimate, irrational leap: propositional meaning and significance is a myth or a fancy; forget it — *except* the denial!

In this situation, any search for ultimate significance, or for final answers is utterly futile since the *a priori* assumption denies the possibility: so don't even think the concepts or ask the questions. Here, the principle of the self-fulfilling prophecy rules: what we don't believe will happen, will not happen — unless we get surprised out of our minds. Somewhere in this reasoning a paradox is imbedded. Do people believe their denials using propositions? Yes, absolutely.

On the basis of personal attachment to secular linguistic philosophy the proponents have decided that propositions and reason will be employed to deny the possibility of ultimate propositions and reason. At the level of our *own* thinking and knowledge, it is basic, but shift it into a higher key and attribute it to deity? Oh no, that's going far too far! We don't want a supernatural God who reveals himself to us in words. He might tell us what to do, which would cut across our own goals, and we might even have to give an account to him. We much prefer to think that could never happen. Anyway, a God who speaks is much too human for our liking.

So speech becomes a social accident of evolution that after aeons of grunts and grimaces happened to work and become an effective tool. If that's all it is, how can it be employed to deny the existence of the living God of Christian theism? — A serious dilemma.

But if only *someone else* out there in the universe would really speak meaningfully to us, — the more money allocated to the research budget, the greater the —: an optimistic, blind leap? Absolutely.

There, for the moment, we have to leave the SETI enthusiasts, including Dawkins, pondering. Their dilemmas are enormous, and reflect the huge tensions that exist in any system of belief that rejects the infinite, rational God of biblical revelation.

Chapter 9

Light in the darkness

We humans give ourselves such airs, even aggrandizing our pokey little 'sins' to the level of cosmic significance!

Richard Dawkins, *The God Delusion*, p 238

As Jesus enters upon his public ministry, the Gospel writers show how he fulfils Old Testament prophecies. In one of these, light dawns in the gloomy shadows: 'the people dwelling in darkness have seen a great light, and those dwelling in the region and shadow of death, on them a light has dawned' (Matthew 4:16). Light and dark are striking analogies from the physical world, often used in a biblical setting to illustrate the sharp contrast between the brilliance of divine truth, and the spiritual darkness of the human heart.

Once, Jesus challenged his gathered listeners by startling them: 'If then the light in you is darkness, how great is the darkness!' (Matt. 6:23). In contrast, John's description of Christ reveals him to be the universal light, flawless and brilliant, when he says, 'The light shines in the darkness, and the darkness has not overcome it' (1:5).[1] Christ's coming has brought great light into the world.

Signature

All people have received the light of natural revelation. Earlier, we noted how the 'light of nature' in our humanity retains remnants of the image of God. By this light, even without any knowledge of the Bible, people are aware of *inward* things like, conscience, human value, selfhood, love to their neighbour, honesty and integrity, and a deep need to be listened to and understood. Also, by looking outwards, we become aware of *external* realities, such as God the Creator, the vast wonder of the universe, and our apparent littleness in it, as these words show: 'When I look at your heavens, the work of your fingers, the moon and the stars, which you have set in place, what is man that you are mindful of him —? (Psalm 8:3-4).

Natural revelation is inescapable, but left to our own devices we, 'suppress [God's] truth' (Romans 1:18). This is a serious, universal indictment on how we stubbornly keep on pushing our knowledge of God below our conscious threshold. Indeed, all of creation displays God's visible signature, and even though our minds are clouded by sin, the message is clear:

> For what can be known about God is plain to them, because God has shown it to them. For his invisible attributes, namely, his eternal power and divine nature, have been clearly perceived, ever since the creation of the world, in the things that have been made. So they are without excuse (Rom. 1:19-20).

In the presence of this display, an atheist like Dawkins has to get busy with his thick Darwinian paint, daubing it over his wide knowledge, much of which reflects the splendour of God.

Creation speaks a universal language: 'The heavens declare the glory of God, and the sky above proclaims his handiwork. Day to day pours out speech — '(Ps. 19:1). Daily, huge volumes of information pour in splendour from the material universe, reflecting God's glory and majesty. The sheer silence of created beauty calls out through space with one penetrating, majestic voice, in comparison with which SETI becomes an extravagant clutching at straws.

Reminders

The light of nature is a witness against us: we stifle its solemn reminders, and rather than groping for God, Robert Reymond describes what happens, 'All it [general revelation] does is leave them in their idolatry without excuse (Rom. 1:20).'[2] Many react to Jesus Christ, the light of the world, in a similar way. Instead of recognising Jesus, 'the world' expressed a determined hostility towards his purity and light — 'He came to that which was his own, but his own did not receive him' (1:12).

Natural revelation is quite distinct from the glorious, divine outshining revealed in the life and death of Christ. People see this glory when God opens blind eyes to a lifegiving sight of Christ. This illumination unveils the truths of written revelation, and particularly the gospel of Christ, when the Holy Spirit awakens us to our lost condition, and enables us to turn from our dark night and trust in Christ.

All of the people to whom Jesus spoke already had some measure of the light of nature, but he never accepted it as a substitute for life-giving illumination. Jesus talked about this when he said to Nicodemus, 'You must be born again' (3:7): when he said that whoever hears his word and trusts in him who sent Jesus — 'does not come into judgement, but has passed from death to life' (5:24): when he taught, 'All that the Father gives me will come to me, and whoever comes to me I will never cast out' (6:37); and when he explained, 'I am the light of the world. Whoever follows me will not walk in darkness, but will have the light of life' (8:12). Now everyone needs *his* 'light of life' to illumine their inner darkness.

Christ's light begins to dispel dark ignorance and radiate a true understanding. As God works upon the soul, he gives life and light, which expands our minds, opening new vistas and undreamt horizons. A spiritual resurrection occurs in the here and now, which Jesus clearly taught: 'I tell you the truth, a time is coming and has now come when the dead will hear the voice of the Son of God and those who hear will live' (5:25).

With this life-giving light comes a confidence in his promise, 'that whoever believes in him shall not perish but have eternal life' (3:16). Christianity is a relationship with God, received through faith in Christ.

Who needs light unless there's darkness? And how dark is dark? 'Maybe I'll find my own way' — is the reaction of many. If you fail to grasp the severity of a problem, your solution will not deal with the inner complexity. If we form shallow impressions of this darkness, we shall underestimate how serious it means to be lost, cut off from God, and the lengths to which he has gone to rescue us from it.

The Bible is clear that from the day of Adam's disobedience in the Garden, mankind was condemned — lost in a dense, spiritually dark jungle; not a romantic, dreamy spiritual twilight, but deep moral darkness in which he was exposed to real dangers. This is the consistent position right through the Old Testament, 'They have all turned aside; together they have become corrupt; there is none who does good, not even one' (Ps. 14:3). And the prophet Jeremiah bluntly reveals the inner intellectual, moral centre of operations, 'The heart' as, 'deceitful above all things, and desperately sick' (Jeremiah 17:9). Spiritual darkness brings a profound degree of confusion, ignorance and sheer hostility to the light. We have no reason to accept Dawkins' view that we, 'aggrandize our pokey little "sins."' Once we begin to see Christ's utter purity and glory, the darkness of our sin is a lot blacker than we had thought! Peter eloquently expresses the powerful light of the good news, when he reminds Christians that God himself is to be praised for having called us, 'out of darkness into his wonderful light' (1 Peter 2:9).

Dawkins would have us believe that atheism is scientific, enlightening and authoritative, so that only prejudiced fools, especially religious ones, would not believe it. Alas, left to his own devices, man remains in the dark, cut off from the light and wisdom revealed in the life and words of Christ, the light of the world.

This is exactly what John has been saying about people loving darkness rather than light because of their prior attachment to moral darkness. Yes, we can twist and turn into every dark crevice of human thought, but there is a dead end at every branch in the maze and we are trapped in utter darkness. Getting caught in a self-made trap in nothing new, 'The nations have sunk in the pit that they made; in the net that they hid their own foot has been caught. The Lord has made himself known; he has executed judgement; the wicked are snared in the work of their own hands' (Ps. 9:15-16). Unbelief involves a subtle self-deception deep in the heart of our fallen human nature.

Hallmarks

For all its intellectual respectability, self-conferred or otherwise, evolutionary atheism exhibits all the hallmarks of the problem of our first parents. When they disobeyed God, everything changed. Now when, 'they heard the sound of the Lord God walking in the garden in the cool of the day, — they hid themselves from the presence of the Lord God among the trees of the garden' (Genesis 3:8). We, their descendants, are still so skilful at dodging behind all the trees of our absolutist atheism, or our relativistic pluralism that we do not see we're caught in a vast web of deception, behind which we slink and slither to hide from the solitary voice of the One who comes to find us.

In this natural condition, cut off from God, we are wise in our own eyes, securely insecure in our independently floating reference point. But this reference point is like a compass with the points erased. Conscience may remember where the points are, but we don't want to know, and work to erase any faltering memory.

Mankind occupies a kingdom of moral confusion, and spiritual death: in short, utter darkness. The book of Proverbs teaches, 'The way of the wicked is like deep darkness; they do not know over what they stumble' (Proverbs 4:19). The moral darkness is so intense we don't see the traps concealed in the pathway and fall into them.

The world is teeming with conundrums, fallacies and contradictions, but many are at home in their atheistic or pluralistic worldviews. Of course, we're still using our attachment to our philosophical beliefs and the validity of our thinking to confer authority to those beliefs. We are self-appointed judges, and so used to it, the thought doesn't really occur to us.

People in this darkness are trapped in the web of their autonomous reason. Such reasoning confers authority to our conviction that denies the existence of absolute truth because we believe the absolute truth of our philosophical convictions that it (absolute truth) doesn't exist. Yes, by nature, we are inveterate circular thinkers, always assuming the validity of what we have decided to believe.

We are trapped in a labyrinthine web from which we need a supernatural deliverance. In comparison with the tortuous reasoning, there is an altogether different set of conditions — when the supernatural light of Christ illumines our self-deceptive thinking by the regenerating work of the Spirit, we accept a new circle. But, instead of our self, now Christ becomes the new centre.

He is the source of our light and the basis for the validity of our thinking, because he has created the categories of perception and rationality with a capacity to grasp what is really there in the objective created reality. Now, with Christ, as our light and Lord, we know what and where we are, because we know who, and where he is, and the nature of our relationship to him.

In the final analysis, the biblical Christian position is irrefutable, because Christ is the origin of truth, meaning, significance, rationality and light — reality itself. As 'the Word,' (1:1) and the eternal Son of God, Christ's word is supremely authoritative. Even so, in the encounter of light with darkness, the Christian position does not advance or overcome unbelief merely on the basis of rational arguments. That the arguments for the absolute truthfulness of Christianity are utterly sufficient, on an intellectual level, to present a compelling and irrefutable case does not mean that people trapped in unbelief will be convinced, without the enlightening and life-giving work of the Holy Spirit.

Biblical Christianity is more than a system of abstract philosophy — it is rooted in the historic Christ, and the application of the truths of his death and resurrection by the Holy Spirit. In the depths we encounter knowledge of the supremacy and reality of God, as the I AM.

The very words that I use to deny final realities mock my crude defences and radiate an unquenchable, transcendental dimension. Through creation, I have received them from the divine Word himself. By nature, we all deny God, and use our God-given reason to do so.

Such denials are at the root of Dawkins' dilemmas that keep bouncing back to challenge him. He may not believe that he is a unique creation, retaining the marred image of God, but that doesn't stop him using God-given reason to think in concepts and categories that project personhood, meaning and significance that stretch far beyond the denials and dilemmas of atheism.

Fragmented

No wonder people feel fragmented and a strange tension between the gentle light of reason and the force and fury with which they hold tenaciously to their own beliefs. John's Gospel says the same, 'men loved darkness instead of light' (3:19). What an enigma! What misplaced honour for the noble quality of love, to be attached to moral darkness!

Thinking like this often finds it hard to stifle the witness of the light of reason, or the light of God's revelation in nature, and has a hard time holding it all down. John Frame shows that: 'The unbeliever knows things at one level of his consciousness that he seeks to banish from other levels — he knows God, he knows what God requires, but he does not want that knowledge to influence his decision, except negatively: knowledge of God's will tells him how to disobey God.'[3]

We have seen how much of Dawkins' protest against biblical theism is precisely that. He will not believe in biblical theism because, as he says, he 'is a dyed in the wool monist.' But in order to deny theism he needs an absolutist presupposition, that, for example, the philosophy of monism is absolutely right. In other words he needs to confer an absolute validity to his own view in order to sustain it, and deny theism. As we noted earlier, this is the same fallacy as saying, 'I believe there are no absolutes'.

Ultimately, everything in a naturalistic universe is explicable in terms that agree with its presuppositions, and the supernatural, by definition, must be excluded. On the other hand, for example, the evidence for Christ's resurrection is substantial, witnessed from multiple sources. Claims for its occurrence may be discussed, denied, or accepted, using categories of historical evidence. Both an inner circle of people who knew Jesus intimately, and a large number of additional eyewitnesses claimed to see Christ after his resurrection. People were well aware of the differences between hallucinations, fabricated stories, (such as his body was stolen) and credible events.

Many detailed studies have forensically evaluated the arguments and sifted the evidence both for and against his resurrection. And very large numbers of people, right up to the present time, have accepted the case that Jesus of Nazareth was crucified under the mandate of Pontius Pilate, that he did not merely swoon, later to revive, but died an awful death, from which, being raised by an act of God, he is alive for evermore.

Basic to John's Gospel is the thought that reaching back to ultimate origins and finding the objective significance of our humanity are completely beyond our reach without special revelation. We need a true word from outside as an absolute reference point; otherwise we fall into the trap of awarding our own significance on the basis of our confused, fallen thinking. But without the light of a revealed, God-given reference point, thinking about our own significance is laden with self-directed bias, dilemmas and uncertainty.

Without an absolute reference for our reason in God the creator of rationality, and the laws of logic we have no basis for the final validity of our reason. McDowell and Williams summarise this in terms of basic alternatives:

> If you reject God as reason's ultimate absolute, you have nowhere else to turn. Deny God as the source and absolute for reason, and you leave reason afloat in a sea of irrationality. — When reason collapses, our certainty of any truth falls with it. To put it simply, either you believe in God or you cannot be sure there is anything to believe in at all.[4]

As we have already seen, a secure God-given basis for the validity of our thinking is more than an exercise in bookwork. We need an inner spiritual transformation that all the man-made offerings to achieve raised consciousness are unable to give. They are spurious wisdom systems that promise much but give nothing. That deny what they need to retain, in order to offer an illusion of reason in which it is fashionable to believe one's unbelief in open denials of Christian theism.

Penetrating the gloom of thick darkness, Jesus radiates the light of his own personal glory. As the light of Christ shines in the moral darkness a judgement occurs in which many shrink back into the shadows, but some, beginning to see the light of Christ's glory, are drawn towards his light. When God, who dwells in unapproachable light, unveils a little of his glory, brighter than the sun, people fall down and shield their faces from the awesome majesty of the living God!

We see this in John's Gospel, where John desires that his readers see Jesus' glory: the radiant outshining of divine majesty in his wonderful person. Speaking about the Word becoming flesh, making his dwelling with men, John says, 'We have seen his glory, glory as of the only Son from the Father, full of grace and truth' (1:14).

After Jesus performed his first miracle, by turning water into wine at the wedding celebrations in Cana, John records, 'He thus revealed his glory, and his disciples put their faith in him' (2:11). The Christ of Scripture comes to dispel the darkness by the radiance of his glory: 'The people dwelling in darkness have seen a great light, and for those dwelling in the region and shadow of death, on them a light has dawned' (Matt. 4:16). In the light of the risen Lord we see a clear basis for the supreme validity of reason.

Chapter 10

Christ and meaning

All of us believe in evidence in our own lives, whatever we may profess with our amateur philosophical hats on.

Richard Dawkins, *The God Delusion*, p 282

In the context of Dawkins' atheism, we need to probe John's Gospel to further develop a final basis for the validity of our reason, which we need to confirm and reinforce our position that atheism has no final meaning.

One of the most surprising things about what John wrote is how up-to-date and penetrating are the ideas he deals with. Here are words with a timeless, universal appeal.

What he wrote in the first century still has the capacity to reach down into our deepest assumptions with life-transforming answers. Verbal revelation is neither contrary to reason, nor above reason, but given by God, the supreme communicator, as his authoritative word.

John's Gospel addresses profound issues by radical, far-reaching claims from the person of Christ. But just what is the relationship, if any, between Christ and the validity of reason, or even meaning itself?

Our answer must be able to confirm that Christ is the source of final, divine truth: meaningful truth that comes to me objectively from *him*, and not merely from the turbulence of my cerebral molecules. Which will it be — Christ or atheism — confusion or meaning?

Spotlight

In John's Gospel, the spotlight falls upon Jesus, his true humanity and deity, his relationship to the Father, his pre-existence, teaching and miracles, and his death and resurrection — all these bring before us a superlative Christ, a totalitarian Commander, towering in his grace and majesty as Sovereign Lord, lowly Servant and divine Redeemer.

Naturally, we are ruled by a fierce self-will. We love influence, power and prestige, and see Jesus as a threat to our private, sovereign territory. There are also many such who, having started out with a deeply hostile mind-set against Christ, have been brought to bow the knee and yield their all to him. Jesus is sufficient to satisfy the yearnings and aspirations of Jew and Gentile, first century slave and master, fisherman and Rabbi, men and women, degraded outcast, or socially elite.

John opens his Gospel with majestic simplicity:

> In the beginning was the Word, and the Word was with God, and the Word was God. He was in the beginning with God. All things were made through him, and without him was not any thing made that was made. In him was life and the life was the light of men (1:1-4).

In these opening words John begins to locate the source and origin of rationality in the divine 'Word' (from the Greek, *Logos*), who dwells with the Father, but who, as he makes clear (in verse 14), in his incarnation, stooped to live among us. In the first sentence alone, John brings before us five profound realities. Here is a brief summary:

1. There was a genesis: a reported beginning of all things.
2. The Word has an identity, and belongs to an uncreated order of being.
3. The Word has a personal, open relationship with God — is a Person, and *not* merely an idea in the mind of God.
4. The Word has a divine nature and confirms that there is an eternal plurality of Persons in the monotheism of Genesis.
5. The Word is the supreme, divine authority through whom everything was created, *ex nihilo*. All creation is dependent upon him, and has an end goal in view that is *his* purpose.

These categories of relationship, deity, self-existence, personal Creator of all things, exclusive monotheism, time and eternity, communication and meaning, cover a huge range of ultimate issues. The language is not anti-scientific, but deals with a different order of information — divine revelation — not available to scientific research, but without which any meaningful enquiry could not exist. Now, personal being, identity, relationship, significance, and so on, pre-exist the cosmos of created reality.

John's mission as a communicator for Christ continues in the stream of biblical revelation and uses *words* to reveal the supreme 'Word,' the *Logos*. At first glance, the use of *Logos* sounds rather abstract, even coldly impersonal. We noted it in an earlier chapter; now we need to look more closely.

Context

Literature never occurs in a vacuum; there is always a context. And while a Hellenistic Jewish dispersion, or Diaspora, had existed for centuries in what had become the Roman Empire, John had, according to early tradition, ventured into the vast Roman Empire. According to Eusebius (born about 260 AD), John had gone, later in his life, to Ephesus in the province of Asia Minor.

Greek philosophy and mystery religions flourished in Ephesus. Here, also the Christian message had taken root and grown. John already knew that the gospel of Christ was for 'all nations' (Matt. 28:19), and from seeing many lives changed, the Jewish apostle had seen for himself the deep relevance of Christ to the Gentiles. Paul had described their natural condition bleakly, 'without hope and without God in the world' (Ephesians 2:12). The two words 'without God' translate a Greek word, *atheoi,* which is the nearest literal, biblical equivalent to the word 'atheist,' and is used to convey the thought of human existence *without* God.

John wrote his Gospel in a setting of Greek thought and where, as Douglas Groothuis comments, *Logos* was already at home and: 'used in a variety of ways in Greek philosophy, but generally referred to an immanent and impersonal ordering principle in the cosmos.'[1]

John does not merely borrow '*Logos*' and give it a *personal* reference to Christ. John is not a creative theologian, but an inspired apostle. There are already close parallels here with Genesis, where it describes how light suddenly appeared out of primeval darkness, 'And God said, "Let there be light", and there was light' (Gen.1:3). Several times, the Genesis creation account records how, 'God said, "Let — and there was"' (Gen.1:3 etc.). Here the Old Testament gives a background to *Logos*, where God uses his *word* to bring everything into being.

John further unfolds what he means by *Logos* when he adds, 'In him was life, and the life was the light of men' (1:4). What John is saying is that the Jesus whom he knew, whose divine majesty had shone with such striking and gentle radiance, is also the Word, the source of this conscious, personal quality we call 'life.' John describes this life 'In him' as, active, powerful, original — without a beginning: eternal in the Trinitarian relationship, but radiated through creation in his image to illuminate humanity with the light of reason and significance.

Carl Henry comments that the biblical use of *Logos* refers to, 'the foundation of all meaning, and the transcendent personal source and support of the rational, moral, and purposive order of created reality.'[2] And Jaroslav Pelikan confirms that using the name *Logos* shows, 'that what had come in Jesus Christ was also the *Reason and Mind of the cosmos*.'[3]

John — and remember he is a man steeped in Jewish monotheism — is moved to share that the same Jesus he had known and watched closely, is none less than the incarnate God of Genesis, the divine *Logos*, the source of mankind's natural, moral, and rational illumination. And John knows this, not by a well-developed spiritual intuition, but by divine revelation.

What a momentous step for a *Jewish* person, like John, to accept that Jesus was Yahweh incarnate, the I AM! Indeed, many were enabled to accept his deity and awed by deep gratitude for his sacrifice upon the cross. But before we accept such a far-reaching conclusion, we will need to accept that the validity of our thinking has a more profound basis than chemistry alone. How we know we know continues to be crucial, and especially in relation to the identity of Jesus.

When Christians talk about Jesus being the Son of God we do *not* mean, nor ever did in the past, that his Sonship means that he is the offspring of a relationship God had with Mary (or anyone else for that matter). This thought is *meaningless* to Christians. The Bible is clear that God is forever ONE indivisible LORD supreme, existing in three equally divine Persons. John's Gospel and the rest of Scripture are supremely monotheistic, and exclude all forms of multi-gods, polytheism or monistic pantheism.

Consistent with his theme, John's apologetic is profoundly logical. (Interestingly, the English language uses many words — two in the previous sentence — derived from the Greek, '*Logos*'). John begins just where you might expect, with creation, the divine reason, and human rationality. If the divine reason is going to be communicable, a corresponding personal mind with reason grounded in the 'image of God' answers to this awesome objective. Divine verbal revelation assumes rational and responsible recipients. The whole Bible is based upon this premise. John then develops this to account for the terrible effects of the Genesis Fall, which led to spiritual blindness, and moral failure.

Relevant

Into this appalling situation he shows the perfect-fit relevance of Christ's coming. John communicates the gospel, explaining new birth by the Spirit, faith and the gift of eternal life. But the reason John goes back to origins is, perhaps, twofold.

First, he believes it's the logical place to begin to set the meaning of redemption and salvation within a coherent framework of one created, cosmic order.

The Trinitarian monotheism of John's Gospel sets the creation of the cosmos as a single canvas large enough to present the Incarnation, and the Person and work of Christ. The good news John presents has ultimate cosmic dimensions and context. All occurs with an eschatological finality, and within a unified field of knowledge.

There is no excuse for mistaken identities. Jesus is, 'the Word [who] became flesh and dwelt among us,' (1:14). Deity in all his majesty now enters this process of becoming — and enters human nature itself in, what was for the Greek mind, its most shocking expression: physical 'flesh.' John's teaching about Christ confirms his utter deity and true humanity. Jesus is God incarnate.

In the final analysis only God discloses God. This is precisely how the Prologue concludes, 'No one has ever seen God; the only God, who is at the Father's side, he has made him known' (1:18). And he has done this in the most intimate way, coming down to our level through birth to reach into our own humanity.

Secondly, John aims to present the glory of Christ as the revelation of the new Genesis, the good news of new beginnings that mark the eschatological new creation inaugurated by the Son of God, who, in direct continuity, is also the divine agent in the first creation. But now the emphasis is spiritual, personal and communal; individuals become new creations in Christ, related by the one Spirit to Christ and to each other.

As the incarnate, divine *Logos,* Jesus undertakes a teaching ministry in which, during the space of about three short years, he speaks the divine word to men. Soon, the high calling of the apostles becomes a mirror of Christ's own mission. Jesus said as much, when in prayer he said, 'As you sent me into the world, I have sent them into the world' (17:18).

He followed this by expressing how people would trust *him* through the apostles' proclamation, 'I pray also for those who will believe in me through their message' (literally, 'through their *word*') (17:20). Indeed, large numbers of people *did* believe during the early, far-flung Christian expansion. Through his faithful witnesses, Christ continues to speak, as much to Greek philosophers as to Roman slaves, to Jewish priests, as to all classes of men and women, throughout history.

Come to our own day and we see how Dawkins' evolutionary atheism is still feverishly working to erase and banish all the light of this same awesome, majestic Christ from its consciousness. While the darkness frantically tries to block all the many leak holes through which the light of Christ shines, his light penetrates the dark recesses, 'The light shines in the darkness, and the darkness has not overcome it' (1:5). The personal relevance of Christ is above and beyond culture.

He comes to us at the level of what we all share: a common Creator, a single solidarity in our humanity, and our corporate and individual sinfulness. The *Logos* who was with God, and who was God comes as the one God-man of whom John says, 'And the Word became flesh and dwelt among us, and we have seen his glory, glory as of the only Son from the Father, full of grace and truth' (1:14).

Seamless

The Jesus we meet in the New Testament is seamless. In John's Gospel, the one who sits beside Jacob's well, hot, tired and thirsty, who talks to a Samaritan woman about her failed marriages, is Jesus of Nazareth, Christ the king of Israel, the Creator of all things — the I AM, who forgives sins, turns water into wine, raises the dead, and who is both the Lamb of God and the Good Shepherd who gives up his own life for the sheep, and then rises as victor over death!

John's description about the Word taking our nature and *dwelling* in the frail tent of our humanity — as the thought of his Greek suggests — continues with, 'In him was life, and the life was the light of men. The light shines in the darkness, and the darkness has not overcome it' (1:4-5). His descriptions of the *Logos* being Christ the divine Son in his lowly humanity and exalted glory as divine Redeemer upon the cross, are very explicit, and presuppose the validity of meaningful thinking about these high themes, a gift that owes its origin to our creation by the *Logos* himself. Here is the basis for the validity of a true knowledge of God, gained from both the light of nature, and his illumination of the sacred page by the Spirit of God.

Ultimately, John's Gospel has a goal, to bring light and life to people separated from the life of God into his family through a new birth, which produces fruit-bearing disciples of Jesus Christ in spiritual union with him.

Search

So just how is John's Gospel able to help us in this search for meaning? There are two types of answers in John's Gospel. One deals with ultimate explanations that reveal Christ the divine *Logos* is the answer to first-cause type questions; that is, answers that satisfy our thirst for meaningful information, and explanations about cosmic and human origins. Now there is a unity, with Christ at the centre.

The second type deals more with how Christ *himself* is the answer to our need for a personal relationship with God, and begin to apply answers to subjects like peace with God, a personal trust in Christ, the forgiveness of sin, and a true knowledge of God.

If Dawkins really believed that what goes on in his head was only chemistry, why does he get so superheated about issues beyond the reach of chemistry? As we have learned from John's Gospel, the darkness presses relentlessly to extinguish the light. Indeed, the battle for the mind continues to rage superheated, but it's more than a battle about chemistry. If you believe that 'the laws of logic' are merely psychological processes derived from molecular activity, but devoid of any 'transcendental necessity,'[4] or personhood in the image of God, then there is no correspondence with objective truth and falsehood, and no final reason why you should trust your own reason. The basis of Dawkins' naturalism is too narrow to account for what we know about reality, and only leads to the enigma that objective meaning ought not to exist.

A biological theory of language posited on a naturalistic basis is unable to secure the validity of reason. We are from the earth — dust, but created as persons according to a divine design. Ultimately, my reason depends upon God, who as Creator designed its complex master plan. From the first page of the Fourth Gospel we learn that the same *Logos* who has 'written' meaning and significance into reality has also created us with the most amazing mental mirrors, able to collect and reflect what is really *there*, including the curiosity to read and express meaning in verbal propositions. Consider that he *spoke* it all into being in the first place. Everything is pregnant with meaning for which we have an unquenchable thirst to understand and explain using — yes, you're right — *words*!

An open book

Reality is like one vast book. All we need to do is learn how to open it, turn the pages, so to speak, and to read it. But what an amazing *a priori* assumption that is! Now, people are beginning to read more of the book of nature than ever before. Some of the 'small print' in DNA codes, and 'terms and conditions' are beginning to show hallmarks of the least expected. Suddenly we begin to recognise paradigms of the already familiar. Things we thought we had invented are already *there*! God leaves his signature in the least expected places, one of the clearest of which is within. So, just as we would expect: intelligence recognises intelligence.

Ultimately, from a biblical perspective, there is one divine 'theory of information' written into everything, and one unified field of knowledge. Why — doesn't even SETI assume the same? I have already noted how Dawkins and other atheists use this correlation to extract true data and information from the natural world using the validity of their reason and evidence-based processes. Dawkins says we all believe in evidence in our own lives, irrespective of our different philosophical hats. Yes, of course, he's right, we all do.

Science is a discipline, which, like others, is in a position to answer questions as repeatable experiments produce verifiable data. The approach assumes that a trained mind is capable of discovering pre-existing data that is waiting concealed 'out there' and that somehow the whole of objective reality is potentially meaningful, an immense store of coded information that may capitulate, at least, some of its secrets to the mental processes of our research.

The whole enterprise, ultimately assumes the validity of evidence-based reasoning and research, upon which the idea of proof itself depends. So we shall need to reckon carefully with what John says about Jesus being the *Logos* and final source of illuminating life. Now, we may accept how the validity of our thinking process, and our ability to make discoveries in the objective reality answers to a profound correlation between observer and the observed: a true correspondence written into reality by the divine *Logos*.

John's Gospel also reveals the connection between the validity of our rationality, conveyed by 'true light,' and the categories of order, truth and beauty in the universe; that awareness of awesome glory and wonder, which although we appreciate them subjectively, are authentic — they don't just happen to be some bizarre, internal response devoid of any relationship to objective reality, but they correspond, not perfectly, but authentically to what is truly there. Here is the basis for truth and meaning — a profound discovery! So, when I am awed by a fantastic sunset, there is a sense in which, in that encounter, my aesthetic capacity, combined with the marvel of my sight, is 'creating' my response to what is objectively there. This is more than a chemical reaction. Derivatively, we are creators. In response, we offer our thanksgiving, including all the fruits of our scientific research back, not first to the creature, but to the Creator and Lord of all. Then, in the light of our stewardship, we offer our knowledge for the benefit of others.

As all the different parts of reality are seen in relation to their significance and value to Christ the *Logos*, we begin to see that the entire cosmos was called into being for his glory. With him it all begins to make sense. Instead of that elusive equation for a unified field theory, for which Einstein searched all his life, now I know that beyond whatever equation may unify the diversity, the one who ultimately integrates reality and, 'upholds the universe by the word of his power' (Hebrews 1:3) is a *Person*.

Which will it be, Christ or atheism, futility or meaning?

With the truths revealed in John's Gospel, we see that the validity of our reason is grounded in our creation by the *Logos*, a truth that we discover through the illumination of God's grace when he shines, 'in our hearts to give the light of the knowledge of the glory of God in the face of Jesus Christ' (2 Corinthians 4:6).

Chapter 11

Reality and redemption

Miracles are events that are extremely improbable.

Richard Dawkins, *The God Delusion*, p 373

Deep foundations support human thought. For a cornerstone we have offered a biblical basis for the validity of reason, and looked at some of Dawkins' dilemmas in the light of this validity. Now, we need to see how this validity is essential to the meaning of the Christian gospel.

As an atheist, Dawkins believes that the gospel is supremely ridiculous. He believes that Christ's death presented as a 'vicarious punishment' is 'barking mad, as well as viciously unpleasant.'[1] Not confined to atheists, Dawkins, like everyone, is naturally offended by the message of the cross of Christ. There are no surprises here — we meet it every day.

Atheists often use the way they understand evil as a reason for their rejection of Christian belief. It's a very old question — asked by a lot of people besides atheists: if your God is supposed to be both good and all-powerful, how come he seems (if he exists) to let evil flow unchecked to spoil what might have been a better world?

Part of the purpose of this chapter will be to see how Christ's death gives an answer; that God never condones evil or sin, but will even use it, and then finally and forever deal with it, in his time and his way. And also, in view of Dawkins' protest, we shall make an effort to show how Christ's death, at the centre of Christian theism, does make profound sense.

In what might appear, at first glance, to be the most unlikely way, the cross of Christ reveals and upholds God's perfect justice. This is a large subject and I will only sketch an outline.

John's Gospel has two connected themes: first, the person of Christ and, secondly, the saving work of Christ, central to which is his death and resurrection. We have introduced the first in the previous chapter, and now focus on the second.

The meaning of the work of Christ as Saviour and Redeemer is given through verbal revelation, and is consistent with reasoned thought. Here are truths that make final sense. We are not talking about emotional flights of fancy, or mythology, or where reason reigns supreme in critical rationalistic theology. Neither are we talking about miracles as extremely improbable events occurring in a naturalistic universe. But, we are talking about gaining an understanding of the meaning of Jesus' death consistent with the revealed truths of Scripture.

Honoured

Beside the apostle John, we are quickly introduced to another John, who is also well known as 'John the Baptist.' His highly honoured role was to 'Make straight the way for the Lord' (1:23). He came to prepare for Christ's ministry, which would soon eclipse John's work. After making his prophetic role very clear, John was ready to speak about the identity and ministry of Jesus. And the next day, when he saw Jesus, John lost no time in announcing, 'Look the Lamb of God, who takes away the sin of the world!' (1:29).

A startling announcement, even on Judean soil, or anywhere else for that matter! What sounds mystifying in today's secular world would have created different resonances in John's first readers. Here in the Fourth Gospel is the first occurrence of the word 'sin.' John will help us see its meaning and its gravity.

A brief reading of the Old Testament would soon give clues that the 'Lamb of God' was metaphorical. Jesus himself was to make the ultimate sacrifice, and to grasp it, like the early disciples, we need clues from what sacrifice meant in the Old Testament. There we see how the sacrificial system was rich in symbols that gave the key to Jesus' death; a meaning explicitly supported by Jesus' own teaching.

The Passover lamb and the Levitical sin offering are prominent. How could worshippers, barred from acceptance with a holy God, have their sin cleansed? How could they draw near to the living God to obtain peace for a clouded conscience? The answer was, by sacrifice, which God had provided.

Think for a moment about the historical-redemptive context of John's announcement. For about four hundred years the voice of the divinely commissioned prophet had been silent — until God sent John as 'the voice crying in the wilderness.' John the Baptist was sent as a prophetic witness, 'the voice' announcing that Jesus is the Lamb of God.

John's Gospel quickly shows that the identity of the exalted *Logos* is also the Christ, *and* the Lamb of God. But the titles and roles don't seem to fit together. We shrink from giving lowly duties to persons of high rank. Let menial tasks be done by lowly servants, not by persons of rank and dignity. But, suddenly the Christ of the New Testament cuts across our tiny boundaries and offers himself as the final sacrifice for sin: 'I am the good shepherd. The good shepherd lays down his life for the sheep' (10:11). If we thought that suffering was a sign of weakness, Jesus' self-giving makes us think again.

Not as a quick afterthought, or that, unforeseen, he must now capitulate to the cruel demands of the angry mob: Jesus is called the Lamb of God at the *start* of his public ministry.

First promise

One particular person, uniquely called, qualified and sent to accomplish the bearing away of sin. This is supremely a sacrifice offered to God with the object in view of settling a vast moral problem. A problem so immense that no one else could ever carry it out. At the cross, we see the moral perfections of God's purity, holiness and righteousness set against the moral darkness of a truly flawed humanity. Only in light of the character of God as the ultimate reference do moral lawbreaking, human responsibility and sin have any meaning. What once appeared to us as mystical nonsense, now the cross of Christ fully answers to the moral guilt of our rebel darkness.

Jesus was crucified at Passover time, close to the annual commemoration when each Jewish household brought a blemish-free lamb for sacrificial slaughter. Powerful memories were evoked of divine judgement and deliverance, innocent sacrificial victim, redemption — deliverance upon payment of costly price — a new identity, a people rescued by the Lord himself, and thanksgiving: all these and more were bound up in the Passover. We may now see, as the One the Passover lamb anticipated, why Jesus was crucified at Passover time, so that no one misses the connection.

However this may all fit together *now*, step back into the disciples' world as they were confronted by Jesus' crucifixion, and we see a different scene. There, in those bleak hours all the Baptist's previous witness, and Jesus' own teaching about him paying the ransom by his death, vanished from their minds. Instead of watching in amazement Jesus die as the sacrificial Lamb bearing away the sin of the world, they stare in grim horror and dismay, their hopes of a restored Jewish kingdom of God with Jesus their Messianic king on David's throne, and their own high rank — shattered. Yes, the first disciples thought that the concept of a suffering king was absurdly humiliating, especially in one supposed to be destined for universal acclaim and triumph! Confronted with the stark reality of Jesus' death, they simply could not take it in.

Immense change

Later, after Christ's resurrection, his ascension and the outpoured Spirit, an immense change occurs. A life from the death of deepest, depressing, unbelieving despair. From our vantage point we can detect a divine purpose in this. The early disciples, and John was one of them, gained a clear insight into the dark nature of unbelief. They had been into the depths of despair — their dreams smashed. Later, having been rescued from its grip by the transforming grace of God, they had great realism and compassion in dealing with unbelief in the lives of others.

If the good news of Jesus could break through the deepest darkness and bring life and hope, so it would do so for a gloomy world. As the Holy Spirit encouraged their grieving minds, they also began to see how the Old Testament had already spoken about the Suffering Servant's death, and its meaning. Puzzling pieces began to connect: how the Messianic Son of David was *also* the Lord of heaven and earth, who had given himself in redeeming sacrifice. All the Levitical ceremonies and sacrifices that had, for so long, pointed forward, came to an end when Jesus cried from the cross, 'It is finished' (19:30).

Not only do all the signs in John's Gospel point clearly to the deity of Christ, but also all the age-long promises and sacrifices, priests, prophets, kings and the forgiving mercy of the covenant Lord of the Old Testament Scriptures. All lead unerringly to one focal point: 'Behold, the Lamb of God, who takes away the sin of the world!' (1:29).

With Christ as their foundation, they see how his death and resurrection were despair and unbelief-defying realities, fixed as the most secure anchors — acts of God in this world. With this bedrock, they became unflinching, through thick and thin, later calmly facing threats of death, and even death itself.

Witnesses

Of all the overpowering truths we learn from John, none is more central than Jesus is the sacrificial Lamb, without moral taint or flaw, who willingly endured the full weight of sins' judgement. And we learn these truths through verbal revelation — the same teaching that Jesus gave to his disciples. A little later John extends this:

> For God did not send his Son into the world to condemn the world, but in order that the world might be saved through him. Whoever believes in him is not condemned, but whoever does not believe is condemned already, because he has not believed in the name of the only Son of God. And this is the judgement: the light has come into the world, and people loved the darkness rather than the light because their deeds were evil (3:17-19).

In these verses we see the purpose for which God sent his Son. An exalted object is in view, but what lowly condescension it involves! A purpose is in view *not* to judge: the final judgement of the Great Day is held back, as if it would have been entirely fitting at his trial before the Sanhedrin and Pilate for the Son of God suddenly to unveil his terrible majesty, reverse the court, and don the robe of Judge, before his horror-struck audience. But instead, he humbly goes the way of suffering, patient love.

In context, these verses are part of a comment on the previous one (3:16), which speaks, not about judgement, but of an almost unspeakable deliverance from it. Immensely more than judgement merely suspended. Perhaps John would have liked his words read in hushed surprise: 'For God so loved the world that he gave his one and only Son, that whoever believes in him shall not perish but have eternal life' (3:16). Here we are brought face to face with the outpoured love of God.

In an open act of self-giving, the living God, the Creator of all things, presents the morally perfect Son of his love into our world to occupy the place of condemnation that justly belonged to sinners. God thus surrenders — in the almost outrageous sense of giving up *his* own, supreme love — his Son, into that dire judgement that others deserved, so that they 'should not perish but have eternal life.'

Perilous condescension

In this self-disclosure, God rips the veil of his own personal privacy and shares, not in laser letters in the sky, or audible announcements, but in the luminous words of revelation, first written on papyrus or parchment, that he has a nature, beyond measure, of self-sacrificing *love*, a love that expends itself in a mission of perilous condescension.

Love travels so far beyond what *we* thought were its outer limits, controlled by decorum. Now divine love commits the ultimate in self-giving: God *so* loved the world, unlovely — shrouded in spiritual, deathly darkness — damned. Not love on a whim, but purposeful, planned from before time, with a goal of rescuing ones that would otherwise 'perish.' Trying to find words to describe such love, I wrote:

> Here he unveils his shocking majesty and humility, declares himself to be the high and lofty One who inhabits eternity, who for our salvation, descends into our humanity and exalts himself upon a Roman cross between two criminals, near the city garbage dump. In the perfect union of his two natures, he manifests boundless divine power in such appalling humiliation! — Here is unfathomable love! [2]

Love is not something new to God, as if it never existed before there was such a vast need, but in the everlasting, eternal present: 'the Father loves the Son —' (5:20). And it is the infinite fullness of this divine, self-giving that is poured out to secure the rescue of those lost and perishing in sin. Here is one of the most striking consequences of a plurality within the unity of biblical monotheism.

Love must have an object. In John's Gospel we see that object supremely in the Father's love for the Son. The Father gave his Son, as the Son gives himself. Sin, which has caused this terrible rupture and breakdown, is a profound reality for God. At the cross of Christ we see, in a remarkable way, God's integrity vindicated in full.

In light of the holiness of God and the sinfulness of sin, a penal view of Christ's death is the only view that sees divine justice satisfied, *and* sinners delivered freely from the penalty of sin. With Paul, we may then affirm, 'I live by faith in the Son of God, who loved me and gave himself for me' (Galatians 2:20). A penal view of Christ's death is not the only way the New Testament throws light on the meaning of the cross, but it is certainly pivotal to God's way of dealing justly and fully with the guilt and penalty of sin.

Jesus the Lamb of God gave himself to suffer the condemnation others deserved. No one is exempt from the ultimate rebellion: all have sinned and need to receive forgiveness and life. Now, there is a way back, and Christ calls for a personal response, 'And as Moses lifted up the serpent in the wilderness, so must the Son of Man be lifted up, that whoever believes in him may have eternal life' (3:14-15). And again: 'I have come into the world as light, so that whoever believes in me may not remain in darkness' (12:46).

Salvation is the undeserved gift of God from beginning to end. Such an accomplishment by such a Person! Christ admits of no peers or rivals. The glory of Christ is the glory of God. Deity leaves no space for other claimants to his throne. A supreme intolerance of rivals is his by right.

When once we make the supreme discovery of whom Christ is, there is no room for competition! His glory fills all things, and his beauty captivates our hearts like nothing on earth. Wherever the living Christ makes himself known, people come out of the shadows, exposed. Stripped of self-deceit, they fall before the Sovereign Lord confessing their rebel hearts, and call upon him for forgiveness.

As the historic Jesus of the New Testament continues to assert his divine glory, many people are also stumbling back into the shadows of their dark heartland. In light of John 3:16 atheism tightens its blindfold. Some may even wish with a fury that they hadn't seen so much.

Rival

In any reading of the Gospel accounts, it quickly becomes plain that many people met Christ, but they met a Stranger and did not recognise him. His demands were too radical. Supreme irony — somehow, *he* did not fit into *their* universe. Some would like to pull the royal Son of God from his throne and replace him with a puppet-god who moves at their command. But the Christ of John's Gospel will not be trammelled into a man-made pantheon of idols sitting bewildered on an idol shelf.

Atheism is a rival to such exclusive belief, because it is intolerant of all rivals and must, on its own terms, rule and reign supreme. Clearly, it does not openly display such imperial garb, but atheistic thinkers adopt this mindset because it fits their rejection of the supreme authority of divine revelation.

For the time being Dawkins describes the cross of Christ as: 'vicious, sado-masochistic and repellant — barking mad.'[3] A reaction shared by many others, probably including Saul the antagonistic Pharisee, who later as the apostle Paul described a different view of Christ's death: 'In him we have redemption through his blood, the forgiveness of our trespasses, according to the riches of his grace' (Ephesians 1:7).

As far as Dawkins was concerned, to attribute personal existence to God was a sufficiently large delusion to warrant his major polemic against it. Here we are going a *long way* beyond that! We are talking about being personally loved by God *and* personal knowledge of God! We are not talking about Dawkins' naturalistic definition of a miracle. We are talking about direct divine interventions.

Locating a biblical basis for the validity of reason was not an end in itself, but prepared the ground for that subsequent fellowship with God through regeneration in which God in Christ grants a rich, saving knowledge of himself.

Personal

What is the nature of this personal knowledge? Early in Jesus' High Priestly Prayer as he intercedes for all those who have been given him by his Father, he says, 'And this is eternal life, that they may know you the only true God, and Jesus Christ whom you have sent' (17:3).

Personal knowledge of God is not the ultimate mysticism, but vital, intimate communion with God, lost in Adam but gained in Christ. This is kinship at its highest. In our fellowship with God we know his person, his Fatherly care and discipline, his utter forgiving faithfulness and tender mercy.

In the final analysis, the redeemed children of God are authentic moral agents, with the attributes of personality that correspond, on a finite scale, with the personal attributes of our Saviour-God, and which issue in interpersonal fellowship — both reality and redemption.

We have seen that the answer from John's Gospel dethrones our wills from the centre of our moral universe, and sees the light of glory that streams from Christ, the Light of the World. He breaks the chains of our captivity, pulls us out of the trap of our own circular reasoning and enables us to accept his grace and truth.

God's word penetrates into the darkest recesses with life and light — truths of our being the image of God, fallen in Adam but restored, forgiven, reconciled and adopted by grace through faith in Christ's atoning death. Saved by grace, we have fellowship with the Father and the Son. This is eternal life.

Chapter 12

Let's face it

But my belief in evolution is not fundamentalism, and it is not faith, because I know what it would take to change my mind, and I would gladly do so if the necessary evidence were forthcoming.

Richard Dawkins, *The God Delusion*, p 283

My main goal was to show how atheism has no final validity, because to begin with and underlying everything it may claim, it lacks a final validity for reason. The belief that one, understandable, objective reality exists and that our own rationality is a true correlation of that reality, is grounded in biblical theism, but *mirrored* on inconsistent presuppositions in atheism. As we have seen, this rational correlation is the most fundamental assumption of scientific research and discovery — with it atheists carry out genuine research — without it their research lacks coherence, or the means to secure rational proof.

The atheism of Richard Dawkins is an anti-philosophy, which establishes its central identity by saying what it is *not*. Atheism is not a final, unifying worldview, because it has no intrinsic meaning, and no final frame of reference, except the one that it denies.

I suggest it is a fair appraisal of Dawkins' position in *The God Delusion* to say that he presents his atheism as a vehement protest against theism, because he is an anti-theist. If 'atheism' refers to the belief system that denies theism, because it is believed to be invalid, superstitious, irrational, and so on, then 'anti-theist' refers to the nature of an opposition against the legitimacy of theism. Dawkins anti-theistic protest is both vehement and vitriolic.

Atheism is thus on the horns of a giant dilemma that Dawkins may not readily acknowledge: that when he works to deny theism he assumes the legitimacy of reason, and final significance that flow from biblical theism. Atheism must define itself in terms of the theism that it denies.

Atheism draws the apparent legitimacy of its denials from the position it attacks. It has no final legitimacy in its own right, or final base upon which to stand. This is very significant.

Exceptional

Atheism is no ordinary sort of belief! It is unable to advance its own vision of reality without framing it in terms of the one it denies. Atheism cannot stand-alone, and while it claims to be a final, integrating reference point, it must always sustain itself from its central denial. The stance of atheism is reactionary, and continuously energised by the theism that repulses it. Atheism exists in the overarching light of the theism that repels it.

Atheism is characterised by being the arch-opponent, who always keeps his hostility focused on the main goal of denying the final validity of theism! Atheism has no intrinsic basis for the validity of reason from within its own system, and when it denies the final validity of reason grounded on biblical theism, atheism *uses* that *same* validity to deny it *in* theism! Atheistic reasoning refutes itself. Atheism needs to retain what it needs to deny.

When, on atheistic presuppositions, you say there is no final basis beyond chemistry for your reasoning processes, you say more than you intend, because you need a final basis for your reason to make a meaningful denial of theism. When atheism denies the central position of theism it is just as absolutist as the position it denies — that is what atheism is — the supreme anti-thesis, because it intends to deny the final validity of theism without possessing any intrinsic validity of its own! The assumed validity of atheism is a logical fallacy.

On its own terms atheism is irrational, because it rejects the validity of theism but cannot reason against it without using the validity of final and ultimate meaning, which it denies. And if nothing has any final meaning, atheism is also included. You are trapped in the ultimate paradox where truth and falsehood don't have any final meaning, because you need objective truth to deny falsehood.

In consequence, atheism lacks final objectivity and an independent basis for its own validity from which to attack theism. I suggest that Dawkins has not seen the nature of this dilemma, or if he has, he wishes to use the illusion of reason, (probably without seeing it's an illusion of reason), to enhance the plausibility of his arguments.

Perhaps he has seen it in the nature of the 'either/or' — the true or false, based on the classical reasoning of antithesis. He knows secular philosophy has moved on from this sort of thinking and accepts pluralism in a frame where nothing is either finally true or false. But he also knows that pluralism is not going to help him attack theism in the antithetical way he wishes.

There is another very simple explanation for this conundrum. Dawkins is a man in God's world, who breathes theistic air and, in spite of postmodernism, uses the validity of reason that is written into his humanity. This way he will deny that he 'borrows' from theism what, as a man made in the image of God, is already intrinsic to his humanity.

But Dawkins knows that if he is going to deny theism, he must reverse-image all that he knows about God and turn it into denials. It's not surprising, then, to see why Dawkins gets so passionate about trying to demolish theism, because atheists must work hard, trying to block out all of the theistic light that shines in God's world, including the light in their own minds and consciences.

Leaky vessel

Atheism is a leaky vessel, and Dawkins has his work cut out in trying man all the pumps and stop up all the fast-leaking holes. But in spite of which, Dawkins still loves life because so much of it is full of the goodness and wisdom of God. Atheists see it everywhere — in their wonder at the marvels of creation, in their joy of friendship and family, and in their strong, one might nearly say, 'absolute' preference of honesty, loyalty, to be valued, and understood by others. Atheists breathe God's air, take the gifts for granted, and learn to live with the tensions and dilemmas, because being committed to their reaction leaves them no choice.

Deep down, does Dawkins show us a compelling case that atheism is utterly reasonable? Think it through with him and soon most sensible people will cut free from their pernicious nonsense and begin to enjoy the exhilarating air of atheism's pure reasonableness. Mind you, that's not his style, and I seriously doubt whether Dawkins is out to convert people to atheism on the basis of its utter reasonableness, because that's precisely where the central proposition is most vulnerable — just where he hoped it wouldn't let him down.

Indeed, from the way Dawkins writes, there is something still deeper going on. He goes for the jugular, and calls the people he hopes to reason with, 'faith-heads' and 'wingnuts' suffering from 'a pernicious delusion' — hardly a well thought-out polemical strategy. Is this his last resort at shock treatment before the eminent doctor admits the nature of the delusion is utterly impervious to his kind of 'reason'? Perhaps, but ultimately Dawkins' neo-Darwinian atheism, that had seemed to be such an incredibly clever synthesis, isn't the wonderful panacea for all the world's ills that his dreams have cherished. Instead of it being final truth, it has rejected final truth, and must live with the consequences of moral cause and effect.

The more that Darwin raises his consciousness, and the ideas of anthropic principles, luck, and atheistic interpretations of reality, permeate Dawkins' thinking, the more he needs to meditate, especially, on natural selection and 'swim about in it.'[1] As he does so, he moves deeper into a fragmenting worldview and meaninglessness.

Mis-diagnosis

The more he ponders the meaning of his beliefs, and looks out on such a deeply flawed world, the less able he is to find a rational unity for objective reality and human life, and any final meaning in atheism. Trying to resolve this, he targets his anger and frustration against religion, and especially Christian theism. This seems to be the worst culprit!

Whether or not you believe that the moral order is related to a final reference, and that what we now see is abnormal says much about your worldview. Dawkins would certainly reject any final reference, but he also knows something has gone wrong with the world — seriously adrift — but abnormal is going too far for him, because he lacks a 'normal' reference standard of comparison, except himself.

However much he works to squeeze the supposed causes and explanations for the contradictions, and all the immoral religious corruptions into his evolutionary system, they're not at home in it — it's such a wildly speculative force-fit that doesn't give an adequate explanation for such terrible abnormality. Evolution was supposed to deal with it all, but it hasn't.

So, he lashes out at Religion, the universal mother of all grief, madness and folly, the curse of mankind. But how does he *know* the world is so *wrong*? From which deep-seated intuition does he invoke moral law? And against which moral standard does he determine his judgements? The ideals of atheistic humanism? Or just the result of a slight chemical imbalance in his brain, or an unusual gene — if there are no absolutes, it cannot have any moral, objective meaning in his atheism.

Why isn't he simply at peace with all the wonders that evolution has bestowed? Why this blatant misfit, 'Religion,' that wrecks the model of reality he is trying to build? It would have all been so wonderful without Religion — yes, and as 'religion' is mankind's self-made, dark response to his real moral dilemmas, the Christian *agrees* that this continues to blight the world. But, atheism cannot tell Dawkins why he believes there is so much that's wrong; it can only give him a false panacea, and tell him what *not* to believe because it rejects the biblical account of the Genesis Fall.

In the final analysis, the death of all absolutes leads to the death of final meaning. And without an irrational optimistic leap into a future of new, inspired creativity Dawkins has little hope. But from the way he writes, perhaps he is slowly coming to the conclusion, that using the validity of his reason, atheism has no final meaning.

Awesome truth?

After all, if matter is the final reality, did that awesome truth just drop out of the random collision of molecules or subatomic particles? On what basis does Dawkins gather sufficient information to interpret matter and form this final conclusion, to be sure that he knows what's final and what's not? Is it empirically verifiable that matter is the *only* final reality? No, it's a tenet of naturalistic philosophy. A consistently atheistic belief system doesn't exist — it would inescapably borrow theistic assumptions, but the central denial of atheism, the refusal to accept the infinite, rational God, inevitably leads to the death of rational proof and objective meaning.

Certainly, based on a lot of what Dawkins writes in *The God Delusion*, I would not be surprised if this conclusion has already stared him in the face. Atheism essentially is the *big* denial. Personal belief systems are rarely static, especially in active thinkers. As well as being a man on a mission, Dawkins is also a man on a journey.

He knows, just as much as the rest of us that delusions are complex, usually deep-seated and impervious to reason. And yet he thinks that the reasons he advances are going to be so impressive, so overwhelmingly cogent that only a few of the worst cases will ever be able to withstand his powerful rhetoric, and balanced phrases.

He believes any theistic belief, especially biblical Christian theism, to be one of the worst delusions ever to afflict the human race and blithely thinks it will be amenable to a conversion experience to atheism. Especially as he thinks his reasons are grounded on evidence-based science.

Whatever gives him cause for such optimism? Is Dawkins justified in stigmatising a different worldview from his own as a delusion? How does he know we are suffering such a head-in-the-sand, delusory condition, blocking out reality? Dawkins is an optimist, without a foundation, who believes that when the universal validity of reason (which he enjoys, but denies is a gift from God) is pressed into the service of his atheism, even deluded theists will see the light.

Like Saul of Tarsus, shut up in the box of his traditional conservatism, fumed and ranted against the innovators who dared to proclaim the resurrection of Jesus and salvation through him, Dawkins prefers the cover of his atheism, because that's the way he wants to think.

To be a man like Richard Dawkins, trapped inside the box of his schizophrenic naturalism, who can only vent his fury at the madness — where nothing has any ultimate sense, leaves him with terrible dilemmas every day.

Central

I have also explained that the validity of reason, as I have used the expression, in no way refers to the rationalist's belief in the supremacy of reason. But, I have aimed to show how the absolute validity of reason is grounded in biblical theism, which reveals that we were made to listen to God and to love him with all of our *minds*. Our faith is *not* in reason, but in the living God who has given it us to be used for him! This was central to my case.

My key purpose was to show how atheism invalidates its own position by having no intrinsic final basis for the validity of the reasons advanced to support it. This exercise was intended to show that lacking a reasoned base, Dawkins' atheism was self-contradictory.

Early in his argument, Dawkins sets out some basic definitions, and advises that he is 'a dyed-in-the-wool monist,' a view that necessarily denies the supernatural God of theism. As he develops his case, he crosses the line of his monism and grants his opponents the benefit of the doubt by saying, in effect, 'let's accept that God — the *supernatural* God either exists or does not exist,' and goes on to assign high probabilities to atheism, because he already believes in it. He moves away from the antithesis of true or false and tries the probability route, perhaps because he thinks it will appear more reasonable, to those of his many readers who think in postmodern, less absolutist terms than he.

I have already taken some time in showing some of the inner, logical weaknesses of 'probability.' In essence it's similar to the old inadequate 'proofs' for the existence of God, turned around in an effort to support atheism. What does the argument show? That the conclusion you wish to reach is implicit in your starting assumption: the argument appears to prove what you intended because the conclusion, or 'proof' was already taken for granted at the outset. The exercise in 'Probability' shows that Dawkins is an atheistic monist whose naturalistic science-based arguments rely on *a priori* ideological assumptions.

In part of his argument, Dawkins suggests that he was going to have a relatively straightforward job demolishing the belief of those whose 'god' was all of a piece with the religious delusions of mankind, little different from the fairies at the bottom of the garden. But if this demolition is all so rational and straightforward, why so much invective?

If his argument has a coherent and rational basis, why not advance it on that basis so that we may all see it and evaluate its cogency, but to hit out with so much hostility and *angst* against such — in his view — trivial little non-entities seems a trifle short of a proportionate and reasonable response. Is his anger directed at God in a *truly* flawed world, or at a simulated model produced by his thoughts, unrelated to a final reality? He is unable to give up either one or the other — because he really is a man in the image of God. So, he cannot resolve his dilemma, and tells us he is an atheist, angry at how religion is wrecking human civilisation. Has Dawkins a faint suspicion lurking at the back of his mind that he is up against 'someone' rather larger than he cares to let on?

Subjective absolute

Dawkins appears to know which character traits are most appropriate for God. But, if everything is thrown up by evolution, why does he care about objectively ideal character traits? Whatever his reason, he projects his human idealism onto an ideal deity and displays his bias for a 'God' whose moral attributes, he — Dawkins will determine are more appropriate for a mature and moderate God, even if he *doesn't* exist. Why waste your breath describing an ideal 'figment of the imagination'?

Without batting an eyelid, Dawkins establishes himself as the measure of all things, (classical humanism) able to assess the most likely virtues a God ought to possess and the main criteria by which the probability or otherwise of his existence should be evaluated, if he were to be assigned an improbable existence by Dawkins. Of course, Dawkins knows this is par for the course, and that as the God of the Bible is so severely censured by Dawkins' moral code, and fails so miserably, it is not too difficult, as a moral consequence, to award him the least likelihood of possessing objective existence. (Here, for convenience, Dawkins obligingly decides, based on how he invokes moral law that the God whom he most dislikes, correlates with the least probable existence).

Don't forget, Dawkins sets out to try theism by *his* moral scheme of values: a theism he intends to find wanting on the basis of criteria that he — the atheistic judge, will select.

Also, don't forget that Dawkins' central allegation — because that's what it amounted to, that theists were the subjects of a pernicious delusion, was based on the assumption of the validity of his own thinking as a chemical reaction. He believed the results of his own thought processes to be imbued with sufficient validity to reach into the nature of reality and confirm the highly probable, final truth of atheistic monism. And this was all supposed to be empirical science, the opponents of which were 'faith-heads.'

The crunch

Dawkins' central goal was to enlist the services of science to deny the existence of God. Beneath each position, his and mine, are two incompatible worldviews — biblical Christian belief and neo-Darwinian, evolutionary atheism. This is the supreme either/or issue. Now it's time to face the big question. Has he advanced plausible reasons for the high probability of the non-existence of the supernatural God?

He did, after all, tell us in his second chapter (on page 31) that he was later going to 'show' that belief in a supernatural God was 'a pernicious delusion.' Certainly, he has shared his atheistic *belief* that to believe in a supernatural God was a pernicious delusion, but that's a far cry from showing us rational grounds that such a belief *is* a pernicious delusion.

This was the whole point of his book. How shall we fairly evaluate Dawkins' success or otherwise? His most basic assumption was that the validity of *your reason* was sufficient to evaluate his arguments, and sufficient to accept his persuasive case. — Yes, it is rather stating the obvious, but presumably you kept it in mind when you read his book.

Now, if you already think your reasoning and beliefs have a correlation with final realities, *that* basis assumes the validity revealed in biblical theism. But, if you deny the transcendental dimension of human reasoning, I suggest that you have no way of knowing that atheism is either true or false, or that theism is either true or false — or anything else, absolutely, for that matter. Atheists live with the tension of using their knowledge of a transcendental dimension to deny it.

Complex cerebral chemical reactions are unable to give a basis outside of cerebral chemical reactions for a valid thinking process able to reach final absolutes. On the other hand, I have not been trying to demonstrate or prove the existence of God using reason. I have denied that reason is either fitted to attain such goals of logical proof, or disproof. Rather, because we are able to rest our minds on the rational, living God of Christian theism, we are then able to reason and think, knowing that as persons we have minds that transcend materialism.

We have offered a brief defence of the historic Christian position on the verbal inspiration of Scripture. Quite simply, if God has not spoken on subjects such as origins, human failure, destiny, the person of Christ, and his death and resurrection, men and women will remain trapped in utter darkness, baffled and angry, trapped in the web of their own paradoxical rationality.

We have noted how the Genesis Fall brought spiritual and moral ruin upon mankind, leaving us without any self-energising powers of recovery, but notwithstanding this, the remnants of true light, though muffled and distorted, still twinkle and shine inside our own personalities like stars on a dark night. Intelligent Design witnesses that we already know God *is* and that, 'in him we live and move and have our being' (Acts 17:28). But, natural revelation never communicates the content of the gospel as the final remedy for sin: for that we need supernatural revelation.

Valid validity

We have advanced how biblical theism reveals the God-given basis for the validity of thinking. Central is the identification of the divine Logos with the historic person of Jesus Christ and the meaning of his death and resurrection, enlightened by the Holy Spirit. That the *Logos* is the fount of all true meaning communicated both by nature and by sovereign grace, provides a secure and final foundation for the validity of human reason.

From the Prologue of John's Gospel we have seen that Christ the *Logos* has imbued reality with rich significance, and also created us with astonishing mental mirrors, able to collect and reflect objective reality, including the curiosity to possess, interpret and communicate that reality, using complex streams of logos-imbued symbolic code.

Scripture reveals *one* God-given basis the validity of reason and true knowledge. All attempts to find an independent basis for the validity of reason end up with autonomous reason awarding its *own* credibility. God does not depend on my reason — my reason depends on him. And so, I have tried to show that only in biblical theism has the validity of reason a final and secure basis. With one final base for the validity of all true knowledge, we have one universal field of knowledge, of which Christ himself is the source.

We have offered how God-given revelation has supremely described the meaning and relevance of Jesus' death as a completed work and how it effectively deals with sin and guilt. Verbally inspired, divine revelation has touched the depths and scaled the heights of such a great salvation.

3:16

That God should somehow have time for moral rebels speaks about his patience. That he should go to such lengths in forgiving the violations of his perfect justice speaks of undeserved mercy. And that he should do it through the death of his Son reveals the awesome demands of divine justice, and the unspeakable self-sacrificing love of God. That death is a divine sentence due to true moral rebels reveals that Christ's substitutionary death for those with real moral guilt vindicates the integrity of God, and shows his willingness to pay even the supreme price to uphold that integrity.

That he should rescue condemned rebels at such a cost to himself begins to reveal the depths to which God was willing to go to deal with sin, and to have his family with him forever, to behold the glory of the Redeemer's face, the One who loved them before the foundation of the world. On biblical presuppositions there *is* a final answer to the enigma of how I know there is eternal love.

As one coherent, self-disclosure of God, biblical revelation is able to stand by itself. The infinite, rational God has revealed in Scripture final truth about the beginning of the cosmos, a deeply troubled world, and salvation through Christ. With this revelation, reality makes final sense.

'Science'?

Authentic science always takes place within a biblical, theistic worldview with its careful sifting of evidence-based conclusions, however much thinkers, who at heart are rebels against the living God of biblical theism, borrow the assumed validity of their reason for their work.

Where does Dawkins fit into all this? I have no doubt that Richard Dawkins cares passionately about the world. That is beyond dispute. But, for all that, he has been unable to demonstrate the final, rational validity of atheism, and admits that Darwinian evolutionary theory needs some luck when it is applied to account for the cosmological origin of something out of nothing.

In this light, Dawkins knows he might be seen as an innovator of cosmological mythology, but knows the chances of such luck appearing out of nowhere are zero, unless he admits to a baseless optimism. But this was supposed to be 'science.' At the core of atheistic Darwinism is a humanistic ideology — the forward march of humanity without a final goal. Atheism, whether married to neo-Darwinism, or not, is essentially irrational — it is a flight from reality.

I submit, then, for your reasoned reflection (but be careful upon what you rest its validity) that Dawkins' atheism is the ultimate denial of reason, light and truth that flow from biblical theism — and that he knows enough of the same reason, light and truth to turn against them with a marked hostility.

But he also knows that without reason, light and the knowledge of God, he cannot argue, with the appearance of reason, against God and for atheism. His dilemma is deep and profound because he knows that by itself his atheistic thinking leads only to futility. And a position of futility held by a person with a rational mind produces deep tensions and anger.

One resolution
Dawkins gives away his serious dilemma about the ultimate identity when he dismisses God as a 'figment' and then heaps up his invective against Christian theism. Do people usually get so superheated about 'figments of the imagination' that don't fit their worldview? Dawkins shows a marked hostility towards the utter realism of the historic Christian position for a truly flawed world, and confirms it.

I won't ask, 'What *chance* is there for any who may be so hostile?' But I know there is abundant hope for all who will turn and lay down their arms, and turn to Christ. Even such as Saul of Tarsus, who led such a frenzied campaign against the risen Lord and his people, became the apostle Paul, who in later life, could write, 'though formerly I was a blasphemer, — I received mercy' (1 Timothy 1:13).

Here again, are the questions I posed at the end of chapter five, after recalling that the main part of the definition of 'delusion' that Dawkins' accepted was, 'a persistent false belief held in the face of strong contradictory evidence.'

Which leaves Richard Dawkins with a large dilemma: if his case for atheism lacks a rational basis, will he continue to believe the unbelievable? And if his reason and rational correlation with objective reality come from the reason and mind of the living God, why does he use them to deny the undeniable? But, if they don't, why does he work so hard using them as if they did?

What do *you* think?

Notes

Introduction Why Argue?
[1] Richard Dawkins, *The God Delusion*, Bantam Press, London, (The Random House Group Ltd.) 2006, p 5
[2] Dawkins, p 6

Chapter 1 Dawkins and Atheism
[1] Dawkins, p 31
[2] Dawkins, p 5, quoting a Microsoft Word dictionary definition.
[3] Dawkins, p 18
[4] Dawkins, p 31
[5] Dawkins, p 54
[6] Dawkins, p 180
[7] Dawkins, p 180
[8] cited by Dawkins, pp. 13-14 from, *Atheism: A Very Short Introduction*, by Baggini J (2003). By permission of Oxford University Press
[9] Dawkins, p 48
[10] Dawkins, pp. 58-59
[11] Dawkins, p 14
[12] Dawkins, p 50
[13] Dawkins, pp. 2, 3, 114, 115
[14] Dawkins, p 36

[15] *Rationalistic* or *Rationalism* refer to the belief that reality is naturalistic and consists of nothing more than what the senses can perceive and reason apprehend — all is, or potentially is, scientific fact, while *Rationality* refers to the capacity of reasoned or rational thinking that derives, ultimately, from biblical theistic foundations.
[16] Dawkins, p 121
[17] Dawkins, pp. 163-164
[18] Dawkins, p 35

Chapter 2 Christian Theism

[1] R. C. Sproul, *Getting the Gospel Right — The Tie that Binds Evangelicals Together*, Baker Books, Grand Rapids, 1999, p 101
[2] Ronald H. Nash, *Faith and Reason*, Zondervan, Grand Rapids, 1988, p 24
[3] J. I. Packer, *Fundamentalism and the Word of God*, IVF, London, 1958, p 162
[4] Colin Brown, *Philosophy and the Christian Faith*, The Tyndale Press, London, 1969, p 276
[5] David Gooding, *An Unshakeable Kingdom, The Letter of the Hebrews for today*, IVP, 1989
[6] Robert M. Horn, *The book that speaks for itself*, Inter-Varsity Press, London, 1969, p 14
[7] Horn, p 88
[8] Peter Hammond, http://www.frontline.org.za/articles/howreformation_changedworld.htm
[9] Francis Schaeffer, *Escape from Reason*, IVP, London, 1968, pp. 30-31

Chapter 3 The dilemma of a flawed world

[1] Greg L. Bahnsen, ed. Robert R. Booth, *Always Ready — Directions for Defending the Faith*, Covenant Media Foundation, Arkansas, 1996, p 96

[2] Francis Schaeffer, *The God Who Is There*, Hodder and Stoughton, London, 1968, p 99
[3] Schaeffer, pp. 99-100

Chapter 4 The dilemma of humanity

[1] Josh D. McDowell & Thomas Williams, *In Search of Certainty*, Tyndale House Publishers, Wheaton, 2006, p 38
[2] Bruce Milne, *Know the Truth — A handbook of Christian Belief*, Inter-Varsity Press, Leicester, 1982, p 55
[3] C. S. Lewis, *MIRACLES* © C. S. Lewis Pte. Ltd. 1947, 1960, pp. 18-19
[4] Alex McDonald, *Love Minus Zero*, Christian Focus, Fearn, Ross-shire, Scotland, 1989, p 10
[5] McDonald, p 10
[6] McDonald, p 11
[7] Herman Bavinck, *Our Reasonable Faith*, Eerdmans, Michigan, 1956, pp. 205-206
[8] Robert L. Reymond, *New Systematic Theology of the Christian Faith*, Thomas Nelson, Nashville, 1998, p 147 (Hereafter referred to as, *NST*)
[9] Douglas Vickers, *Divine Redemption and the Refuge of Faith*, Reformation Heritage Books, Michigan, 2005, p 113

Chapter 5 Almost certainly

[1] Dawkins, p 113
[2] Dawkins, p 54
[3] Dawkins, p 50
[4] Dawkins, p 113
[5] Dawkins, pp. 119-120
[6] Dawkins, p 120
[7] Dawkins, p 121

[8] Dawkins, p 120
[9] Dawkins, p 121
[10] Dawkins, p 114
[11] Dawkins, p 141
[12] Dawkins, p 143
[13] Dawkins, p 114
[14] Dawkins, p 120
[15] Dawkins, p 50
[16] Edgar Powell, *On Giant's Shoulders*, Day One, 1999, p 130
[17] Powell, p 130
[18] J. B. S. Haldane, (*Possible Worlds*, p 209) quoted by C. S. Lewis in *MIRACLES* © C. S. Lewis Pte. Ltd. 1947, 1960, p 19
[19] Powell, p 130
[20] Dawkins, p 113

Chapter 6 The dilemma of which 'god' to deny
[1] Dawkins, p 158
[2] Dawkins, p 35

Chapter 7 The ultimate paradox
[1] C. S. Lewis, *MERE CHRISTIANITY* © C. S. Lewis Pte. Ltd. 1942, 1943, 1944, 1952, p 42
[2] Cornelius Van Til, *The Defense of the Faith*, Presbyterian and Reformed, Phillipsburg, NJ, 1955, p 396
[3] Dawkins, p 73

Chapter 8 SETI — the search for meaning and significance

Chapter 9 Light in the darkness
[1] All Bible references given by numbers only in this and subsequent chapters refer to John's Gospel.
[2] Robert L. Reymond, *NST*, pp. 56-57

[3] John F. Frame, *Apologetics to the Glory of God*, Presbyterian & Reformed, Phillipsburg, NJ, 1994, p 8, (quoted by Robert L. Reymond in *NST*, footnote, p 57)
[4] McDowell and Williams, *In Search of Certainty*, Tyndale House publishers, Wheaton, 2003, pp. 42-43

Chapter 10 Christ and meaning
[1] Douglas Groothuis, *Revealing the New Age Jesus*, IVP, 1990, p 223
[2] Carl Henry, *God, Revelation and Authority*, Word Books, Waco, Tex., 1979, p 195
[3] Jaroslav Pelikan, *Jesus through the Centuries*, Harper and Row, San Francisco, Calif., p 62, (emphasis his).
[4] Greg L. Bahnsen, *The Great Debate: Does God Exist?* Covenant Media Foundation (CD), 1985

Chapter 11 Reality and redemption
[1] Dawkins, p 253
[2] Michael Austin, *Looking at the Cross — viewing Jesus' death Today*, Exposure Publishing, Cornwall, 2007, pp. 119-120
[3] Dawkins, p 253

Chapter 12 Let's face it
[1] Dawkins, p 117

Printed in the United Kingdom
by Lightning Source UK Ltd.
132315UK00001B/134/P

Head Teacher in Your Pocket

The Essential Guide to Your Prep School Journey

Merinda D'Aprano
with contributions by Elizabeth O'Shea

"One can say too much, even on the best of subjects."
Michel de Montaigne

Published by Merinda D'Aprano

© Merinda D'Aprano 2016
Elizabeth O'Shea comments © Elizabeth O'Shea 2016

ISBN: 978-0-9935503-0-0

All rights reserved. No part of this publication may be
reproduced, stored in a retrieval system, or transmitted
in any form or by any means, without the prior written
permission of the copyright holder.

The right of Merinda D'Aprano to be identified as the
author of this work has been asserted by her in accordance
with the Copyright, Designs and Patents Act, 1988.
The views shared here are entirely those of the author and
contributors, and not those of any organisation to which
they are connected.

Designed by Red Giant, London; rglondon.co.uk
Printed in the UK by Latimer Trend Ltd, Plymouth

Contents

About the author: Merinda D'Aprano iv
About the contributor: Elizabeth O'Shea vi
Acknowledgements vii
Introduction viii

1   Why should I accompany my child through school? 1
2   What should I look for in a quality education? 5
3   How can a school be both holistic and academic? 10
4   Should I choose a single-sex or co-educational school? 13
5   How can I help my child to settle into a new school? 17
6   How can I create a good partnership with the class teacher? 21
7   What is the role of the Head Teacher, and when should I contact them? .. 29
8   What are the rights of my child? 35
9   Why are children so demanding? 40
10 Why is reading so important? 43
11 How can I promote a brave learner? 48
12 Why should I encourage my child to persevere and be committed to things? ... 53
13 Why is it essential to allow my child to experience failure? 60
14 How can I help my child to learn to think? 63
15 How can I build good listening skills in me and my child? 67
16 Do good manners really matter? 71
17 How can I stop my child being bullied by her friends? 76
18 Why does the school think my child is cheating? 82
19 Do I need to get a home tutor? 84
20 Why is it important to be bored? 88
21 What does a school expect from homework? 93
22 What can I do at home to help with basic maths skills? 99
23 Is the Internet safe for my child? 102
24 What do test results mean? 106
25 What should I do if grades are lower than expected? 110
26 How should I read a school report? 115
27 How do I manage parents' evening? 118
28 Why specifically teach life skills to children? 123
29 What is the point of a Forest School or outdoor learning? 127
30 Why and how should I support learning a musical instrument? 130
31 Why are celebration days (or feast days) important? 135
32 What can we do in the holidays? 138

About the author

Merinda D'Aprano

Merinda D'Aprano was born and brought up in Wimbledon, attended Holy Family Convent for Infants, as her mother had done, then Holy Cross Prep School, in Kingston. She then went to St Maur's Convent in Weybridge for her senior education. Her ambition was always to be a teacher, because she loved finding things out and explaining them to others. Her teacher training was at Whitelands College, Roehampton Institute (now Roehampton University), where she returned in 1990 for a Master's degree in Education, and 2013 to begin a Professional Doctorate.

Merinda has had a very varied teaching career, starting out in Brixton and Wandsworth working for the Inner London Education Authority, before moving to the independent sector in 1990, to the Ursuline Prep School in Wimbledon. In 1995, she joined Notre Dame Prep School as Year 4 class teacher and Head of Science. She has followed an interesting career path in the school, holding the posts of Head of RE, Child Protection Officer, Director of Studies and Deputy Head. She was promoted to Head in 2013. During her time at the school, Merinda conceived and developed the humanities programme for the prep school, called TASK, and spoke on this to IAPS heads and Directors of Studies in the local area. In 2012 she was invited to speak internationally in California, and conducted a brief lecture tour in the Company of Mary

> **MERINDA IS AN EXPERIENCED ISI INSPECTOR AS WELL AS A WELL-RESPECTED EDUCATIONALIST. SHE HAS BEEN RECRUITED TO SUPPORT SCHOOLS AND COLLEAGUES IN RUNNING COURSES, HEAD'S RECRUITMENT AND EDUCATIONAL CONSULTANCY**

Our Lady Schools, speaking to a range of educators about approaches to teaching.

Merinda is an experienced ISI inspector as well as a well-respected educationalist. She has been recruited to support schools and colleagues in running courses, Head's recruitment and educational consultancy. She writes a regular blog and articles for magazines, some of which are collected in this book.

In her daily life, Merinda is also a musician, composer and chorister, singing regularly in cathedrals and churches. Her musical works have been performed by choral societies, semi-professional choirs and churches as well as at school. She regularly plays her bodhrán (an Irish frame drum) in gigs and at church. Merinda is also a self-confessed foodie, and loves to cook and entertain, especially for her wonderful friends and family, including five nieces and nephews. She grows her own fruit and vegetables, forages for ingredients on the local common, and makes wine, cider and beer in her kitchen. On rainy days, she paints seascapes in oil, watched by her naughty cat, Florin.

You can read her educational blog at http://ndpsedblog.blogspot.co.uk

"Learned we may be with another's learning: we can only be wise with our own thoughts."
Michel de Montaigne

About the contributor

Elizabeth O'Shea

Elizabeth is a parenting specialist who lives with her husband, Maurice, near Horsham. She has four children – Emily, Sophie, George and Katie. When her youngest child was born she had four children aged 0, 2, 4 and 6!

Born in Wimbledon, Elizabeth was raised in Chertsey, Surrey. After completing her degree in Nursing at Kings College, London, she worked as a nurse, later becoming a Nursing Sister at Dulwich hospital.

After taking a career break to raise her children, she went on to teach Positively Parenting classes in 2000, and returned to nursing to help nurses back to the NHS, and to work in Accident and Emergency. She worked for more than five years for Home-Start, then with the YMCA helping parents-to-be who had suffered abuse or neglect in the past to break the cycle. She also trained to run four different types of parenting courses.

In 2011 Elizabeth set up her own business, Parent 4 Success.

As a parenting specialist, Elizabeth appears regularly on BBC TV and Radio. She appeared on BBC1 *Breakfast* (with Charlie and Louise on the sofa), has been interviewed on Radio 4 *Woman's Hour*, The BBC World Service, and appears regularly on Sky News. She has also been featured in the *Guardian Weekend* magazine with other top negotiators showing parents how to negotiate with children.

Elizabeth mainly works with parents to help them manage issues with their children's behaviour, such as sleep, aggression, homework, bullying, friendship issues, sibling rivalry, difficult teenagers, stealing, children going off the rails, and helping children cope with divorce or working parents. She also runs parenting courses and workshops in schools, and is invited as a speaker to talk to parents and professionals about parenting issues.

You can read Elizabeth's parenting blogs on her website *www.parent4success.com* which attracts thousands of visitors each month.

Acknowledgements

With grateful thanks to...

Previous portions of this book have appeared as a blog written by me, 'EdChef' – *http://ndpsedblog.blogspot.co.uk* – and published on the Internet.

I would like to thank all who have helped to bring this book to fruition, especially:

Tamsin Cousins for editing the text, helping and encouraging me, Helen Evans for correcting my dreadful spelling and missing words, and generally knowing what I am trying to say, Stephen Cviic for checking the text, and Ian Bond for making the whole thing greater than the sum of its parts.

Contributors: Elizabeth O'Shea, for leaping into the project with such enthusiasm, Anne Thompson, for help with the chapter on reading – and generally pointing me in the way of helpful literature, Julie Shaw, for the chapter pertaining to music, and Melanie Lehmann for helping me to understand more about EYFS and Forest schools. Fellow Heads Judith Fremont-Barnes and Samantha Sawyer, for their useful advice and ideas for future projects.

I am sincerely grateful to David and Louise Plummer, Millie Hart, Anna King, Tracy Jones and all the staff at Notre Dame School who have read and digested, suggested changes and ideas, and encouraged the conversion of my blogs into a proper book!

Thanks also to the Sisters of the Company of Mary Our Lady, and Governors of Notre Dame School, for all their generous help and support.

Finally, of course, rather belated thanks to my late father, Frank D'Aprano, and my long-suffering mother, Terry D'Aprano, and my siblings Marisa and John who were my first and best educators, and who inadvertently made a teacher out of me.

You will find occasional short quotes throughout the book attributed to Michel de Montaigne, a sixteenth century French philosopher whose outlook and much of whose writing about the education of children has had a strong influence on modern educational theory. He was also uncle of St Jeanne de Lestonnac, the foundress of the first schools specifically for the education of girls in the seventeenth century (including my own school, Notre Dame). His words have a very special relevance for me and for schools seeking to educate for life rather than just for the next set of qualifications.

Introduction

Helping you on your journey...

This book is intended to support parents considering or embarking on a prep school career with their children. My own school is a girls' prep school, but with boys welcome up to age seven, as was common in prep schools in the past. This allows for convenience in the 'infant' (sometimes called 'pre-prep') years, when parents may want to be close by and with the reassurance that all siblings are together. My school then moves on to be a school which is focused on the attainment of girls as they go through the 'junior' classes (aged 7–11) in preparing for 11+ and secondary education. More often than not in the text I will refer to 'daughters' – but the information tends to be the same for sons. You are sure to be able to interpret this.

My own teaching career has spanned thirty years in several different types of schools, accompanying thousands of children in their learning journeys, firstly as a play leader, then a class teacher and later as Head of Department and Deputy Head. Now, as a Head Teacher, I believe my most critical and crucial role is in helping whole families on our shared journey, allowing their children to achieve their best in all areas of life and to grow into wonderful people. I have been helped in my training by hundreds of children, parents and wise colleagues, as well as by reading a great deal of educational research and shared examples of good and bad practice that fascinate me and enhance my educational view. I am not a parent myself, but I am a dedicated, enthusiastic and experienced educator, and I am constantly grateful to all who have shown me how to be the best teacher I can be.

You will also see comments from my trusted friend and advisor, Elizabeth O'Shea, who works professionally with parents and children from the other side of the educational fence. Between us I believe we can offer friendly and accessible advice to anyone negotiating the complex communication channels between home and school, and enable you to shape your expectations in line with what a school should be expected to offer (and a few clues as to what they should not, as professionals, reasonably be expected to do…).

Any mistakes here are my own, and the opinions expressed are kindly meant and intended to be reassuring or helpful. I do hope that some of my insight into school, the language that teachers speak, and the learning behaviours of your children will be useful in some small way as you navigate the twisting paths you are made to walk as you accompany your children through school.

Chapter 1

Why should I accompany my child through school?

1. Why should I accompany my child through school?

School is a long and daunting journey for the whole family.

It is to be hoped that your chosen school has all the things that make you feel reassured and confident that all bases have been taken care of. More of this in the next chapter but, for now, consider that you are on a roller-coaster journey, bringing your child to adulthood.

You obviously want him or her to really enjoy school and for the experience to be the best possible with all the advantages you can muster, including a happy daily life, kind and interesting friends, good experiences, excellent results, and smooth problem-free relationships with teachers and adults. Through this fantastic school experience she will become an incredible member of society: fulfilled, happy, compassionate, articulate, interested, inquisitive, competent and highly qualified. However, this clever, flexible, well-adjusted young person is unlikely to exist if she has not been allowed to find her own paths, to become an independent learner and thinker, to have had the chance to take the reins, to manage first on guided paths and then to choose her own way with skill and confidence. Your presence is essential, creating a partnership between home and school, and helping your child to understand that the road is consistent, reasonable and that you are there to support. Nevertheless, it is their journey and they need to take over as often as possible throughout the 15 years of school life, so that university or the world of work are places that your young adult can take by storm.

Consequently, you are called on to accompany this journey, because along the way you will need to guide, support, encourage and sometimes to challenge. You will need to know when to wade in and when to step away. You will need to discern when your child is holding back, doing her best or using her natural self-centred view of the road to seek your attention, or to manipulate the outcome. You will need to learn to praise effort rather than just results, and to listen and listen and listen (until you are exhausted) to the good, the bad, the improbable and the incredible. You will need to trust the school and learn to communicate with them quickly and calmly when you need help, and to accept their suggestions for dealing with issues that you may not see or experience at home.

Children are wonderful creatures: funny, creative, clever and imaginative, but also demanding in the pursuit of self-interested 'fairness' or self-acclaim. The best help you can often give is to love them and encourage them, and take their anxieties and frustrations in your stride with a kind word as they strive to find their way on that journey. Challenging character traits are natural and, unless you are superhuman, you will be swept up easily by your nearest and dearest into fighting their battles and seeing the world from their perspective (some of which is good, and some of which will teach them that the world can be controlled with tears, tantrums or half-truths). The more intellectual your child, the more likely he or she is to need training in wise judgement or even objective honesty, because those important years of imagining that she is a princess (or he is a superhero) will linger when he or she is challenged or annoyed, especially if you have given in at times or fought their corner for them just to make immediate life a little easier. As a general rule, I do hope children will come to understand that fairness sometimes needs to be put aside in the interests of kindness, and that a little compassion and forbearance will make life far easier than an insistence on justice.

We read of 'tiger mothers' who fight their children's battles for them, 'helicopter parents' who cannot stay away and hover over the classroom to check up on the teacher, and 'snowplough' families who remove every obstacle to success for their children. Sadly, their children will be impoverished by their experience of the world and will be well behind their peers in independence, ability to cope with change or challenge. These children will be afraid to perform in case of failure and disinterested in responsibility in their own lives, because it is apparent to them that their problems really belong to and are controlled by their parents. They may appear to be highly successful, and they may attain A* grades, but their achievement ▶

> "THIS CLEVER, FLEXIBLE, WELL-ADJUSTED YOUNG PERSON IS UNLIKELY TO EXIST IF SHE HAS NOT BEEN ALLOWED TO FIND HER OWN PATHS."

1. Why should I accompany my child through school?

will be short-lived if it is shallow-rooted and their self-esteem is based on a parent wading in with a rescue. Minimising all risk and hiding from failure will lead to reduced learning.

If children cannot take responsibility for making improvements, they will instead blame circumstances and situations for what goes wrong, or will see life as unfair, rather than trying to solve problems for themselves and grasping drawbacks as signposts to new pathways and opportunities. Thus, the greatest efforts to love and help your children need to be tempered by the understanding that you are accompanying the journey, not carrying your child or making them walk in your footsteps or on paths you have cleared for them. Let them fearlessly take the lead over the trip hazards and the cracks, secure in the knowledge you will advise, listen, encourage and praise, and that they can always run back to you for help, but that it is their journey.

Supporting academic work is obviously important, but is not an end in itself, because creating an intellectually discriminating learner will mean encouraging co-curricular (extra-curricular) activities, games and clubs, physical health and social development. All these are referred to in the next few chapters, and the titles of each will guide you to areas you may wish to consider. ■

ELIZABETH SAYS…

It's really important for parents to help their children learn to cope with adversity and disappointments. There will be many times in your daughter's life where she will need to experience failure. When that happens, let her feel the frustration, get through it, dust herself down and learn from the experience. Hopefully with the determination to improve the next time. Every time you blame someone else for your daughter's disappointment, make light of it, or try to distract her out of it, you deny her the opportunity to learn coping skills that she'll need later in life.

Chapter 2

What should I look for in a quality education?

2. What should I look for in a quality education?

> **Every parent wants a quality school for their child; a school offering high academic attainment, excellent pastoral care, outstanding facilities, and opportunities for each child to stand out from the crowd.**

Searching for a school, therefore, becomes a quest for the Holy Grail, where glossy prospectuses and league tables become the artificial, and somewhat unreliable, lens through which schools are examined. However, long experience as an educator has taught me that unequivocal lifelong success is dependent upon good teaching, great relationships between pupils and dedicated and capable teachers, and the parents, and an emphasis by the whole school on creating learning experiences that challenge and shape the pupils. These things matter far more than former pupils' exam results or the presence of a school golf course! What every parent is right to want is success in the true sense. I have learnt that, for children, this comes from the development of a number of personal qualities, which advance academic skills, and allow for good judgement, creativity, compassion, problem solving and determination. These qualities result in a kind, self-motivated, reliable, wise adult.

Good schools understand this, and offer vibrant education in depth, the quality of which is evident in the range of subjects and activities. This type of education comes into its own by developing the sort of excitement, abilities and skills that enable children to succeed at anything and everything, or at least to have a very good attempt in any sphere, with confidence, perseverance, resilience and enthusiasm. Children who have benefited from the best education have a prime advantage in life, because they succeed at the transformation from pupil to professional to person – not just from child to examination candidate. Schools are the stepping stone to a future in which learning will be ongoing; one where knowledge, skills and creativity form the backbone of effective work, but where rationality, creativity, imagination and confidence are already well established. The workplace of the future is by no means a predictable place, and transferable, flexible skills and a firm foundation in how to find the necessary information will be far more use than rote-learned or regurgitated

> "TOO MANY CHILDREN ARE CRIPPLED BY FEAR OF FAILURE, ESPECIALLY GIRLS, AND THEY NEED THE SUPPORT TO KNOW THAT CLEVER THINKING, WILD IDEAS AND IMAGINATION ARE AS IMPORTANT AS FINDING THE RIGHT ANSWER."

correct answers. In my own school I place a strong emphasis in the primary phase on cross-curricular teaching to strengthen the connections between skills and knowledge that enable pupils to make concrete sense of the world. Teaching in my 'all girls' setting also takes account of the way the female brain works, particularly as children start to reach the abstract stages of thinking in the junior classes (Years 3–6) and encourages an engagement with risk and failure, both of which are a valuable part of any rich and effective learning process.

If I were looking for a good school to undertake the vital process of educating a child for the future, I would look for the following aspects:

- **An emphasis on learning rather than attaining:** a joyful disregard for failure is essential if children are to become independent and confident learners. Too many children are crippled by fear of failure, especially girls, and they need the support to know that clever thinking, wild ideas and imagination are as important as finding the right answer. In my life as a Head Teacher I am often asked to be wise in a crisis. That wisdom comes from encountering failure, untangling complex issues and making judgements through rational and moral critical thinking tempered by human warmth and kindness. Look for cross-curricular projects, a range of clubs, team sports, good music provision, programmes for ▶

2. What should I look for in a quality education?

the gifted and talented and the moral or ethical training within the curriculum. These will show that the school wants your child to become wise.

- **A commitment to collaboration:** recognising ability and effort through collaborative and team activity allows children to develop self-belief, and to recognise relative strengths and weaknesses. All too often parents tell me that their children need more praise to improve their self-esteem before they can succeed. This is a false premise: children already benefit simply from knowing that they have a valuable place in life and that their contribution and participation is valued. Self-esteem grows when children recognise how their own individual effort contributes to the success of the whole. Success follows easily when children feel that they belong, that they have a share in working alongside others, and that their talents and gifts are recognised, useful and valued. Friendship and happiness also rely on collaboration, and doubtless that will also be a priority for all parents. In the modern post-school world, collaborative working is considered the norm, so all to the good if children have some experience of it in their own education. Look for extra-curricular team sports, choirs and orchestras – these will help a great deal, and make sure that classrooms feel purposeful and busy when you visit. A permanently silent classroom is not a good learning environment for anyone.

- **A commitment to high expectations:** it is no good expecting children to do their best unless the school is committed to understanding your child's strengths and weaknesses, striving to build on good foundations, plugging little gaps and regularly communicating with the child to allow them to develop pride in their work, understanding of what their own responsibilities are and cultivating

> "THESE THINGS MATTER FAR MORE THAN FORMER PUPILS' EXAM RESULTS OR THE PRESENCE OF A SCHOOL GOLF COURSE!"

a desire to do well. Obsessive testing is counterproductive, but ask about regular assessment or quizzes, self-evaluation systems, rewards and awards, assemblies praising all kinds of achievements and house systems or competitions which encourage participation and effort as well as success. A good school will also track the scores and data so that they can share realistic expectations with you, confident that their evaluation is evidenced and not just an opinion.

Finding the right school can also depend on the right school aims, so be clear what the school believes it is doing and why. It is not just a servant to your memory of what school was in your day, nor an institution that you can pay to meet your own expectation – usually you can find a mission statement on the website before you visit. It is worth remembering that you are buying into a long-term educational process, not paying for results. Most independent schools (but also local schools, free schools, academies and many nurseries) have that mission statement, and may be 'faith schools' or attached to particular educational philosophies. Even if you have come from a different style of educational background or culture, do not let this put you off. Successful schools may well be using a carefully developed educational or moral philosophy that actually works, have their roots in educational tradition or good international practice, and are worth exploring. All schools are inspected these days too, so you have some objective data in these reports, although it is worth remembering that any inspection only views what is on the report itinerary and may not comment on the things that matter most to you or your child. Use caution in relying on forums and social media for feedback – it is a well-known fact that unhappy moaning about anything happens publicly but happiness tends to be celebrated quietly.

A visit is the best way to see what a school is like – go on an open day to chat to other parents, and then make an appointment to return in order to meet the Head Teacher one-to-one, to see the children in situ, to see how the children view the teachers, to see if you can feel the happy ethos that all will promise. Then you will be able to make a reasoned decision – although it is likely that your heart will tell you more than your head! ∎

Chapter 3

How can a school be both holistic and academic?

3. How can a school be both holistic and academic?

Parents often ask me, with genuine puzzlement, how I can claim that any school can be both holistic and academic.

For many, the concepts are as different from one another as cats and dogs – related to education but fundamentally meaning different things. But I do not believe that to be the case.

In my opinion, the two are essential symbiotic requirements of a first-class quality education: you can only have genuine academic success in an academic tradition that values roundedness, thinking, breadth of understanding, nurture, compassion, physical fitness, flavour of the world beyond the present, aesthetic appreciation, extensive vocabulary, and a well stretched and experienced brain. Similarly, a thoughtful, well-formed, experienced, knowledgeable, well-read, curious, flexible, excited mind must be stretched, and academic disciplines are important in the post-formative years to lead to real success.

It is clear to me that most children have the potential to be whole, thoughtful, academically successful people – members of society who could make a real difference for good in the world. We must enable this in all our children by developing the capacity to be wise, clever and good communicators first, and then inculcating them in the disciplines of the academic world.

Of course, these skills cannot be taught in lessons alone, but must be developed by balancing the ingredients of education for all pupils. It is clear that Educational theory backs up the notion that young children who have been challenged in every direction, and expected to make their way through mixed and multi-disciplined approaches, can later be channelled to use their well-developed learning behaviours to succeed in the more traditional academic areas. Becoming a confident self-starter is essential, and needs perseverance, resilience and an ability to use playfulness, experience and failure as learning tools to make that possible. Once mastered, these skills are in the toolkit for life. It is no coincidence that this is what employers of the future will also be seeking.

This is why, in any good school, there will be a shift in emphasis between prep and senior, because the academic path cannot be adequately and successfully followed if children have had a narrow way leading to ▶

3. How can a school be both holistic and academic?

it, or if they are not later properly focused and prepared to work independently when they are ready. Put simply, children need to be equipped to learn by a great all-round primary phase, and then to have the experiences and knowledge presented to them incrementally throughout the upper junior years and beyond. That will lead to much higher examination attainments than pressing for academic results in the primary phase. Real academic success in education is not about artificially bolstered results in the young; it is about slow maturing and developing to aim for a peak at GCSE and A Levels and on to a brighter future made secure by firm and broad foundations. ∎

> "YOU CAN ONLY HAVE GENUINE ACADEMIC SUCCESS IN AN ACADEMIC TRADITION THAT VALUES ROUNDEDNESS, THINKING, BREADTH OF UNDERSTANDING, NURTURE, COMPASSION, PHYSICAL FITNESS, FLAVOUR OF THE WORLD BEYOND THE PRESENT, AESTHETIC APPRECIATION, EXTENSIVE VOCABULARY, AND A WELL STRETCHED AND EXPERIENCED BRAIN."

Chapter 4
Should I choose a single-sex or co-educational school?

4. Should I choose a single-sex or co-educational school?

In some ways this question has a very simple answer. Research shows that girls do better in single-sex schools (in particular for the secondary phase of education) and boys do better in co-ed (mixed) environments.

It is my belief that for youngest pupils (those up to six or seven), being in a mixed environment does more good than harm. These early experiential years are valuable times for sharing and learning to be human. Children can test their parameters, share educational opportunities, and siblings can remain together, allowing security and reassurance for parents as well as convenience.

So why do girls perform better in single-sex environments? This makes sense for several reasons. Firstly, girls tend towards a more communicative, articulate and less physical style of learning in the classroom and, secondly, they are likely to be made self-conscious or shy by the more physical and assertive learning styles used by older boys. Developmentally, girls mature both physically and neurologically more rapidly than boys, with better fine motor control, and ability to concentrate on small tasks for longer periods of time, and a useful ability to listen actively whilst absorbing information. Single-sex schools for boys and girls make the most of these diverse attributes and, although children do not arrive with stereotyped personalities and skills, the differences are worth noting so that the styles of teaching can be tailored to suit. The gender stereotyping that can occur in mixed schools can be avoided, instead building on the genuine interests of the child and finding her true strengths rather than perceived ones. Girls mature emotionally faster than boys and, while this often means there is a need to address the resultant issues head on and to understand the anxieties, it does help to know that there is at least a level of emotional intelligence and some common ground among their peers that enable girls to develop emotional tools for the future.

Girls' schools have a responsibility to develop the whole person, emotionally and physically as well as academically, and to create aspirations to head for the most highly sought-after professions and places in society. Therefore, confidence is high on the agenda, with added sport, drama, dance and public speaking to allow girls to develop a sense of themselves and to become assertive in the right way when it matters. They aim to take girls beyond what gender stereotypes would imagine.

The curriculum also needs careful management, so that subjects which in the past were considered 'best for boys' such as science, mathematics, design technology and digital technologies are elevated and introduced early and encouraged through the girls' emotional, communicative and creative attributes – all of which come more naturally to girls as a group.

At Notre Dame Preparatory School, the girls are encouraged to undertake a combined humanities and arts approach to learning, using the tools of digital technology, including iPads, data logging, and interactive whiteboards. This is in addition to an education rich in the sciences, which are taught practically but with a curve towards the needs of society. For example, in Year 6 all the girls in my setting undertake a Young First Aider Certificate, learn how to create and deliver presentations on technical scientific knowledge, and learn to set up and manage a debate on ethical issues, as well as following the broader National Curriculum. This initiative is called TASK, with the ▶

> "THE CURRICULUM ALSO NEEDS CAREFUL MANAGEMENT, SO THAT SUBJECTS WHICH IN THE PAST WERE CONSIDERED 'BEST FOR BOYS' SUCH AS SCIENCE, MATHEMATICS, DESIGN TECHNOLOGY AND DIGITAL TECHNOLOGIES ARE ELEVATED AND INTRODUCED EARLY."

4. Should I choose a single-sex or co-educational school?

T standing for thinking – certainly the most important thing for any girl to learn.

In the sporting arena my school offers 'sport for all' sessions, as many girls love participating in team or accuracy sports, but begin by being far less confident than their brothers about experiencing unfamiliar activities or trying out for a team. The idea here is that the more competitive children, as well as those quietly competent, have the freedom to participate and to 'be themselves', which can spur the remaining few into enjoyment and success. The school is then able to offer both competitive and non-competitive sports for the girls to enjoy, and to develop life-long fitness and well-being, away from the enthusiastic proactivity of physically confident boys. Sports ranging from racket sports such as badminton and tennis, to team sports such as hockey, football, lacrosse and netball to other activities such as golf or cross country are offered to bring out the best in each girl. Success breeds success, and girls need to be taught this in order to overcome their reticence and to develop their skills to try new things. The football clubs are particularly popular in girls' schools, because there is no stereotype to confuse those who want to join in and have a great time.

Music and drama have a very immediate pull for girls, and drama groups, choirs, orchestras, ensembles and class activities are able to pick up on themes in other lessons as well as teaching beyond the basic skills and giving them poise. Their relative emotional maturity allows for thoughtful improvising and a nurturing of the different aspects of personality. Girls enjoy humour in the classroom but are less able to cope with sarcasm or jokes that put them into the limelight. Creative lessons allow them to explore this as well as leading to fantastic performances and success in the future. The idea is to capitalise on the feminine side and to develop the skills needed to become an all-round amazing person.

A fear often expressed to me is that girls in single-sex schools will not have the opportunity to get to know boys. However, I ask these people to consider what that might mean for some girls: less chance to play stereotypical boys' sports, a leaning away from sciences and certain technical subjects, a reluctance to be noticed in a classroom and often being uncomfortable in a physically active (and, as many girls see it, aggressive) environment. Boys are a fact of life, and there will be plenty of opportunities throughout life to play and work alongside them. Schools are aware of this, taking care to present role models of successful male teachers alongside the women. However, for some girls, the sanctuary of an all-female class offers the most positive and effective start to the educational journey. ■

Chapter 5

How can I help my child to settle into a new school?

5. How can I help my child to settle into a new school?

> **Most prep schools will be used to children joining the school throughout every year group.**

In some ways, the younger the child the more anxious the parent, although the worry and protectiveness will never really go away and older children may be able to rationalise their feelings more with their parents. Nonetheless, both parents and children are likely to have a few sleepless nights due to a mixture of anxiety and excitement. Nothing solves that worry like a good first day, and that can be supported by a little bit of preparation beforehand.

Most schools will allow a taster day so that your child can make friends in advance, and be familiar with the setting. Many schools do a session in the new classroom before the year ends (for a September start), and will be happy to welcome your child on that day to meet the new teacher and be part of the anticipatory process. There may well be induction days and coffee mornings for you to see the school in action, while your child visits. Make use of all you can, but try not to be worried if you are abroad and cannot visit. Schools want you to feel welcome whenever you arrive, and will do their best to make children feel at home whatever the circumstances.

If there is any way of meeting children from the class and making contact with their families, then do so. Play dates will mean that your child will at least have one existing friend before the first day.

Sleep is essential, so a run of late nights and high excitement at the end of the holiday is likely to be very unhelpful. Try to settle back into the pattern of going to bed and getting up closer to the times required for the school routine. Even teachers feel dreadful if their lie-in is only interrupted on the first day of term.

Finally, and most importantly, try to keep your own anxiety out of sight, because that will affect your child more than anything. If you are worried then they will think there is something to worry about. On the first morning, be as cool as you can be, and try your best to step away from your child's panic by reassuring, laughing with them and reinforcing your excitement because 'this is going to be great'. Your reaction at the end of the day will also be important: try not to grill them about their experience, and do understand that children's response to something overwhelming may be tears.

In my experience children often cry once a parent collects, because they feel relief and/or exhaustion. If you then follow up with questions about what went wrong, then you will have missed the chance to reinforce what went right, and create an excitement about the next and subsequent days. It is worth remembering that if you ask children what was wrong, then they will naturally assume that something must be, and focus on that. Reward them instead for trying hard and for counting the positives. ■

Turn the page to see what Elizabeth says

> "MOST SCHOOLS WILL ALLOW A TASTER DAY SO THAT YOUR CHILD CAN MAKE FRIENDS IN ADVANCE, AND BE FAMILIAR WITH THE SETTING. MANY SCHOOLS DO A SESSION IN THE NEW CLASSROOM BEFORE THE YEAR ENDS (FOR A SEPTEMBER START), AND WILL BE HAPPY TO WELCOME YOUR CHILD ON THAT DAY TO MEET THE NEW TEACHER AND BE PART OF THE ANTICIPATORY PROCESS."

5. How can I help my child to settle into a new school?

ELIZABETH SAYS...

If you have a school prospectus or can access a website, look at it with your child. Talk about what you find out and how it may affect them.

Involve your child when you go out to buy their uniform or any equipment (especially lunch boxes) they will need for school. Let your child try on the new school uniform. Don't forget to tell them how grown up and good they look in it!

If your child is starting primary school, practise skills that they will need at school. This may include putting on their shoes and possibly tying shoelaces, getting changed for PE, even wiping their own bottom! If they are struggling, break the skill into small micro-skills and practise each little bit until your child feels confident.

If your child is going to have a cooked lunch, introduce them to some of the food on the menu over the holidays. If this is going to be a big issue, then work out strategies to help your child cope with unfamiliar foods or new tastes they might try. (I love the suggestion of Noel Janis Norton of having a 'first course' of six to eight tiny amounts (the size of about a quarter of a pea) of different foods, which the child needs to eat before eating the second main course.

Be positive when you talk about the experience of school. At the same time, listen to your child's concerns, empathise with them and ask them how they could deal with any situations they are worried about. If you are feeling emotional about your child going to school, do indeed try to keep it to yourself (at least until they are out of sight on their first day!).

Talk to your child about how to be a good friend. Over the holidays, let them practise the skills of meeting new children, smiling, introducing themselves, taking turns, playing with other children, asking another child what they want to play, and thinking up good games to play, having fun and starting interesting conversations.

Teach your child how to join in a game. Do a little role play where you pretend to be doing something, and your child comes up and asks if he or she can join the game.

Chapter 6

How can I create a good partnership with the class teacher?

6. How can I create a good partnership with the class teacher?

This is a perennial and vital question, and is apparently simple to answer: be nice, keep calm, support your child, and remember not to send Chardonnay-soaked emails at midnight expecting an urgent reply over lost kit or reading levels.

Flippancy apart, the relationship you have with a form teacher is central to your sense of security during the year, even though it is the teachers' relationship with your child that really matters. If you are to feel comfortable, then do stay in touch, remember the teacher is a person with feelings like yours, and try not to pounce with the question 'How is my child doing?' as soon as you see her, even if that's what your inner voice is screaming, because her head may be full of one hundred other things that she has to do before returning to her classroom.

The first contact you have should be as relaxed as you can make it. Although you will naturally want to bombard the new teacher with questions, and a list of your child's needs and wonderful abilities, it is best to simply introduce yourself with a smile and step back for the first three weeks or so to let the teacher bond with your child. That bonding will be a key to success, and allows the teacher to do her job of getting to know the child. Unless the child is new to the school, there will be some data from previous years to indicate academic progress, and generally there will be many other adults who know her. However, the teacher will be building that relationship anew and you do not need to worry if your child loved or hated the previous teacher, because this is a new relationship. Teachers in September are very excited about meeting their new classes and they will work very hard on finding out who your child really is. If you have background information that you know will be useful, drop the teacher a line so that she can look at it when she has a proper reflective moment to consider what you are saying.

For the first few weeks, try to avoid questioning your child as to whether they like their teacher, or think she is good. Your question may be well meant, and may be simply a way to try to reassure yourself, but will colour your child's thinking. The very fact that you ask will put some doubt into their mind; I have known several cases when this becomes a vicious cycle, with the same question going out through several parents and undermining confidence in really good teachers. Similarly, checking on struggles or raw nerves as you pick up at the school gate will always result in tears, even if the day has gone well, so wait a bit and refuel with a drink and a snack before tackling the tricky stuff. If you have a genuine personal concern about the teacher herself, then book a confidential chat with the Head Teacher – the horse's mouth is far more use than gate gossip.

A good relationship with the teacher can be developed by a smile and a happy word at drop-off or collection, as well as using all the means for communication that are provided by the school to indicate your engagement with learning, such as reading diaries, homework notebooks or emails. Your child will tell you enough about the day to establish what is probably happening, and this can be confirmed at a parents' meeting or in a booked slot after school.

Expect reasonable time frames, such as 48 hours for an email reply. Try not to stress the teacher by sending details or requests for that very day via email when they are likely to be teaching, because they will be upset that they missed it and were not able to oblige. Teachers are not generally expected to deal with correspondence during the teaching day, and any good Head will encourage them to eat lunch and take a reasonable breather at break, so that they are refreshed for good teaching during the next session. For anything really urgent, call the school office or the contact that the school suggests, so that an actual person can deal with anything pressing. Similarly, catching the teacher on the way into school as she collects her class can cause accidental chaos. In most schools if there ▶

> "FOR THE FIRST FEW WEEKS, TRY TO AVOID QUESTIONING YOUR CHILD AS TO WHETHER THEY LIKE THEIR TEACHER, OR THINK SHE IS GOOD."

6. How can I create a good partnership with the class teacher?

is a genuine crisis, someone will be able to assist you if you go directly to the office and ask for help.

Do contact the teacher of course, but accept that the their job is to teach and to manage a class of children. This means planning, preparing, teaching, supervising, managing the classroom, marking, umpiring a trickle of their children's needs and disputes, dealing with pastoral issues (sometimes complex and harrowing child protection issues) personal needs such as lunch, loo break, staff meetings, paperwork, reports at certain times of year and then, last of all, the emails and messages from parents. There are very few unwilling or lazy teachers (I know of none), and the few times I have had to chase staff to respond, it is because of pressures of time and work on them and, sometimes, because of pressures in their personal lives. My own team starts well before 8am, and the school remains full of teachers and their own tired children late after teatime (and often during the holidays). Indeed, many teachers appear to live under their desks (along with piles of papers, blunt scissors and mugs of cold coffee). These long hours are filled with the trappings of school life and the demands of paperwork, accountability measures and professional development, as well as the bread and butter of teaching your children.

Once your child reaches the infant class, they will be expected to take some responsibility for themselves and their belongings, so do help them as best you can, and ask the teacher for strategies and support if needed. Try not to fall into the trap of requesting that the teacher does things for your child, such as packing their bag for them every afternoon. Although forgetting things is a dreadful frustration

> "ONCE YOUR CHILD REACHES THE INFANT CLASS, THEY WILL BE EXPECTED TO TAKE SOME RESPONSIBILITY FOR THEMSELVES AND THEIR BELONGINGS, SO DO HELP THEM AS BEST YOU CAN."

when you get home without them, it really isn't practical for the teacher to pack everyone's bags. Most of all, it will not help your child in the long run. Try giving your child a list, or taking a stroll back into the classroom (if the school allows) to look through the bag and the desk together with your child.

Sometimes the teacher may contact you and ask you for a chat or a phone call at your convenience. Try not to panic – these days it is considered good practice for schools to involve parents in discussions about what they are doing and why, or to explain anything awkward or untoward going on in class so that you have as full a picture as possible. It is very common in these situations, especially if dealing with a thorny issue such as fighting with another child, not doing homework, shouting out in class, or failing in a particular topic, for parents to become defensive or angry because this is the first time they have heard about the issue. Remember that the teacher is likely to be aware that this is their first discussion of the topic with you. They will want to come together with you calmly to broach the situation, seek your advice, find solutions and nip in the bud any risk of continuing problems or escalation. There always has to be a first contact, and it is likely that the teacher will have done everything in her power (and according to school policies) to choose the right time for this conversation. Therefore, they will be contacting you so that you can work things out together. Whatever the problem might be, rest assured it will not be the first time the teacher or school has dealt with it, so they will not be trying to judge, blame or undermine you. More often than not they will want to talk through how to approach your child in a way that is sensitive to any circumstances at home, or to discuss things that you may be completely unaware of because your child has avoided telling you.

Trust is paramount to the parent-teacher relationship, and both you and the school can develop this trust effectively by talking through the good, the bad and the ugly, as if they are shared problems and you are all owners of the solution. This is likely to be far more effective than denying that your child would ever be involved in whatever has occurred.

Finally, a few helpful tips:
- **Keep abreast of school events:** the school probably has a regular newsletter or magazine that keeps you up to date with what is going on at school, and it naturally helps if you stay on top of these events. Dates and events will be timetabled and published somewhere such as a website or portal. Check this regularly and try to reply to permission ▶

6. How can I create a good partnership with the class teacher?

requests within the requested time-frame. Paperwork is incredibly bureaucratic and onerous for teachers these days, with a sheaf of forms or online databases to complete before they can plan a trip or event and proceed with confirmation. It is helpful if you can reply early, volunteer to help or make sure your child has everything required according to the information you receive.

- **Label every item your child owns:** this will avoid having to ask the teacher to look for unidentifiable or unnamed items (however distinctive you imagine the one with the loose thread at the collar and the missing button is).

- **Offer to help with reading or activities:** if you have time to help out, this can be an immensely rewarding pastime. However, do not expect to be placed with your child or to speak about your child to the class teacher or anyone else on those occasions. Helping in a school has professional expectations but can be helpful in developing an understanding of how a school functions.

- **Discuss any educational worries with the teacher:** remember, though, that she has experience about reading levels and books, and will be seeing your child work unaided during the school day. Teachers are trained to avoid being swayed by competitive pushing from parents and they will make every effort to keep the pace right for your child. What you see one-to-one when you are helping may not be the same as what the class teacher is seeing in the classroom. If you are unsatisfied after speaking with the teacher, then seek a second opinion from a Director of Studies, Head of Department or Deputy Head.

- **Maintain trust in the school:** do discuss with the teacher, as soon as you can, anything that appears to be damaging your confidence or your trust. Otherwise it could spiral out of control. Teachers are not generally telepathic – they may have no idea that you are worried, angry or upset. Discussing with other parents first can also spread dissent or misinformation, so be brave and head into the school for a chat.

- **Keep discussions about your child with their class teacher:** try to keep your engagement about your child with the person who knows them best and is responsible for them – the teacher. Escalating problems to the Director of Studies or Head of Department should be a next step where necessary, especially if you want to check what the teacher has told you and you have evidence to the contrary. If the teachers and senior managers of the school are doing their job in listening to the problems that you encounter and communicate to them, then everything should be quickly and easily resolved before it becomes entrenched and needs the Head's intervention.

- **Encourage your child to talk to any teacher if they have a problem:** all adults (including the Head) in any school should be prepared to listen to and help any child. It is important that you support the school in empowering your child to participate in problem solving. Do not be afraid that there will be repercussions – teachers do want the best for children and work on the basis that everyone needs a proper hearing. Similarly, don't feel your child will be grilled if you make a complaint; teachers have procedures for dealing with these and are good at managing issues confidentially. However, it is very important that children are encouraged to have a voice to express their own anxieties, views and witness to events. In my experience, children are articulate, unafraid and are great agents for improvement through ideas and plans. Most children truly benefit from being involved in the solution to the issues that trouble them. It is entirely appropriate in social issues for a teacher to talk to the child about his or her perspective or experience, and this will be done sensitively. No child or teacher can be disciplined based on an unsubstantiated complaint, so do expect your child to have to talk it through with someone rather than rely on your report. ▶

> "DO DISCUSS WITH THE TEACHER, AS SOON AS YOU CAN, ANYTHING THAT APPEARS TO BE DAMAGING YOUR CONFIDENCE OR YOUR TRUST. OTHERWISE IT COULD SPIRAL OUT OF CONTROL."

6. How can I create a good partnership with the class teacher?

- **Be open about needing external professional help:** if you think you need external professional help, or you are receiving it, or you believe your child has medical, emotional or any other personal difficulties, then please do be honest with the school. You will not be the first parent seeking further assistance and the school will also benefit from the links and partnerships that can be formed around a child.

- **Do not use other parents as a measure of your child's success:** to get a true assessment ask the teacher – it is what she trained for, and she will have a high level of expertise. If in any doubt, make an appointment to talk to the teacher, and do not wait until the next parents' evening. ■

ELIZABETH SAYS...

Your child's academic achievement can be adversely affected if she picks up that you don't like her teacher, or the way the school does things. If you have any concerns, never voice them in front of your child, and contact the school directly to sort out any misunderstandings or differences in opinions.

One thing that I would also add is never, ever be tempted to do your child's homework. No matter how tired, upset or demanding she is. Teachers need to know that the homework completed is the child's own work. Your role is to provide an environment where you child can complete her homework, with all the equipment they need. And to make sure that your child has sufficient time to complete it. One thing you can do is ask your child to explain what they need to do at the beginning, and to set a timer, so they know that when the time is up her homework is complete. It helps teachers gauge your child's progress if you write a note when your child has spent sufficient time on the piece of work.

If you provide too much help, the teachers are not able to see how well your child has understood the work, and how well she is coping with the homework. But, even more worrying is that your child may become over-reliant on you to help her complete her homework, and that may undermine your child's confidence in being able to do homework independently as they go through the school.

Chapter 7

What is the role of the Head Teacher, and when should I contact the them?

7. What is the role of the Head Teacher, and when should I contact the them?

The Head is the lead professional in the school.

Heads are accountable for the educational, social, and financial outcomes of the school. They are effectively the chief executives of a large and complex organisation, and have overall responsibility for leadership and vision, staffing and managing the school, and for budgets and financial security. Heads work for the governing body, and will have been appointed for their expertise in the educational field, and an aptitude for seeing a whole organisation that needs to be guided and steered to success in a host of ways. A good Head will understand the cogs that need to turn in order to create a successful learning environment for all pupils, and will know that the daily expertise for financial management and smooth running of the school needs to be delegated into the safe hands of competent, confident and trusted senior colleagues whom they will oversee and meet with regularly. The school is an educational establishment, although it is in fact a business which has successful education at its core. Decision making, critical thinking, wise judgement and leadership are the backbone of a good Headship – not presence at every event or rapid agreement to the latest idea or things that work in other schools, nor trying to please themselves or other individual stakeholders.

Heads are expected to manage all staff indirectly or directly, including developing teaching and other responsibilities, maintaining effective systems and planning into the future. They need to ensure that there is adequate challenge and experience for the succession of new leaders in the school in every department. Many schools will employ hundreds of people even though the teaching staff may be relatively small, and the Head is effectively the face of the employer.

Children are of course central to the Head's mission, and it is likely that many hours will be spent reviewing pupil progress, teaching plans and child welfare with the Director of Studies and the teachers. In addition, they will spend time visiting classes, doing weekly learning walks and talking to children. This also extends to seeing children who have excelled in any way so they can be praised and congratulated personally (and also those who need a sterner word!).

The educational direction of the school, underpinned by research and experience,

> "A GOOD HEAD WILL UNDERSTAND THE COGS THAT NEED TO TURN IN ORDER TO CREATE A SUCCESSFUL LEARNING ENVIRONMENT FOR ALL PUPILS."

as well as deep knowledge of the learning in each classroom, is firmly under the direction of the Head. They will be supported by a leadership team for educational aspects – often someone in charge of academics, someone with pastoral responsibilities and perhaps someone with responsibility for particular age groups such as nursery or sixth form. These people will meet regularly, often formally, more than once a week, to share issues and to make decisions. Outcomes will also be discussed and at each meeting the key questions, 'What is best for the children?' and, 'What might enhance the learning?' are asked and considered. Parental concerns or individual pupils may well be discussed, but the team has a responsibility to all children in the school, and will seek to understand the widest possible picture.

As the lead teacher of the school, the Head will usually take assemblies and give a strong lead in behaviour management. In a faith school, alongside the chaplain, the Head will be a faith leader, and will give witness to those beliefs valued by the school. Often they will be central to any services and faith groups.

Heads also manage staff, including performance management, quality assurance and disciplinary or capability issues. The Head will have a team led by the Bursar (or Financial Controller, or similar title) who runs financial, administrative and estates management, and a team of support staff and maintenance workers, as well as contract staff for catering and cleaning. The Head will also oversee and evaluate the work of these non-teaching groups ▶

7. What is the role of the Head Teacher, and when should I contact the them?

◀ through regular briefings and updates. Any building work, planning, facilities and contract changes are likely also to fall under this purview. It is vital that the Head be fully up to date with anything that spends the budget provided by parents' fees, to ensure that everything is of acceptable educational merit and will work for the best advantage of all pupils. Independent schools are charitable foundations, and so the achievement of the school's charitable aims and its public benefit also fall under the remit of the Head.

Thus, the Head's day is likely to be filled with regular meetings regarding the various aspects of running a school as well as dealing with queries from stakeholders within the school. It is important that a Head is able to build relationships of trust with all they work with, to enable them to delegate tasks, ensure that everything is properly completed in line with school policy, and ensure that nothing slips between the cracks. Often there are offsite meetings with professional bodies (eg, GSA, CISC, IAPS, ISI) which Heads are expected to attend in order to remain within those organisations. In addition, there are regular formal internal meetings with a series of Governors' committees in each area that enable a constant and accurate report to the entire governing body. Sadly, the days of knocking on the Head's door and finding them free to see someone on an ad-hoc basis are gone.

On occasion, an issue that is raised to a member of the leadership team (or the Head's PA) by a parent, staff member or child is sufficiently concerning to be brought immediately to the Head. They will then investigate the issue and act as appropriate, and within very clear

> "A GOOD HEAD'S PA IS A REALLY INVALUABLE PERSON, AND WILL KNOW WHEN IT IS THE BEST TIME FOR THE HEAD TO CONSIDER PARTICULAR REQUESTS."

regulatory guidelines. In cases of difficulty, the governors' advice may be sought, or that of professional bodies to which the school belongs, such as GSA or IAPS. Child protection is key, and at any one time the Head could be dealing with a number of painful and complex cases with the Child Protection Officer of the school and with external agencies. All of these tasks are likely to fill the gaps in a very busy schedule.

Heads will contend with hundreds of emails each day, which require focused attention, and response or redirection, if the school is to remain at the cutting edge of educational success. If you send an email to the Head it is probably best to send it via the Head's PA. This way it can either be forwarded to the Head or passed to someone who is available at shorter notice or is more able to answer your query. Do not be too surprised if the reply to a concern or query therefore comes from another respondent; the Head and PA will always make sure that the person best suited to answer is the person who does so. This is done not to push items away but to ensure that the organisation has good leadership. If everything was channelled via the Head, this would impede reasonable decision making, proper accountability and certainly delay prompt action. Similarly, most Heads will welcome feedback, but are unlikely to make sweeping changes to systems that already suit the school's way of working and that match the aims of what is best and expected for the children.

It is useful to have feedback from parents, which can be considered carefully, so do make the best of any opportunities to chat and suggest what you can to the Head, or to send emails with positive comments and ideas as well as negatives or improvements.

A good Head's PA is a really invaluable person, and will know when it is the best time for the Head to consider particular requests, so emailing or ringing the Head's PA may be your best measure of when to tackle something. Typically, a Head will be fully booked a week ahead, so generally only the most urgent issues will be able to be fitted in sooner and the Head will be keen to allow for this. Critical issues such as teacher conduct, child protection or safety should always be brought immediately to the Head's attention via the PA. Urgent academic or pastoral concerns should be taken immediately to the pastoral/academic deputies or Assistant Head(s) or Director of Studies/Head of Department as appropriate, who will deal with these, involving the Head as necessary. Again, if in any doubt, the Head's PA is the best place to start.

Heads are expected to read, review and analyse educational research and literature ▶

7. What is the role of the Head Teacher, and when should I contact the them?

to allow progress and improvement. This knowledge is used to shape the academic vision through short- and long-term plans and changes in the school. It will form part of the agenda for weekly meetings with teaching staff which allow educational ideas to come to fruition, and can then be properly evaluated and adapted.

Heads' professional, legal and ethical responsibilities are laid down in professional standards regulations, and Heads are accountable for all that happens in the school. Therefore, monitoring, evaluating and critical thinking will be part of each Head's week too, since ensuring success, consistency and rigour in the school is a key professional expectation. The Head usually joins in with parent committee meetings when possible, and will be involved in marketing, writing articles and attending courses, as well as in local educational initiatives with maintained schools and feeder schools. Many Heads like to meet and/or tour prospective parents and to visit any establishments that send children to the school. If the Head is widely known and respected, they will be expected to serve on other governing bodies as educationalists, and offer consultancy and assorted wisdom and support to other Heads and professionals, including recruitment and wider training and quality assurance.

Beyond this, Heads always enjoy seeing their own pupils on the sports field and in the theatre and concert arena, wherever and whenever possible. If you are lucky, you may catch the Head as they escape from their office early or late in the day to greet pupils and parents, partly because they remember how much they liked teaching in the first place! They will naturally be pleased to see you and always look forward to a chance to hear your views. However, while it may be reassuring to see the Head and to have a chance to catch them and chat it is worth remembering that when they are not seen it is still the case that the Head is working on behalf of you and your children to their fullest ability. ∎

> "IT IS IMPORTANT THAT A HEAD IS ABLE TO BUILD RELATIONSHIPS OF TRUST WITH ALL THEY WORK WITH."

Chapter 8
What are the rights of my child?

8. What are the rights of my child?

For a good education in a school to be properly child-focused, the whole staff, including the teachers and everyone else working in the school, must understand and be determined that children are valued, loved, appreciated.

Their needs and abilities must be taken into account as part of the planning of their educational experience. This is a right that should be enshrined in the teaching and learning policies of the school.

There are some corresponding rights that the child has at home and at school that will also make their experience positive, allowing them to get the very best out of the educational encounter:

- Firstly, they have the right to structure and consistency in their lives. Without this they can become uncertain and even afraid, and will find it hard to cope with the timetable and systems of school life and the world beyond.
- The right to a good night's sleep. Make them go to bed regularly at whatever time this needs to be for them – and probably earlier than you may imagine. Teachers see far too many tired children during the day, who get tearful very easily or find it difficult to listen or follow instructions. Tired nursery-aged children will find socialising very difficult, and can appear bad tempered or overly timid.
- The right to be prepared for the next day at school. Help your child sort their things out before bed, and go through with them what might be happening and what they might need to have packed.
- The right to understand that their actions have consequences – not next time, but this time – and a discussion to help them understand what to do next time. This helps children to understand and set their own boundaries. Be wary of harsh or ongoing punishment that creates resentment, but don't be afraid to make a clear statement about what is acceptable and what is not. Unfortunately, you do need to be consistent with carrying out these consequences and stick to them – every time you give in will lead to another attempt to create boundaries and potentially make your word or opinion worth a bit less.

- The right to learn to work hard, in order to achieve what they are capable of, without the handicap of excuses that hinder their progress rather than help.
- The right to be rewarded for the good things they do and say and think.
- The right to hear 'yes', when their requests are reasonable.
- The right to hear 'no' when they are being unreasonable, to help them to make sense of their place in the world.
- The right to become increasingly responsible for the things in their lives; with your support and with appropriate age-related scaffolding to support them.
- The right to have another go, make a fresh start and to be given the benefit of the doubt.
- The right to be listened to with a pinch of salt, to help them to understand that their truths may not be the most accurate perspective on an event.
- The right to be given tools and strategies to manage issues on their own, with supportive coaching rather than having the path cleared for them.

These rights are often counter-intuitive to parents and sometimes to teachers, as they don't represent the easiest course of action in a busy day. But we should commit to helping each other. Because a school education is all about helping each child realise that she is one among many, and that he or she has amazing potential, but that his or her gifts and talents will be wasted if they are not used well and wisely, at the right time and with some confidence.

Along the way, teachers will expect children's rights to be balanced by the responsibilities of the pupils (and the families they go home to every night). Pupils must learn that they cannot achieve just because they have an eye on what they hope to achieve. Children will have to learn that hard work is essential. They need to be reassured that help is always available and that they must know how to ask for it. You can help and encourage them with this. They will be expected to recognise opportunities, even if they seem as if they may be initially more work than fun, such ▶

> "I BELIEVE THAT CHILDREN HAVE A RIGHT TO LEARN TO ACCEPT (IF NOT TO WELCOME) FAILURE."

8. What are the rights of my child?

as taking up musical instruments that require practice. They need to know that learning to cope with failure is enriching; that persistence is essential, and that success is rarely instant. It will help them to understand that practice does indeed make better if not always perfect. At home a good attempt to set up routines of homework and practice will really help, and a little bribery goes a long way in making the dull things seem a little more attractive. Young people will also go further in life if they realise that courtesy does matter, that 'please' and 'thank you' are non-negotiable, that listening is essential and that measured responses are good. Successful people know that struggle and effort develop character and self-esteem and accomplishment, and that along the way there are many hands that will hold them when they slip or fall.

I believe that children have a right to learn to accept (if not to welcome) failure. FAIL can stand for First Attempt In Learning. It is in fact the route to success. We all need to be wary of how cultural examples such as Saturday night singing shows can fool our young people into thinking that they can achieve without talent or hard work, just because they really desperately want to, or because a dying grandmother wishes it. As adults, we know how unrealistic an expectation that is, but we often resist upsetting our children young, and we want them to have hope, so we don't tell them how empty that route is, often until it is too late.

So, I urge you, consider what these educational rights are for in childhood. It might be a time when they have an

> **"SUCCESSFUL PEOPLE KNOW THAT STRUGGLE AND EFFORT DEVELOP CHARACTER AND SELF-ESTEEM AND ACCOMPLISHMENT, AND THAT ALONG THE WAY THERE ARE MANY HANDS THAT WILL HOLD THEM WHEN THEY SLIP OR FALL."**

inalienable right to have fun, to be carefree, to be supported regardless of what they do or say, to occasionally get away with not doing what they are told, to be allowed the freedom to develop independence, to have you fight their battles with them (not for them), and to have showered upon them the things that you may not have had in your childhood. It is all of those, but it is also a right to be trained to be productive, thoughtful and empowered individuals. The truth is that, like making sourdough bread, or fine wine, it takes time, it takes expertise and it takes effort on the part of us all working in partnership, including your children. I would remind us all, however, that training needs to start as soon as the child can listen to you and act for him or herself away from your presence – at school – so do not leave it too late. ■

ELIZABETH SAYS...

Descriptive praise is very useful to enhance a child's self-esteem. 'Descriptive praise' is a description of the exact behaviour you liked, rather than 'evaluative praise' using words like 'fantastic, brilliant, excellent, fabulous, amazing etc. etc.', which don't give your child much information about exactly what they've done to deserve your good opinion.

Using descriptive praise, you might say:
'I like your handwriting. The words are well-spaced, and all the letters are the same size.'
'I just glanced in your bedroom and noticed that you made your bed, opened your curtains and put your pyjamas under your pillow. You're learning to get yourself really organised in the morning!'

Chapter 9

Why are children so demanding?

9. Why are children so demanding?

Recently, I listened to a helpful short article on a magazine programme on the radio about biological imperatives.

This explained that human children are genetically programmed to want, desire and demand far more than they need. This was due to the fact that human parents in past eras had to divide their offerings among many children, and to face difficult circumstances, including lack of food and material belongings. Thus the 'survival of the fittest' in human terms meant a genetic requirement to seek more of the share of what the family had to offer. Therefore, making increasing demands, regardless of what is given, is inbuilt in the child's DNA.

Right up to the present day this demand imperative is inbuilt in our children, and continues to mean that children will make demands based on their needs, but also their desires. In our global, virtual world, this means especially what they perceive others might have that they simply want. This is their human nature. To learn to be great human adults they will have to learn at some point that their expectations are higher than can be reasonably met, and that it is fine to want something they can't have – it is part of life. However, the problem has been somewhat turned on its head by a culture that creates guilt in parents who feel they need to keep up with demands, or at least with the neighbours, and are pressured to offer more and more to their children. Biology tells us that the demands will never end, so we need to find ways to manage expectations and realise that the most important word a child can hear in the right context is 'NO'. You also don't need to feel guilty when you coach your child on what is acceptable.

During Christmas or approaching birthdays the fever of expectation can reach a peak. ▶

> "HUMAN CHILDREN ARE GENETICALLY PROGRAMMED TO WANT, DESIRE AND DEMAND FAR MORE THAN THEY NEED."

9. Why are children so demanding?

◀ Here are a few suggestions to help:
- Enable your child to desire something for someone else – let them choose presents with you for other people.
- Give them the responsibility, a budget and a hint list, and encourage them to keep within its boundaries.
- Help your child to manage delayed gratification – let them want something they cannot have immediately, perhaps they have to save up for it, or do tasks to earn it.
- Make your promises realistic too – children love your time and, if you can organise it, then it can be given freely – without the need for bought entertainment. Most children would love a walk around the park with you listening to them, and an ice cream or a hot chocolate if they can choose. Even a library visit can prove useful by ticking the educational box at the same time.
- Above all, when you say 'no', mean it. Demanding children will in time become demanding teenagers (rude) and demanding adults (lonely) – the power is in your hands! ■

ELIZABETH SAYS...

Parents are also under immense pressure to provide electronic gadgets and time on computer games and programs. While some of these may be educational, make sure you limit your child's use of electronics. Have sensible guidelines and stick to them. Computer games are designed to be addictive. So your child needs your help to learn the self-control they'll need as they progress through school.

Chapter 10

Why is reading so important?

10. Why is reading so important?

Reading is the most important educational skill any child can have.

Throughout history and across many cultures, to be able to read is to be educated. Furthermore, to access a school curriculum, the child's functional reading ability should be at least at the same level as their chronological age:

'Benefits include an increased breadth of vocabulary, pleasure in reading in later life, a better understanding of other cultures, better general knowledge and even a greater insight into human nature.'
(Reading for Pleasure, a research overview, National Literacy Trust 2006)

Good schools have a coherent policy on reading for all pupils, such as 'drop everything and read' lessons, support for weaker readers (including shared reading and additional individual sessions), and reading aloud by teachers to children as often as possible.

In terms of rankings across the globe, children who read more for pleasure are the ones who achieve significantly better than their peers. Furthermore, reading ability in the primary school is the highest indicator of success in public examinations, according to research carried out by the Institute of Education at the University of London. This is true across all subjects, and true regardless of the social or economic group of the families involved. It is also clear that maths and science cannot be taught effectively if reading ability at the appropriate level is limited. Human beings think using language, and information is generated, stored and communicated in written forms as a matter of course in schools. Therefore, without good reading ability, managing to read independently as soon as possible, success in written school subjects including mathematics will be severely hampered.

All of this is unequivocal – if children can read well they will do well. Thus, in most schools the focus on reading is highlighted by a number of regular initiatives reflective of the research findings above, and by occasional events such as celebrating a book week, or World Book Day.

Reading aloud to the child is one strategy that has been demonstrated through research as being particularly effective. This should go on for as many years as possible, certainly throughout the primary school years, but ideally on into secondary. The School Library Association, at the cutting edge of reading research, highlights the fact that reading aloud to children at the end of the day goes far beyond entertainment.

Much of what children learn is what they experience from us. Therefore, we need to be critically aware that we must model reading behaviour as often as possible. Sending a child to bed to read, without your interest or support, may make it appear something unimportant and unworthy of sharing. Additionally, although we all enjoy reading for pleasure at the end of a day, a child may be worn out. It is not a great time for a learning challenge – reading at the end of the day should be strictly an extra pleasure. For tired children, listening to a parent reading is a deeply personal and pleasurable bonding experience, worth fitting in as often as possible.

Do not be fooled by an expressive tone of voice. Your child will learn to do this very early on, with no regard to the content. Words may be skipped, invented or changed, and you will never know because they sound bright and aware. Sharing the text is vital, and so is discussing with the child what they have read. Teachers are all too familiar with competent well-expressed decoding from the children, without any apparent understanding of the context, the plot, or the content. On more than one occasion a child has said to me that she didn't know what was happening in the story, because she wasn't listening as she was reading. The Rose Report in 2006 (national report on success in the curriculum) called this 'barking at print' because decoding phonics (the sounds of the letters) cannot always help the child ▶

> "ON MORE THAN ONE OCCASION A CHILD HAS SAID TO ME THAT SHE DIDN'T KNOW WHAT WAS HAPPENING IN THE STORY, BECAUSE SHE WASN'T LISTENING AS SHE WAS READING."

10. Why is reading so important?

sufficiently unravel the meaning of a piece of writing. This lack of understanding of the written word becomes particularly tricky when it relates to school activities such as comprehension, research or maths problem solving.

Success is impossible if the child cannot read, interpret, internalise and respond. Unfortunately, it is very common for children to be pushed far too fast through reading schemes in a competitive way, which means they are never allowed to develop skills and vocabulary at their own pace. This is the same as building without foundations. Most children will flounder if they are not encouraged to make reading part of a daily routine. Similarly, they may well be mystified about why they are doing badly in class when they are working as hard as they can. Indeed, they might not realise that the tools they have at their disposal simply aren't fit for the job.

There are a few things to look out for at school that will help with reading:
- weekly lessons of reading in class.
- weekly visits to the library.
- library as a lunchtime club or as a place available for regular visits.
- class readers for shared reading aloud.
- teachers reading stories to the classes.
- accelerated reader programmes to motivate and support the most- and least-able readers.
- regular monitoring to ensure reading progress.
- personal encouragement by teachers (and the librarian if there is one), to develop reading choices and interest in different genres.
- individual reading sessions at least weekly throughout pre-prep and lower juniors.
- 'reading for pleasure' promotional activities such as theme days and author visits.

> "UNFORTUNATELY, IT IS VERY COMMON FOR CHILDREN TO BE PUSHED FAR TOO FAST THROUGH READING SCHEMES IN A COMPETITIVE WAY."

What you can do to help:
- Promote and highlight reading through modelling your own reading behaviour.
- Read aloud to your child as often as possible.
- Share the reading books that your child brings home with them, but without distraction.
- Place the focus on reading for pleasure, not on attaining the next level.
- Try to choose books of the right interest level, avoiding anything that will put your child off (use retold classics, not originals).
- Visit the local library regularly and make use of their holiday activities.
- Do let your child choose her own books alongside ones she is given or has been recommended. Don't expect him or her to manage unaided with long, hard books, even if they are at the top of the charts. Perhaps read alternate chapters, or summarise if you have time to read alongside.
- Do not be afraid of big print books, picture books and comics – these are all valid reading materials and all extend ability (for reluctant readers these are particularly useful).
- Make reading a regular part of daily life, not an extended session once a week, and do fill in any book or sheet that informs the teacher of what you have read.
- Use the holidays as a focus time for more reading activities, such as visits to libraries or by encouraging your child to take responsibility for reading information to you on visits to museums and on other trips.
- E-readers, iPads and Kindles are great for presenting books for some children, but try to mix and match with printed books. Handling beautiful books is a pleasure to be shared.
- Finally, top tips for engaging with the pleasure of a book always include making enough time to become immersed. For children who find reading more difficult this can usefully be comics, picture books and children's magazines, rather than the off-putting demand to sit and slog over something that is too hard and cannot be managed independently. I am not talking about reading to improve, or reading to impress, or reading to depress… I am talking about developing the belief that reading can be fun, that stories can have a life of their own, can amuse, entertain, educate and transform. ■

Chapter 11

How can I promote a brave learner?

11. How can I promote a brave learner?

After speaking to the children at my school for several weeks about bravery in learning, I was delighted to have a return match from a class who shared their own stories of bravery with me in an assembly.

They were clearly pleased with their courage and success, and bravery is certainly worth considering in a little more detail.

Being brave is something that was, in all likelihood, introduced to us as toddlers as a negative concept. We were expected to be brave about things that seemed frightening, painful or unknown, such as spiders, grazes or vaccinations. The fearful feelings that being brave gave us will have been difficult to shake ever since. It is, therefore, human nature to protect ourselves from activities that go beyond our confidence, comfort or enjoyment. It is trained into us from a very young age that being brave should always be considered in the light of a possible harmful outcome, pain or failure. Girls are particularly adept at this, and will by school age have developed sophisticated strategies (including being inconsolably upset until the second you give in) to avoid an unwanted challenge.

However, we also know that our own success is likely to be limited if we don't shake ourselves from our comfort zone, embrace things we are not certain about, and make ourselves have a go. Very few people have the ability to take risks comfortably. Some do however and, I must say, it is with great admiration that I watch people undertaking extreme sports, pressurised challenges or developing inventive or even crazy ideas. For most of us, bravery means having a go at something small, measured and slightly unfamiliar. We live in a world of due diligence, calculated risk and critical evaluation. It is no wonder that our children expect to be provided with solid answers and proven paths rather than have to think for themselves, or be challenged to create new knowledge. It is also no surprise that we, in our own insecurity, urge them to follow our paths and not their own.

In fact, giving praise only for producing correct and accurate work has become ▶

11. How can I promote a brave learner?

so horribly endemic in our education process that we have effectively sidelined real creative thinking and getting things right by getting them wrong. We no longer adequately prize working on new concepts, or having mad ideas. We have eschewed inspiration, wild imagining and unlikely connections made in lightning flashes, for more prosaic standard and 'correct' answers, with the onus on the teacher to cover and inculcate every possibility rather than allowing the child to explore.

I fear for children who cannot see past the need to be taught the right answer, who choose not to be brave in their learning, who are afraid to have a go or to face the possibility of short-term failure as one of the reasonable options for what might happen – and cope with that. I worry that we, as teachers and parents, reinforce these fears (perhaps because of our own training), despite the fact that we probably know that real independence, valuable learning and true entrepreneurship comes from being brave, striking out independently and doing something, or even thinking something, that might be seen as different. Bravery allows that leap of faith into the unknown, into the world of potential success and into that essential place where we can, as human learners, really come to know

> "I FEAR FOR CHILDREN WHO CANNOT SEE PAST THE NEED TO BE TAUGHT THE RIGHT ANSWER, WHO CHOOSE NOT TO BE BRAVE IN THEIR LEARNING, WHO ARE AFRAID TO HAVE A GO OR TO FACE THE POSSIBILITY OF SHORT-TERM FAILURE AS ONE OF THE REASONABLE OPTIONS FOR WHAT MIGHT HAPPEN – AND COPE WITH THAT."

ourselves and our strengths and see what needs to be overcome. Only by being brave and by experiencing the consequences with courage, can we develop into whole and incredible people.

I'm not talking here of foolhardiness, of wanton danger, or of misplaced confidence. I'm simply talking about opening the mind to something new, rather than closing it due to inexperience, or by placing too much store on outward success by only attempting what can easily be achieved. In terms of learning behaviour, it is sadly all too common to see children hang back, to say they are not sure when asked a question, or to be coy when expected to express an opinion, rather than having the courage to give it a go. Often a teacher knows full well that a child has the ability and intellect to do more, and it is a real sadness when that child is waiting for one of her peers to answer instead. Girls in particular are very invested in a teacher's praise, and this holds them back from responding if there is any risk of getting it wrong.

In order to help your child, or at least to share the experience, it is worth considering doing something that requires brave learning behaviour. Make or find some opportunities to do something that you wouldn't usually do, or accept a learning challenge that feels a little bit mad. You could embark on this experience with your child, or just quietly on your own. I spoke to a mum recently who was attempting her first marathon and to a teacher who had agreed to prepare and lead a training session although she has never done such a thing before. I have admired members of my staff who signed up to the staff choir to learn to sing together for a public performance (alongside the children) with no previous music reading ability, and spoke to a child about to go to her first ski school with a great fear of heights. I try to encourage the teachers to have a go at new things and to share with their classes the highs and lows of their experiences in order to promote and share good learning behaviours. ▶

> **"IT IS HUMAN NATURE TO PROTECT OURSELVES FROM ACTIVITIES THAT GO BEYOND OUR CONFIDENCE."**

11. How can I promote a brave learner?

In the classroom I have enjoyed listening to six-year-olds trying to reply to their teacher in Spanish amid much hilarity and some fabulous accents, with real bravery in action, especially from a new girl who had only attended one lesson and wanted to take her turn. I was shamed from my position as wallflower and had a go. Although my accent was not as good as the children's, they applauded me, and I was delighted that I had left my anxiety on the side to show my nerve. What these people have in common isn't just wilful bravery; it is the anticipation of great enjoyment, satisfaction and confidence in themselves, and is a fantastic learning experience.

To conclude, you can encourage brave learning by example and by encouragement. The really important thing about bravery is that it allows children to stare at failure and dismiss it as part of the learning process. Praise the bravery and encourage efforts to try new ideas and to follow them through. ■

ELIZABETH SAYS...

If you are interested in really helping your child achieve their full potential and try new things, please read Carol Dweck's book *Mindset: How You Can Fulfil Your Potential* (published by Robinson, 2012). In it she explains that success depends on whether we can help children approach goals with a fixed or growth mindset. And that parents and teachers can foster learning and nurture resilience by helping children to realise that they don't have a fixed level of intelligence. When you stop praising your child for results they achieve and praise them for effort, attitude and perseverance, it will help them perform better academically, and help them to try new things (rather than make them refuse to do something they are not sure they'll do well at.)

Chapter 12

Why should I encourage my child to persevere and to be committed to things?

12. Why should I encourage my child to persevere and to be committed to things?

'Oh, I've quit,' is one of the most disheartening and, sadly, one of the most common things that teachers have to hear from their pupils.

Usually it is in regard to a voluntary club or activity, which the teacher has given up time to organise, and which the child is at liberty to join or to leave at will. Sometimes, however, it is about reading a book, undertaking a project or belonging to a group. No child would be pushed into continuing indefinitely with an activity (especially if causing misery or proving to be too difficult), but the casualness of starting activities that become superseded by other ones on a shifting and regular basis needs careful thought and management. We live in an era of choices, of trying things for size and of changing our minds based on a whim. While it may not be wise to take on new activities such as learning an expensive instrument untried, there is a balance. All of life cannot be simply based on what we really feel like doing today and not doing tomorrow. This is also important if we are to have due regard and respect for the other people involved in the activity, and for the leader or coach who spends time and effort organising it, putting aside time for others rather than putting themselves first.

On the radio recently I heard about a cathedral that was cutting its professional choir by a third to save money. Since I know something about choral music I realised before the presenter did that the choir would be unable to perform adequately, and the choir would soon be thought of as something that was not successful enough to warrant existing at all. It started me thinking about commitment, because keeping up any activities in the school where I am Head is a juggling act of keeping pupils focused and on task, while ensuring they enjoy themselves and understand their contribution to the whole school. Not every moment can be fun, but the collaboration, co-operation and learning that takes place in these activities is second to none, and is indeed often better training for being successful in the future than working under direction in lessons.

Added to which, orchestras, clubs, choirs, sports squads, training squads, reading circles and drama activities cannot continue if each week another child sends a curt message saying: 'I've quit'. New joiners are always welcome, but they cannot be encouraged and developed if the size of the group fluctuates and there is a sliding scale of popularity week-by-week, affecting whether the club is required or desired at all.

In my opinion, commitment and perseverance are two of the most important values we can share in life. Commitment holds the key to so many relationships in life: to our nearest and dearest, to the organisations we join and continue to support, to the jobs we undertake, to our work ethic, our interests, and to all of the other people we accompany on our day-to-day journeys. Some commitments are about obligation – tax returns and bills are commitments we cannot avoid. Others are about the way we take our place in life, balancing the needs of the many societies and people with whom we circulate each day, while other commitments are about our own choices and preferences. Commitment engenders trust and achievement, and this is something that makes life feel worthwhile. Commitment is the thing that enables belonging, purpose and friendship. It also plays a pivotal role in how other people view, judge and value us.

Perseverance is also a vital attribute, as it is the skill that allows children to maintain that commitment to things they may begin to find difficult. Without the will to succeed, to have another go, to deal with challenge, children do find it hard to remain committed to things. They will also need resilience if they are to push through the mistakes and the plateau phase to really become masters of what they are learning.

In schools the teachers have a commitment to the education of the children. They exercise this commitment in front of their classes, but also into the late hours when they are planning, marking and organising for their lessons, and in liaison with others in order to share good practice and develop expertise. They develop committed relationships with the children in their care, on the one hand instructing, guiding ▶

> "COMMITMENT AND PERSEVERANCE ARE TWO OF THE MOST IMPORTANT VALUES WE CAN SHARE IN LIFE."

12. Why should I encourage my child to persevere and to be committed to things?

and teaching, and on the other giving moral support and accompaniment that helps children to grow.

Teachers create partnerships with parents so that children's learning is holistic and is backed up at home for consolidation. Beyond this each teacher has a commitment to the well-being of the children in the whole school and the care of the other staff too. Many teaching staff run extra-curricular clubs (often several) to extend the educational experiences of the pupils, and all share in the daily duties of care of the children. They remain committed to the aims of the school and to the future of each of the young people, regardless of how long- or short-lived that relationship might be. If this sounds grand and idealistic, then that is unapologetic. A commitment to a school and its pupils is not a mere 8.30am–4.30pm workday commitment in line with payment and contract; it is far more, encompassing heartfelt responsibility, generosity, compassion and sense of purpose. The vast majority of teachers take great joy, pride and care in what they do.

Hopefully, with this level of care and commitment, and the love they receive in their families, children will grow up to understand that commitment is partly about duty, partly about contribution and partly about pleasure and enjoyment (often from the collaboration and team effort as much as from the thing itself). Sometimes there is a great requirement for personal commitment and perseverance in order to feed back into the activity, such as music practice or word learning, and although this may not be as much fun, it is part of

> **"TEACHERS CREATE PARTNERSHIPS WITH PARENTS SO THAT CHILDREN'S LEARNING IS HOLISTIC AND IS BACKED UP AT HOME FOR CONSOLIDATION."**

the whole. Thus doggedness, resilience, self-motivation, desire to complete things and a sense of personal achievement can all be earned and enhanced by developing an understanding of commitment.

Hence, I cannot help but worry when I see so many children who believe that success means seeing immediate results, and thus failure is also instantaneous. These children prefer to avoid commitment in case it should not bear fruit, or because it has not borne fruit soon enough. Many children want to participate in activities until it impacts on their social lives, so children 'quit for this week' simply because they don't fancy being included that day (a disaster for longer-term goals that take weekly rehearsals, such as concerts or team training). Here, perseverance is important because hanging onto something brings the benefit of success. Perseverance needs practice, and it is a mistake to think that natural perseverance will kick in when it is important. In my experience, children that flit between things will find it extra hard to settle to working at longer-term goals.

Some children (and their parents) only want to participate if the activity carries kudos. For example, a first-team place is snatched with glee, but a place in squad is declined as unimportant, despite the fact that teams can only be made up from those who learn and improve through practising. Elite activities are good, but nobody can become Leader of the Orchestra without years of training individually and playing in the back rows. It is always worth pointing out to children how a little extra perseverance can develop success, and that being in the first team is not the goal in itself.

I believe you can really help by having loving conversations which enable your child to understand why they need to be committed, to bridge the gap between the efforts of perseverance and the long-term benefits of having another go. Alongside this, with your help, your child can consider respect for others involved with them in their activities, and the people who strive for their enjoyment and fulfilment by organising events for them.

It would always be useful if you could encourage them to do an extra week before 'quitting', or if you tell them to speak to the person in charge themselves, to say why they wish to give up. These are positive ways to develop good manners and a more measured approach to participation. These methods also reinforce your view of perseverance, that staying with things, having another go and delaying the walk-away is important and relevant to you. The skills developed will be good companions ▶

12. Why should I encourage my child to persevere and to be committed to things?

on their learning journey. Adding pressure to make it into the first team is fine if your child is first-team material, but this needs a reasonable assessment, and cannot be pursued if it is going to knock the self-esteem of a child who cannot perform on cue. Many schools will run training squads or clubs for fun, and sometimes even second or third teams if possible (although they need to find partner schools who also do this or weaker teams will always lose). It is worth considering that these training activities may be a more appropriate place for your child until he or she is either ready to progress or can find something else to participate in.

It is easy to imagine that children might improve if they are placed in a higher set, or team, and parents often demand this in error. My experience is that this creates stress and anxiety, and can make your child feel undervalued or put off. In terms of ability sets, in class the vast majority of pupils do vastly better at the top of a lower-ability set than the bottom of a high-ability one, and their confidence will be higher. My best advice is to listen to the school's recommendation, rather than insisting your child be faced with learning new content at a pace that will cause anxiety and poor self-image. Most schools will want to review these decisions regularly enough to make sure they are moved up when appropriate. That is not to say that there should be no pressure or support from you. Of course, there are times when you know your child could do more or is capable of better, and that is really important. However, make sure that effort goes into helping your child to improve in the short term, rather than simply placing them in a situation that they cannot handle.

I suffer personally from an overdeveloped sense of duty, but with it has come deep satisfaction with having joined and benefited from many clubs and activities. This has included working through the boring or sticky patches and being able to persevere happily even when I haven't really been particularly good at whatever it is. I have also experienced great joy in wholehearted participation in many things. In fact, the sense of camaraderie, achievement and friendship that has grown through my perseverance with challenging activities is truly life-enhancing. That is a life lesson for happiness I would dearly love to share with all children. Instead of, 'I've quit', it would be wonderful to hear more children say, 'I'll stick with it!'. ■

"We ruin ourselves with impatience."
Michel de Montaigne

ELIZABETH SAYS...

Every time your child shows perseverance tell them:

'Do you realise that you've been doing hockey for a whole term? I'm sure that there have been times that you didn't enjoy it so much, but you carried on. That showed real perseverance.'

'You only needed to spend 10 minutes on your spellings, but you've spent 20 minutes, and you haven't complained. You're getting really good at persevering at things.'

The more you praise your child for trying new things, making an effort, keeping going and sticking at things, the more they'll think of those qualities as being part of their personality.

Chapter 13

Why is it essential to allow my child to experience failure?

13. Why is it essential to allow my child to experience failure?

There are many things we do in life that make us feel rather overawed, or even afraid.

Not because they are life-changing or will make a real difference in the sum of human endeavour, but simply because we are afraid we might not do as well as we hoped, or as well as someone else. This often means that we cannot really do our best, that we are made jittery with nerves, or that we simply choose to opt out. Given that most of the world's most important inventions are by-products of failure, it is time to revisit how we allow this to work in the successful education of our children.

Courage in what we do sounds perfectly reasonable. It is easy to think of being brave, taking a leap or running a risk, but the truth is we are often held back by the simple notion that we might fail. Children are no different. If they are under pressure always to succeed, and encouraged or helped to do so by someone else taking control, then they learn that failure is a bad, sad or dangerous thing. In turn this makes each task laden with fear that things might not go according to plan. Too much pressure ironically causes this fear of failure to be reflected in underachieving. Most of the underachieving children I discuss with anxious parents are under pressure, a pressure that creates failure through fear rather than driving achievement. Parental anxiety is the child's best indicator that they are not succeeding sufficiently, so beware of the signals you display. Many parents who tell me that they don't pressure their children are simply unaware of the signs they give out. An anxious tone of voice, asking too quickly about how something went, or letting your child know you are talking to the teacher are all things that your child will pick up and use to create their own pressure. Sometimes, 'Let's not worry, is there something I can help you with for next time,' will help to break the panic and pressure cycle. Ridicule, which is something I have also seen used to make children resist failure, is unkind and counterproductive. If you tease a child about failure they will believe that you have no respect for their efforts, and will either become deeply anxious, or fear that your faith in them is related only to what they can simply and unimaginatively achieve.

I was reminded of this when discussing an examination result with a parent of a bright and lively eight-year-old. The child works hard, achieves very good class and homework results, but recently had not ▶

13. Why is it essential to allow my child to experience failure?

done so well in an assessment test. Her mum was terribly worried about this, and so was the child. I asked the mum what she thought would happen if the child really failed (as I did not see this as a failure), and I had to hand out the tissues. The child said she worried about failing because it meant she was letting her family down, and she would fail her exams in the senior school and not get into university or get a good job. This child is well above average, usually happy, and usually shows both initiative and perseverance. However, based on one slipped grade, here they were crying in my office and wondering where the dream had gone awry. I believe very firmly that this lovely girl is not really underachieving, nor failing, nor destined for disaster – unless her fear of failure is allowed to develop further. I tried hard to counsel on the minimal impact of one grade and the need to persevere, to identify what specifically needed more work (or even dismissing this result as unlucky).

Picking up, dusting down and carrying on is the best way to deal with setbacks, errors, mishaps and other forms of perceived failure. Without the ability to learn from failure, and to embrace what it teaches us, learning will have a very definite low ceiling, and attainment will be greatly reduced. Wanting to do our best need not equate to being anxious about the opposite, especially if it is actually going to make things worse. Our best should always be good enough.

Therefore, think very carefully about the messages you give to your child when she comes home with a less than excellent result. Failing allows us to take stock, to see that the sky doesn't fall in, and that something needs changing. It can allow children who have relied on too much help to begin to take responsibility. It can show up practical gaps in understanding and allow work to begin to improve the situation. But it is a balancing act, and it is worth considering carefully before deciding how to tackle each situation with your child. Some children will never be good at certain things and that is OK. Failure is a life lesson. It is a useful reminder that we need to do our best, but with no fear. If failure is one of the possible outcomes we can look at squarely, then the fear of failure doesn't need to impede our efforts. ■

> **"OUR BEST SHOULD ALWAYS BE GOOD ENOUGH."**

"One must be a little foolish if one does not want to be even more stupid."

Michel de Montaigne

Chapter 14
How can I help my child to learn to think?

14. How can I help my child to learn to think?

I was very interested to read about the recent rebirth of a learning and teaching strategy called 'the mantle of the expert', an approach first proposed by Dorothy Heathcote in the 1960s.

The basis was somewhere between drama and role play, but with a real thinking experience to develop interest, perseverance and real learning. The theory has children assuming 'the mantle of the expert' for themselves, and taking responsibility for absorbing the problem, finding all that is needed to meet the task, doing research, imagining the issue from as many angles as possible in order to fully understand it and finding creative solutions. For example, children asked to plan a holiday will need to consider a destination, a travel plan, packing list, financial requirements, itinerary etc. These tasks develop real deep thinking, research skills and a whole host of abilities, connecting ideas into a viable reality that will be needed for life.

These types of activities are generally presented as a project, often for homework or for preparation to be done at home. To support your child engaged in this really valuable learning experience, I recommend that you also expect your child to assume 'the mantle of the expert' and only use the mildest of hints to get them going. If you can sit on your hands while they work, let them bounce ideas off you and ask them for their new expert opinions and thoughts. From a teacher's perspective, one of the most difficult things to encourage children to do is to give their own informed opinion. When asked 'What do you think?' most children, especially girls, will say 'I don't know what I think', expecting the teacher to tell them the right answer so that they can represent it as what they think. It is vital that children are jolted out of this powerless state. If you prefer to be involved in the work itself as a family project, then do let your child lead you, and guide her when absolutely necessary rather than tell her what to do. This is one of those activities where you can really accompany.

It is worth adding that teachers are very wary of parents completing homework projects, because this really does not help in the development and learning of the child. Learn to be brave about letting the work look a little child-driven, as this will also encourage your child to take pride in their own work. Try to hold uppermost in your mind the fact that these projects are about developing thinking and life skills, not about competing with another child's parents (who may be mistakenly producing their child's project professionally). Your child learning with you in this way will make her gain most out of the experience in the long run. In addition, these types of work can also be huge, collaborative fun. Do seize the opportunity to be involved in a way that shows your child that you value their thinking and enjoy working with them, while not taking over the project. It is a great opportunity to build in library visits, trips or excursions you think might promote interest which at the same time will create some wonderful personal time with your child.

It is so easy for us all to forget that the school curriculum can mean very little in educational terms if it fails to challenge the child in a way that develops cognition, wisdom or intelligence. Without the engagement of thinking processes, adequate challenge, high expectations, fascination, time to problem solve, a chance to play with ideas, encouragement to think independently and to evaluate with real honesty and resilience, then learning will be very limited. Learning, certainly for primary and younger secondary-aged pupils, really means developing thinking skills, extending and enhancing vocabulary, improving thinking speed, working on listening skills, and building on the ability to concentrate in a variety of situations.

The heartening evidence of this is that children who learn to love the world of books and imagination do better in public examinations. Pupils who ultimately need to retain facts and manipulate these to answer questions for GCSE and A Level perform far better if they have mastered that knowledge through being taught in a way that demands something of them rather than handing it to them on a plate.

Recently, a visitor to my school spoke to me in broken English and, rather quaintly, referred to adults being 'implicated' in the education of their children. However, he was utterly right and I believe this to be a brilliant description. We (teachers and parents) are all implicated in the process of educating a child. But that must, if it is to be of any long-term use, place upon us the responsibility to implicate the child in their own thinking. ■

Turn the page to see what Elizabeth says

14. How can I help my child to learn to think?

ELIZABETH SAYS...

You can encourage your child's thinking skills at home too. Many parents (myself included!) tend to have our 'fix it' hats on when our children come to us with a problem. We immediately think that it's our job to come up with a solution and give them our (unsolicited but very well intentioned) advice! However, it's important to help our children to find solutions to their own problems. So that when they are in the classroom or school playground, they are confident they can think of solutions and make good choices.

So, how can you help your child with problem solving?

At a good time, ask your child to state the problem they have. Or explain the problem you have. Say it in a neutral way without blaming your child. And ask for your child's help to solve it. Do it casually, or:

- Write the problem at the top of the page in a neutral way that doesn't imply you're blaming your child.
- Ask your child to come up with 10 to 15 possible solutions (to really get their creativity flowing).
- Write down all their answers. Even the funny or silly ones.
- If you have any other ideas, ask if you can add them at the end.
- Cross off the ideas that are not acceptable. (Anything that involves maiming, killing or unlawful activities!)
- Ask your child to choose what solution (or combination of solutions) they'd like to try first.

It's surprising how this simple process can help children to realise that they have some great ideas. It can also help them recognise that they can come up with really creative solutions to dilemmas or difficulties with a little guidance and encouragement.

Chapter 15

How can I build good listening skills in me and my child?

15. How can I build good listening skills in me and my child?

How much active listening do we actually do?

Every day we hear thousands of sounds, some in the background, many that we are supposedly attending to, but only some that we actively listen to. We expect the children in our care to listen to instructions, filter out the important sounds from the rest, and then do what they have been told. In the background they also have conversations of their own and ambient noises to deal with. We tell them they must listen, but how well do we train them to know what they must listen to?

Hearing is an extremely acute sense. It is generally understood that it is the last sense to disappear, and that unconscious patients can still hear sounds and voices. Hearing is an evocative sense, and at its most basic acts as an alarm system for danger, alerting us and preparing the body for fight or flight. That's why a sharp sound will make our hearts race and unexpected noises in the night spring us into alertness. Even someone adding your name when speaking to you will naturally increase your attention.

However, in the visually rich culture in which we live now, how do we give our children the opportunity to develop this valuable sense? Listening is the ability to process what is heard using the brain's conscious rather than automatic functions. If we allow children to see that we are only half listening to them, if they think we are constantly listening to the same music, and if we fill their lives with artificial noise then we are limiting the discriminatory powers that intelligent listening can give them.

To develop listening skills, it is important to create some peace to hear the sounds that naturally surround us. For me, providing constant external sound from the radio, TV, or MP3 player runs the risk of reducing my thinking, and cuts off my relationship with the outside world. Some people feel they need the noise to help them work, or use the sound to act as company. But try a morning without extra sound – just a patch of peace and quiet – to see how background noise can calm you and help to reduce the pressure that noise places on the thinking systems. Creating a bit of peace and quiet also enables us to hear our own inner voice; a chance to listen to ourselves!

In the old days we said to children 'look at me when I'm talking'. This instruction has become very unfashionable, but it does have some effectiveness in a classroom, or even at home, and helps to underpin with the child that what we say needs to be attended to, not just be allowed to wash over. It is worth developing your child's listening skills, taking the time to listen to the sounds around and to talk about them, to teach them to look at the person speaking and to engage in meaningful conversation. It is a good idea to encourage your child to actually take time away from the multitasking madness of our visual world to listen, uninterrupted, to something new – a piece of music, a story, or a different style of each.

I know that I am guilty of doing other things while people are talking to me, and have learnt (the hard way!) that I am not really capable of taking in sufficient information if I am multitasking. However, I also know that we all do this to children, from hearing reading while being busy ourselves to just sidestepping the constantly bubbling ideas that flow from a happy child. And so, naturally, our children learn from us that listening is something that can be happily compromised. To make things worse, we then get cross if they don't listen to us barking instructions or if they don't remember what we have just said.

To encourage good listening skills, how about making an effort to listen to things with your child, and making time to enjoy the sounds around you? Make space for a family conversation, listen to something new rather than the same old music, and take those earphones out so that listening can be a valuable shared experience. An activity that your child might enjoy is the 'add an instruction' game (although they will love any game that guarantees your attention). The premise of this game is to send them several instructions to remember and follow before returning successfully to you. Start with one instruction (for example, 'run upstairs and bring me a hairbrush') then add one more instruction at a time (for example, 'run upstairs and fetch me a hairbrush, and then go to the kitchen and get me a spoon before returning'). Then, let them dictate the terms to you for you to have a go. You may think this is just training the memory, but 'not remembering' is often just an excuse to cover up the fact that real intelligent listening did not take place. ■

> **"TO ENCOURAGE GOOD LISTENING SKILLS, MAKE AN EFFORT TO LISTEN TO THINGS WITH YOUR CHILD."**

15. How can I build good listening skills in me and my child?

ELIZABETH SAYS...

It is very important to recognise that sometimes we want our children to do things when they are already engaged in another activity. When you want your child to do something, rather than shouting your instruction from another room, it is best to go to your child. If they're engaged in an activity, you can talk to them about what they're doing. Then, when you have their attention and they're looking at you, give your instruction, clearly and simply, and only once. If they don't respond in 10 seconds or so, ask what you just asked them to do and let them respond in their own words. Then, just stand and wait until they do what you've asked. This is a really effective way of getting your child to do what you ask the first time.

Steven R Covey, author of *The 7 Habits of Highly Effective People,* said:
'Most people do not listen with the intent to understand; they listen with the intent to reply.'

Another good habit to get into is to really listen to what your child is saying. A great way to do this is when your child comes to talk to you, stop what you're doing, look at your child, and try to summarise or paraphrase what they're saying to show you've heard and understood them. And, here's the crucial bit, without trying to offer any advice, judgement or criticism! It's hard for busy parents do this, but when a child feels listened to, they feel valued and important. And it will really help their ability to sort out their own problems, and improve their behaviour and attitude.

Chapter 16

Do good manners really matter?

16. Do good manners really matter?

Why do good manners matter at all in this competitive day and age? What use are they to an education?

For some people good manners may appear to be about old-fashioned courtesy, saying 'please' and 'thank you', holding doors open, or helping old ladies across the street. Perhaps by doing a few formulaic things we can offer apparent kindness and make our little worlds run more smoothly. Is this little bit of altruism actually about making things work for ourselves or for other people? For me, good manners demonstrate how I want to engage with the world; finding a place to belong with the other people who live on this planet.

I have found it useful to ponder the question 'Who is the nicest person I know? Someone I value and who values me. A person who I could go to with anything that troubled me, someone I trust, who will gently help me to the truth, who will "be there" for me dispensing joy, wisdom and kindness'. Of course, we may hope it is ourselves who are viewed as such. It might be that is how you see your loved ones, or your special or old friend. You will know who that person is in your life; someone who knows and cares for you just as you are. Whoever they are, I know they are someone with good manners. I expect they listen, make time for you, appear interested, are happy to pass the time of day, and are solicitous, kind and warm. I hope that I might be so regarded, although I know I am guilty of not making time (and always checking my phone or having somewhere else to be). Most of all, I hope the children that I teach might grow up to be that person, and I hope you want that for your child too.

I believe we can make our children into the wonderful adults they could be by starting with simple good manners. Children are naturally egocentric and they see the world through self-centred eyes. Children at play will naturally push past each other, avoid sharing and try to gain the main advantage in give and take. With little encouragement they are naturally competitive, like to be better (faster, brighter, stronger) than their peers, and enjoy demonstrating their talents and gifts, even to the detriment of their dearest friends. In order to help them to become popular friends to others, they need to learn to be thoughtful, sensitive and understanding of the perspectives that others might have of them and the way others might feel.

Empathy starts with good manners, understanding that an engagement with someone else has a meaning and a purpose beyond the business of functional communication. We want them to learn to say 'please' and 'thank you' because it offers dignity and value to the person to whom they are speaking. Stepping back or holding a door open to allow someone else to pass reminds your child that she has a role to play in making life pleasant for others. It also shows respect to the other person. Saying 'good morning' and looking at the person they are speaking to can create a bond of communication. We all know that a smile shared can lift a grey day! It is important for your child to learn this.

Good manners might make a busy life a bit more pleasant for all, but they also support the day-to-day exchanges that characterise learning. In the classroom, respect for what is happening is important, learning to take turns, to manage the routine of answering questions without shouting out is vital, as is give and take in any collaborative sharing and learning. Listening to others is partly about respect but is also a vital ingredient of good classroom behaviour. Courtesy towards others is helpful, as is respect for space and belongings. All these are about good manners. Within the classroom it seems obvious to any teacher that the best learners often have the best manners; they are able to engage with the task, treading the line between keen interest and managing independently. Not least, those children with good manners tend to be better listeners and communicators, and are therefore less prone to confusion in the lessons and frustration with what they are expected to do.

Children do need lots of encouragement to understand that they are not the very centre of the universe. However, telling ▶

> **"SAYING 'GOOD MORNING' AND LOOKING AT THE PERSON THEY ARE SPEAKING TO CAN CREATE A BOND OF COMMUNICATION. WE ALL KNOW THAT A SMILE SHARED CAN LIFT A GREY DAY!"**

16. Do good manners really matter?

your child this is unlikely to change that, and it can be unhelpful to their developing self-esteem. A better starting point is to train them (by copying us) to take simple actions that validate others and that enable them to understand how to respect people by small acts of kindness and courtesy. To grow up with a warm understanding of others and an ability to be a good friend brings its own happiness. Perhaps this is unfashionable when thinking about success, but being rich and fulfilled is about far more than money.

What I hear referred to as 'bullying' is more often than not simply a rough-and-tumble lack of simple, kind good manners (more of this in a later chapter). Children who push others or themselves to the front to assert themselves or their will over others are often unaware of the impact they are having on their peers. Rather than a consistent calculated attitude of nastiness, they trip into it by overenthusiastic or thoughtless approaches to other people that speak of lack of understanding of what they might want or be feeling. Sadly, these are the very children that end up mystified when they have few close friends, and cannot see why they are considered unkind or rough. In these cases, I tell them that if they want to have a friend, then they must be a friend. I continue by saying that they need to start by showing good manners: sharing, caring, listening, standing back and saying 'please' and 'thank you'.

I wonder whether we confuse our children. We know they have rights and we fight for them. We want them to get ahead and we tell them so. We let them hear us compete with each other, or even bend the truth in front of them (or on the telephone when we forget they are listening) as we manage our own lives. They learn from any self-motivated actions we take that deny the importance of someone else. If we do everything for our children, it is no wonder they take little responsibility for their own actions. If we let them believe they are the most important person in the solar system, they won't understand the co-operative compassion and respect that makes the world go round, and contributes to their own happiness. Do try to encourage good manners from very young, because many families leave the learning of good manners until too late, thinking that schools will teach it instead of insisting on it at home.

I would go so far as to say that teaching good manners, helping children to share cheerfully and to have respect, are more useful tools to give your child to take to school than 99.9% of the objects you can put into their schoolbags. ■

ELIZABETH SAYS...

It's really important as parents that you play with your children. Many parents think that only children 'play'. But they miss the crucial role they have in helping their children learn how to take turns, to share, to be a good winner and to lose graciously. You will be gentler on your child than some of the children in the playground. So make it a habit to play games to help your child learn what to do and say when they win a game, or when they lose. Don't be afraid to take the time for your full turn to help them learn the skill of waiting. Don't always 'let' them win so they can learn how to be a good loser. And gently teach them how to manage their frustration when they realise they can't actually win a game!

If your child is overly competitive, they may feel their self-worth is only validated if they 'win'. If that's the case, it's important to keep telling them each day all the little things they do well or just OK. Tell them all the things you love about them. Give your child at least 15 minutes a day of your undivided time and attention to play or do whatever they want, so they know they're valuable and important. And gradually they'll learn that they don't have to 'win' to get their sense of significance. And that all you ask is that they try hard and do their best.

Lastly, you don't teach compassion by giving your child everything. Paradoxically, people are happier when they help others. If you continue to do everything for your child and give them everything, you are denying your child the chance to feel the true, deep happiness that comes from giving and helping other people. A very useful exercise is to challenge everyone in the family to do 'one random act of kindness' every day. Help your child find little things they can do to help out or make people happy. And you will gradually see your child become happier, more generous, and they will therefore attract more friends!

Chapter 17

How can I stop my child being bullied by her friends?

17. How can I stop my child being bullied by her friends?

I am often asked how a school might deal with bullying.

All schools these days are expected to have careful and systematic policies for dealing with bullying, and most will have made arrangements to have children carefully supervised to minimise opportunities for bullying. If you think your child is involved in a proper bullying situation, is ambushed by unkind children lying in wait for her, is persistently called unkind names, is deliberately excluded, verbally abused, or physically attacked, then do not wait – contact the school immediately. Similarly, if your child is hurt in persistent boisterous play then do inform the school.

These are extreme forms of bullying. However, what most parents mean when we discuss it more fully, is how do schools avoid the unhappiness, low-level unkindness, isolation and petty confrontation that exists between children as they find their way in the pecking order of the classroom? Unfortunately, this jostling for position is completely natural behaviour, because children are (in many ways) pack animals. They want to have a place in the group that accords with their natural inclinations: leaders will want to lead, followers will want to follow, characters will want to be noticed, competitive children will want to be the best, and all are in some form of competition with each other as is human nature. Leaders like to be in charge, to control the games and who is included, and to have willing lieutenants who always agree with them and play with them and who secure their popular position. Young leaders will often naturally resent anyone else who has shared characteristics because it threatens their position. Most classes will have a handful of natural young leaders, and they will always need support to work together harmoniously no matter how lovely and kind they are as people. Teachers generally spend a lot of time trying to iron out mini-disputes to enable pupils to learn appropriate ways to work and live together.

Some children like to be loyal supporters, and the approval of the leader will encourage them into excluding anyone who might take their place in the more dominant child's affections. These less-dominant children will be helped by teachers to see how they might help each other and learn to collaborate, and to develop the confidence to take charge sometimes.

Children seeking centre stage may need the teacher's attention more than that of their ▶

17. How can I stop my child being bullied by her friends?

peers, and thus may unthinkingly disrupt lessons or activities and cause irritation to their classmates, something which they themselves may find hard to comprehend. Some children are mystified by the reactions they cause and need patient help to understand them, not denial or blame elsewhere. Highly competitive children can sometimes react harshly or sarcastically to others who do well (or badly) in class, but may not intend at all (or even appreciate) the shock and upset their comments or disdain can cause. Gentle class discussions are useful to develop awareness, because these behaviours are unhelpful despite being entirely normal.

But most normal and most difficult of all to deal with are 'frenemies' (friends/enemies). This refers to children who are dearest best friends and also at the same time competitive with each other or squabbling over a third friend. They are comfortable enough with each other to squabble in unkind language and are easily upset by the actions of the other. These children may have been friends since nursery, have parents who go on holiday together and have a shared history or they may have fallen upon each other very young and at first appeared to be inseparable. These normally happy children create the most common face of classroom 'bullying', and are likely on a daily basis to fall in and out of friendship and to stir other friends into taking sides.

Often, a teacher may be approached by both sets of parents separately claiming serious upset, bullying and victimisation. They

> "LEADERS LIKE TO BE IN CHARGE, TO CONTROL THE GAMES AND WHO IS INCLUDED, AND TO HAVE WILLING LIEUTENANTS WHO ALWAYS AGREE WITH THEM AND PLAY WITH THEM AND WHO SECURE THEIR POPULAR POSITION."

blame the other child and at the same time express their sadness because the families have become friends or socialise in the same circles. The situation is often exacerbated when parents have approached each other outside the school to blame each other's offspring for attacking their child, resulting in the parents also falling out. Sometimes other children will have become embroiled in the situation, and there may be a schism in the classroom between factions of children and parents. This is particularly relevant in smaller Prep School classes, where the social circle is relatively tight.

This is not simple for any teacher to manage, requiring patience and forbearance on everyone's part, as well as parental support. The children do need to learn to cope and to manage to sort themselves out with lots of empathy and support from the adults around them. A teacher dealing with this every day and managing accusations of not caring or not solving the problem can feel somewhat harassed too. Feelings of jealousy, envy, abandonment, longing and love of a friend are entirely natural, and these critical situations are how children learn to manage such deep and important human feelings. Teachers of young children deal with these issues every single day of their careers, but cannot completely prevent this behaviour happening or happening again with different children because it is such a fundamental part of a child's emotional development and learning.

None of the characteristics described here are unusual, peculiar, bad or wicked. Nor do they make a child a bully, because these are necessary learning experiences for anyone who wants to create deep, abiding, equal friendships. Hard as it is, it is often important to understand that both children are likely to be protagonists on occasion, and victims on others. The best way forward is to allow children to speak together, perhaps mediated by the teacher, so that they have some control over the situation. The children themselves need to be empowered to deal with tricky situations and to learn that they can take control when the conditions are set out.

You should try to allow the school to deal with the flashpoint situations, informing them of the facts when necessary. Comfort your child as much as possible when she is upset, particularly at night when tiredness can create feelings of desolation at being abandoned by the friend whose love and approval they are desperate to have. These tangled relationships can be long-lasting too, so your patience will be sorely tried. Empathy and listening, without being too quick to anger and judge, is important and will lower your frustration levels. If the ▶

17. How can I stop my child being bullied by her friends?

school feels it necessary, then the children may be separated or sanctions applied. Beware, though, that this can also cause serious heartache in your child, so do have rational discussions with teachers if these might be an option.

It is also helpful to remember that both children involved in this love/hate relationship bear almost equal responsibility for the outcome (although the more dominant child may appear to be in a better situation). These children are likely to be deeply attracted to the relationship with the other regardless of whether this is warm friendship or a moment of torment (or a repeating cycle of each). This is also natural – it is part of learning to own a friendship and to develop meaningful longer-term, balanced relationships, as well as finding a place in those relationships. Such relationships are at their most unequal when one child matures faster than the other (certain years can be particularly difficult as the maturity balance in the class changes). This imbalance can also occur when new children join the class and disrupt previously exclusive friendships. It is unlikely that either child will willingly walk away from this relationship even if you say they should 'just stay away'. They will also continue to care about what the other child says regardless of your opinion.

It may seem as if they actively seek out the unkindness that they describe. Often the worse it is, the stronger their apparent need to cling to the friendship and to chase the more reluctant child. Elizabeth has some excellent suggestions at the end of this chapter for managing more conventional bullying.

In describing some of these situations above I can imagine you will start to recognise adult behaviours, which of course the child is struggling to learn. There is really no easy solution. Just beware the bullying label and seek to maintain a healthy social life outside school with lots of other children so that new bonds can develop to slowly replace painful ones. The last thing one would ever want to do with a child is keep naming them as a victim, as that will damage their self-esteem. Be sympathetic, but make it clear you see them as strong when you discuss with them options for managing the situation. Allow them to suggest ways to address the situation so that they own the solution as well as the problem. ■

ELIZABETH SAYS…

As a parent, you can help your child learn 'bully proof' skills:

- Help your child to understand that just because someone says something nasty about them, they don't have to believe it. Maybe you could help your child imagine wearing a 'bully proof vest' that nasty comments just bounce off.
- Also, help your child to develop casual responses to comments that are meant to be hurtful. Phrases like: 'You think so? Yes, you're right. I'm not really interested. Thanks for telling me. So? Really? You don't say! Yes, but I'm good at it!' Or your child might ask 'Why would you call me …an idiot… and try to hurt my feelings?' Or 'Have I done something to hurt or upset you?' (And if your child has done something to provoke the other child they can apologise!)
- If your child talks to you about issues they're having with friendships or bullying, it's important to empower your child to deal with it so you can teach your child that they are not victims in life, but are strong and confident and able to deal with issues. There is an online programme *'10 steps to bully proof your child'* that can take you through the steps to teach your child how to avoid being a victim of bullying for life.

There are seven steps you can teach a child, to enable them to solve an argument with a friend or in the playground:

1. Check how the other person is feeling. Ask: 'Can you explain your side and how you're feeling?' And listen to what they're saying.
2. Summarise their point of view and empathise with their emotions: 'So you're feeling a bit… about that.'
3. Check they've understood properly: 'So you feel… have I got that right?'
4. Ask: 'Now is it OK to say how I feel?'
5. Explain how they feel assertively: 'I feel… When… And I'd like…'
6. Explore ideas: Ask: 'How could we sort it out? What ideas do you have? Maybe we could…?'
7. Find a solution. 'What shall we do then?' (And try to find a solution that they're both happy with).

This is a 'life skill' and will help your child handle disagreements throughout school. Sadly, many adults haven't learned the skill of how to resolve arguments respectfully, politely and assertively!

Chapter 18

Why does the school think my child is cheating?

18. Why does the school think my child is cheating?

Firstly, remember that cheating is one word for a behaviour that we all naturally do in order to learn in the first place: we copy, imitate and mimic.

Teachers and parents model behaviour, language and attitude, which children use as tools to become articulate, thinking beings. We spend a great deal of time hoping that children will learn from example, learn from what we show them and reflect or copy the behaviour that enables them to fit into society.

Then we place them into situations where it is unacceptable to copy: from other children's work, from text written by another author or from the Internet.

If the school thinks your child is cheating, then they are probably suggesting that your child needs a little help understanding what producing her own work means, and is struggling to apply the 'when to copy' rules.

In a classroom, the teachers are good at spotting copying and will jump on any instances. However, the biggest danger is plagiarism in homework that is done on the computer, when children will happily copy and paste the words or pictures created and owned by other people, presenting them as their own.

Although it may be very tempting to feel criticised and judged when a teacher tackles you about this, it is important to stay calm and to be clear what the issue might be. In this way, you can help your child to understand what has gone wrong, and how to know when copying is helpful and when it is not.

In my experience, girls especially will copy each other's work in order to please a teacher, and to avoid showing what they cannot do. In the chapter on failure (chapter 13) I outline the fact that confidence comes from getting things wrong and then sorting them out properly. Try not to deny the copying if the teacher feels there is evidence. It may be useful to expose the incident(s) as this may be hiding a lack of confidence which will need to be tackled head on so that independent success can become possible. ■

Chapter 19

Do I need to get a home tutor?

19. Do I need to get a home tutor?

> **One of the most frequent questions asked at parents' evenings these days is 'Should I get her a tutor?'**

Although I believe that suitably qualified tutors can be helpful for children with specific learning differences or difficulties either outside or at school, I have become concerned about the prevalence of engaging 'academic' tutors as a matter of course. I have known some teachers who I'm sure would be wonderful tutors, but there are others who have not been high-achieving in the classroom and would not be offering your child excellence or giving you value for money.

One-to-one tuition at home, according to recent reports in the media, is as common as attending school. There are now more people offering private tuition than there are teachers in schools. None of these tutors need to be qualified or to conform to reasonable standards. Having a Mrs Doubtfire demeanour or a track record as a tutor for many years is not good enough. Companies exist to offer tuition at particular stages in the school career – to assist with 11+ entry, to prepare for public examinations, or just to top up what is being done at school. Many of these cannot guarantee results. Indeed, an analysis of their success rates, for example in grammar school entry, correlate to the child's natural ability and the amount of rigorous rehearsal (which they can do with you or by themselves using resources bought from high-street shops) rather than to something magical these tutors have added in the many hours of paid extra tuition. I have been frustrated by parents wondering why their children are making poor progress towards independent learning, when most of their child's 'individual' learning is coached by someone sitting beside them. While tuition can work for some, it is certainly not a panacea for academic improvement.

It is worth remembering that tuition may actually be counterproductive:
- Children who regularly work alongside a tutor soon learn that there is no expectation that they can, or should, manage independently.
- Children who are used to tuition have a fear of getting things wrong and become reliant on instant praise, feedback, correction and support, failing to develop the resilience that is essential for effective learning. ▶

19. Do I need to get a home tutor?

- Children who have intensive coaching for examinations often feel de-skilled and deeply demoralised if the tuition has simply raised them to an academic level, set or school where they cannot really manage by themselves.
- Tutors have no regulation. They may be wonderful, but there is no control over what they teach, how current their knowledge might be, or how effectively they work with children.
- Ex-teachers may not be up to date with ever-changing methods and syllabuses, and can sometimes confuse their tutees, or give them conflicting methods or information to worry about.
- Tutors are unlikely to have the same view of progression and continuity that the class or subject teachers have. At school, the teaching team will be working together to create something coherent in terms of learning strategies, linked knowledge and experience across the curriculum.
- Home tutors will not be working from the school's plans for the year, and may worry you or your child about gaps and aspects of the syllabus that have simply not been covered yet for very sound reasons.
- Tutors offering individual lessons often overstate or overestimate the ability of your child. They may cope extremely well in one-to-one sessions, but not necessarily in a classroom, or when later expected to work independently or under exam conditions. The confidence that a child shows the tutor because of close questioning, lots of praise, strong educational scaffolding and a coaching relationship is very different from how they might perform in a school environment.
- Be aware that there are no safeguarding guarantees about an unregulated and unchecked person in your home.

My advice as a Head Teacher is to use tuition only when advised to by the school for clear reasons: to support strategies for learning, to manage learning difficulties or in the short term for children who struggle, to keep the brain awake over long holidays. If your child just needs to be unstuck from a particular problem, talk to the class teacher about some temporary targeted support or for suitable homework strategies or practice. Make sure you have up-to-date references for anyone you invite into your home, and check on the qualifications and experience of the tutor. Great results regarding other people's children (even if you know them well) are not helpful – that child may have a completely different set of abilities, skills and needs from those of your own child. Tell the school if you have engaged a tutor, because the most fruitful experiences will be those that mirror and complement the school curriculum. Visit every session to see what is happening. If your child is overwhelmed, confused, tired or becoming reliant on too much 'tuition', support, praise or encouragement, then stop the lessons – they are simply not helping.

Children who are doing perfectly well at school do not need to be discouraged by having extra work in their free time. Nor do they need another adult questioning their ability, impeding their ability to develop independent strategies and pressuring them over their results.

A parent I have known for many years spoke to me recently about why she had stopped her child's tuition after 18 months with a very nice tutor. She said that she popped in on a session to discover, not for the first time, that the tutor was simply helping with the homework the class teacher had set and already prepared, no more, and no less – for £45 an hour. She confessed to me that she had felt pressured into organising tuition because all her friends had a tutor for their children. I asked if she had booked the lessons so that her child could have different work, more help or just more practice, but she said she had left it all in the hands of the tutor who was well-qualified and came highly recommended. She said she had not informed the school because she didn't want us to think her daughter was getting help. She told me that she had just come to the realisation that her child was actually doing fine, and that she was no longer going to worry about the extra mark or two the tutor could wring from each piece of work. I applaud her, and I hope that the saved money is used for a really enjoyable family activity.

Education is a holistic thing. Would your child benefit from a tutor? Probably not as much as she would benefit from you reading to her each evening if she is young, or taking her on a weekly trip to the library. Or, if your child is older, taking the time to discuss coursework, promoting rational argument at the dinner table and engendering an interest in current affairs. ∎

> "MY ADVICE AS A HEAD TEACHER IS TO USE TUITION ONLY WHEN ADVISED TO BY THE SCHOOL FOR CLEAR REASONS."

Chapter 20

Why is it important for my child to be bored?

20. Why is it important for my child to be bored?

> '**A spirited mind never stops within itself; it is always aspiring**'
>
> *Michel de Montaigne*

There have been many articles in the popular press about allowing children to be bored. It might be useful for us as educators and parents to have a chance to consider the educational reasons why allowing children unstructured time is not only important but also essential.

Firstly, we all know the adage that 'necessity is the mother of invention'. This may well be true, but invention and indeed all of human endeavour is only possible if it can be imagined. Imagination is something that we can feed with ideas and technical understanding, but imagination is only truly possible in a space where we can be openly reflective. Imagination is an active internal process which connects concrete ideas, past experience, diverse inspiration and personal creativity to create something new. It takes perseverance, time and self-motivation. In truth, imagination is the mother of invention. It is a critical faculty for learning and for success in life. The best time for imagination is not the pressure of requiring a solution, it is the time when you have nothing else to do.

As human beings we inhabit many spheres, but it is useful in this case to imagine the difference between an inner creative thinking and imagining sphere, and an external world of learning stimuli, activities and experiences. It is the relationship between the two that creates a whole person. However, we have become accustomed to listening to the noise of that external world as if it holds all the keys to life, and to rejecting the internal voice. How many of us put on music or television to stave off those moments when we might have to engage with our inner selves and run the risk of feeling bored? Two seconds of relative peace and we take out a phone to check, or to text or to chat with someone else. We have become so afraid of boredom that we frantically fill all of our time, and feel guilty if we don't. We also want to save our own children from boredom and, in doing so, we are stealing away their inner lives and their vital connections to themselves. If we fear that without external activities they may in fact become nothing, then we will be impelled to fill their lives for them. We will be creating in them a greater fear of being alone and being unoccupied, and of being unable to cope with just thinking and being themselves. We will have made them dependent and, in fact, we may even have enabled them to become lonely, unfulfilled and unhappy in later life. ▶

20. Why is it important for my child to be bored?

Many experts refer to the need for unstructured time because children have so many activities to complete, often one or two on each night of the week after a full, structured day at school, as well as homework. Structured time can close off the imagination and the ability to be self-determining, and it can make children lack confidence in their own abilities and unable to be independent. The result of keeping children fully immersed in set activities is that it teaches them that they can only succeed or have fun in structured ways. In these situations, they have little control and not much need for self-motivation, other than to compete (hopefully successfully) against the other children placed there to do the same. While it can, of course, promote skills and a team spirit, there needs to be a balance if that same child is ever going to have the imagination to develop strategic play or to be able to transfer skills to other situations. Being always involved in structured activity and games can stifle individuality and reinforces the need to comply rather than to innovate.

Boredom is a creative state. It can initially feel like an uncomfortable state, especially as modern life makes us unused to it. But by giving in to that feeling (in the same way as we give in to that extra chocolate or to any other unhealthy habit) we take a further step away from developing the creativity we would all love to have, through a quick fix.

> "IN TRUTH, IMAGINATION IS THE MOTHER OF INVENTION. IT IS A CRITICAL FACULTY FOR LEARNING AND FOR SUCCESS IN LIFE. THE BEST TIME FOR IMAGINATION IS NOT THE PRESSURE OF REQUIRING A SOLUTION, IT IS THE TIME YOU HAVE NOTHING ELSE TO DO."

Sadly on the other hand, we do have to get used to doing things that are boring, even necessary things, but we have to develop inner resources to cope. I am sure many of you will agree that there are many chores we have to just get on and do despite very low interest level – I often long for a Sunday night without having to do the ironing!

It is easy to fall into that trap of feeling guilty about not doing enough for your child, and therefore plan activities and events to ensure they are fully occupied in all of their free time. Filling the house with music and noise equally provides a (welcome?) distraction from one's own thoughts. It is no wonder then, that screen time (of every sort) has become a useful filler for those empty seconds of the day and evening. As a teacher with 28 years' experience I would say that children in general have shorter attention spans and a greater requirement to be helped, supported and constantly stimulated than ever before. Imagination is undervalued, and children expect constant attention and reinforcement even to get on with what they can easily achieve alone. When faced with anything they don't understand or feel to be hard work they say they are bored. This is one of the results of constant stimulation. It becomes an addiction, alongside an underlying nagging tiredness that creeps into children's lives when they don't have time for adequate reflection, rest and recreation.

Maria Montessori wrote about free play (which modern children often claim is boring) enabling children to become active and in an alert and receptive frame of mind. She demonstrated that children are adept at self-regulating and managing their own rules, and that they performed better in all areas if they were allowed the full scope of their imagination. Children who can play without intervention, and manage their own time, are calmer, more thoughtful and are able to be more articulate because they have time to rehearse ideas and to think things through. They are able to make their own positive decisions and are far less reliant on adult approval before moving on or turning the next page over. Montessori went so far as to say that play is a child's work.

Finally, there are many reasons your child may say she is bored, but an important one to note is that she would actually like a little of your attention. When is the last time, for no real reason other than just for the joy of being together, that you danced with your child? ■

Turn the page to see what Elizabeth says

20. Why is it important for my child to be bored?

ELIZABETH SAYS...

It is very useful to introduce 30 minutes of guilt-free downtime every day into your child's routine. Without a TV, mobile or PlayStation! And to protect that time as a vital part of your child's development. If your child worries about what they can do in that time, help them come up with a list. Then, if your child comes to you and says 'I'm bored' ask them to have a look at the list and decide what they'd like to do.

It's also useful to spend a few hours a week – perhaps on Sunday after lunch or on a Friday evening – where everybody relaxes and gets on with their own thing. Once again, where mobile phones and other screens are turned off. So your child sees you reading a book, pursuing a hobby or writing a journal. Children learn most by the example you set. When you demonstrate the importance of switching off, it helps your child learn to relax and entertain themselves in this frenetic, electronic world we inhabit.

Chapter 21

What does a school expect from homework?

21. What does a school expect from homework?

I am often asked 'what is the purpose of homework at prep level?' and, more specifically, 'why can't it just be completed at school?'.

These are very good questions. Family life on the one hand is so precious that it is a nuisance if it is marred by a daily battle over 'school' work. On the other hand, however, if children wait until their GCSE years to study beyond the classroom then clearly there will be some fundamental issues with their ability to succeed.

A balance is needed, and this is what schools try to address. Schools understand that some children will not have been able to manage the work for a variety of reasons or circumstances, that some will have had a great deal of help and support, and that others will have simply got on and done it, sometimes well and sometimes perfunctorily. This means that teachers are setting work every day that has to be stimulating but well-defined, challenging but independently manageable, meaningful practice without too many twists, not too dull or repetitive, which allows for proper learning and retaining. They are planning homework that is not essential for the next lesson for those who will not be able to complete it, progressive for those who need stretching and extendible for those who have further interests and enthusiasm. However, the homework diet cannot all be cakes and treats. Sometimes it may seem very routine, too easy or too hard, overlong or unpalatable, but that too is part of preparing for life.

Naturally, this is a complex (and, for a teacher, a rather exhausting) set of variables. Whereas some children thrive on exercises and assignments, others find their enthusiasm wanes when faced with work to complete on their own. Learning homework is often viewed as no homework by children and also by their parents. Increasingly, this type of homework is fitted around external clubs, lessons and events, and reading is confined to the last few minutes before bed – never a very good time to do anything that requires thinking!

I am all too familiar with the headache of homework sessions. I remember my frazzled mother standing over the table where my siblings and I were pretending to work each evening. Nowadays I regularly supervise my niece and nephews in their efforts to wriggle away from the mountain of things they bring home. However, I also see how routines help to create an atmosphere and a system that works for the children, and how well they can work when they are settled. Independence is very important, so training children to have those study skills and the resilience and perseverance needed to complete activities will pay dividends in the future. Learning homework may well need your help, and I am a big fan of using non-fiction books to help with information gathering. These can be read together if there is time, to help to broaden the subject at hand.

On some occasions every child will say they don't know how to do the work in front of them, and sometimes this might even be genuine! My advice would be to put a note to the teacher at the bottom of their work, or wherever the school has asked for you to communicate, saying just that. Then stop – go and do something relaxing. Confusion of methods and frustration at mum and dad turning into teacher mode is not conducive to a happy family life, and the teachers are there to help. If your child is too overwrought or too tired to work well, then you should stop. The purpose of homework is to develop good work habits, so consider carefully what those might be (I suggest a few below). If what is happening during a homework session is not reinforcing those positive skills, then there is little point continuing until you want to throw the whole lot into the bin and turn to strong drink too!

Looking at the homework you can usually see that its purpose is one or more of the following: ▶

> "INDEPENDENCE IS VERY IMPORTANT, SO TRAINING CHILDREN TO HAVE THOSE STUDY SKILLS AND THE RESILIENCE AND PERSEVERANCE NEEDED TO COMPLETE ACTIVITIES WILL PAY DIVIDENDS IN THE FUTURE."

21. What does a school expect from homework?

- To reinforce work that has been taught and needs practising in order to increase speed and accuracy or to remember and retain the skills and knowledge. This work may not be very exciting!
- To enhance knowledge and understanding by extending something taught, or by providing resources for further or richer understanding. This may be quite open-ended and time-consuming.
- To allow time to reflect on concepts or topics, or just to finish an extended piece of work. This may require proper consideration of how to present the work, and a bit of thinking and reflection time beforehand as well as at the end.
- To develop independent skills and good lifelong work habits, which include perseverance, metacognition (ie becoming aware of which work styles work best for herself), self-motivation, time management, determination, pride in presentation and content, and satisfaction upon completion. This may be expanded work and require some support with time planning.

You can help by:

- Providing a regular place where work can be completed undisturbed, with good light, plenty of space and a reasonable time limit.
- Providing a routine time, probably after a light snack and a chance to move around after the rigours of a very busy school day.
- Helping to signal that homework is not a punishment and can be rewarded!
- Offering advice, but not too much assistance.
- Helping to prioritise what needs to be done (I recommend doing the horrid part first, taking a moment for praise and then moving on to complete the rest).
- Trying to keep the evenings as uncluttered with extra events as possible.
- Limiting out-of-school clubs to weekends when possible.
- Making sure siblings are not too distracting. When your child has good habits, allow her to work away from others or away from your direct supervision, so that she knows that you trust her developing work habits.
- Giving a quick check at the end to see that everything is done, sufficient high standards have been retained, and that the bag is repacked with everything required for the next day.

Professionally, the people I work best with are people always ready to tackle a task head on when they get it, not with those who delay to the last minute. There are frustrations in working alongside people who have erratic work patterns. Do remember you are training your child for their future. Pressure can be seen as a useful motivator but it rarely produces the best, most considered or well-crafted work. That is worth bearing in mind when you encourage homework. Start now and establish the requirements of the task, with time to self-correct and revisit, or wait till the last minute and complete in a rush? Of course, all of this assumes that your child has organised the tools she will need to just get on with her homework – but that is a different type of hurdle. ∎

ELIZABETH SAYS...

1. Make homework a regular habit. Try to have a set time for homework every day – or on days when homework is set. This time should preferably be when your child has had a little time to chill – and something to eat and drink – after coming in from school, and before teatime. This helps to make sure that your child knows when 'homework time' will be, and stops those last-minute or late-night homework stints that cause so much upset! If your child has after-school activities some nights, agree with your child the best time to do homework on those evenings.

2. Have a set length of time to complete homework. Sometimes children struggle because the homework seems unending. Knowing exactly how long they have to sit and do homework will stop many battles. Check with the school how much homework your child is required to do. It is the teacher's responsibility to set homework that your child can complete in the time specified by the school. Explain to your child how long they will do homework for.

3. Use a timer. The timer only starts when your child is sitting at the table, with all the equipment and everything they need to complete the homework on the desk. Set the timer to go off after 20 minutes, half an hour, or an hour – however long the school specified. You will be amazed at how this simple step helps children focus and just get on with their homework.

4. Stop homework when the timer goes off. After the timer goes off, unless your child wants to carry on, write on the worksheet or book 'this is what Jenny completed in 20 ▶

21. What does a school expect from homework?

ELIZABETH SAYS...

minutes' – and sign it. Please don't try to persuade your child to carry on and complete the homework. If they have done the right amount of time, let them stop. The simple act of sticking to the set time will give your child an important message: that homework no longer needs to take over their evening, and now they can relax and have some fun! (Often children end up enjoying the assignment, and will ask to complete it, and that's fine. Just don't try to force them.)

You'll be amazed at how much difference these four simple steps will make to your child's willingness to do their homework.

- What if your child doesn't have homework that night? Then the time should be used to do something educational. If your child can't find something suitable to do in the time, then you can choose an activity that would help further their education.
- If presentation or attention to detail is a problem, have a rule whereby, after they do a piece of homework, you find two things your child could improve, and they find two things. Your child then does those four things and then that's it. Homework over!

Chapter 22

What can I do at home to help with basic maths skills?

22. What can I do at home to help with basic maths skills?

Some parents think that maths is a difficult abstract set of activities that need to be learned in order to be good at the subject.

This is a daft idea that denies much of the importance and creativity that make maths an exciting and practical skill for real life.

Understanding quantity is one of the main keys to dealing with numbers inside our heads. If you have difficulty working out the value of numbers and the general size you are considering, then estimating, checking and understanding are going to be difficult. Children find number ordering relatively easy by rote – many nursery children can count to fifty easily – but few have a sense of quantity. Constructing this is an important task.

An activity you can try for yourselves is looking at a crowd of people (in a stadium or on the news) and asking 'how many people can I see?' For children estimating simple numbers is difficult: 20, 30 or 40, do they recognise the relative sizes? Most children assume that large numbers are homogenous and similar to each other instead of vastly different. People who are good at mental arithmetic generally have an accurate picture of the size of numbers to use alongside a quick understanding of the operation required. For those of you who find it hard to add up and divide the bill without a calculator at the end of a restaurant meal, you may not be bad at maths at all, but your mental picture of the numbers and quantity bonds is not well established, and you just do not quite trust it!

Therefore, helping children to develop a notion of quantity is very useful. Try guessing the number of things in a jar, guessing first and then checking, and then playing again with other amounts to consolidate the learning. Counting money is also a truly valuable activity – estimating by recognising the different denominations, and not by the size of the coin heap! I have always used cards with children that find number concepts difficult. Simple games of gathering cards in turn around the group to make up an exact number. This game is fantastic for children on many levels, firstly because children love turn-taking games with their parents, secondly because it is number conservation and quantity practice. Thirdly (and most usefully), playing card games are great because the configurations of numbers on the different suits (diamonds, spades, hearts and clubs) always use the same shape for their numbers. This allows children to develop a mental image of the quantity named by the number.

Once exhausted by number games, how about asking your child the quantity of liquids or capacity of a vessel. For example, can they identify 100ml in a cup or how many litres a bottle holds? Cookery with children is a great introduction to measurement; ask your child to measure and check, all the while reminding her of the sizes she is looking at. How tall are your children? How long is your dog? Make a guess before you get out the tape measure – and ask them to guess too. If they copy your guesses, then write them down or make them go first. You will be surprised how quickly your estimates become accurate. ■

> "HELPING CHILDREN TO DEVELOP A NOTION OF QUANTITY IS VERY USEFUL. TRY GUESSING THE NUMBER OF THINGS IN A JAR, GUESSING FIRST AND THEN CHECKING, AND THEN PLAYING AGAIN WITH OTHER AMOUNTS TO CONSOLIDATE THE LEARNING. COUNTING MONEY IS ALSO A TRULY VALUABLE ACTIVITY – ESTIMATING BY RECOGNISING THE DIFFERENT DENOMINATIONS, AND NOT BY THE SIZE OF THE COIN HEAP!"

Chapter 23

Is the Internet safe for my child?

23. Is the Internet safe for my child?

There are two quick answers to this question: *Yes* and *No*.

- **Yes**, if the children can be directed to use safe sites.
- **Yes**, if they know that they should never give out their own personal information.
- **Yes**, if they learn to check with or inform an adult if they are in doubt.
- **Yes**, if you can supervise and check up on them, look at their browsing history and be sure who they are contacting.
- **Yes**, if you make sure everything copied or pasted is either acknowledged or paraphrased.

However, for many children the Internet presents a tempting maze, which means they easily forget the rules or are seduced to follow links that may take them to inappropriate places. So:

- **No**, if they are not trained in the best ways to do research and use information.
- **No**, if they proceed without understanding the risks at their own level.
- **No**, if they are left unsupervised, because dealing with potential risks requires a level of sophistication that a child simply does not have the maturity to understand.
- **No**, if you allow them to contact anyone they choose without you knowing about it or vetting them.
- **No**, if you allow them to copy and reproduce images or material that don't belong to them (some sites will prosecute for plagiarism).

The virtual world seems safe to children, as safe as being at home or at school where the magical portal physically exists. Furthermore, it is colourful, exciting, apparently child-friendly and full of possibilities. They do not realise that it is also populated with biased or incorrect information, and with people who are looking for contacts for advertising or for other less suitable and more abusive purposes. They don't realise they are being solicited as customers for sponsored sites or that there may be far better child-friendly information available through certain sites designed for children. Most schools will publish these links or make them accessible through some form of Internet portal. Children often don't understand the potential of unkind contact or cyberbullying until it happens to them. The virtual world seems less real and therefore the risks seem detached and minimised.

Children, by their very nature are curious and enthusiastic. It is tempting for them, for example, to type their own names, or yours, into Google or another search engine to see ▶

23. Is the Internet safe for my child?

what appears. It is potentially a harmless activity after all, but what happens if they find a person or a site that is not suitable? It is simply not helpful to ban the looking up of anything or everything. Instead, it is better to be frank with them that they might find things that are not appropriate and that they should call you and explain what they have seen. They will also understand that this enables other children to be protected. At my own school we have a 'safe surf' program that eliminates inappropriate words or images. However, the children at my school often don't consider the reasons for this and have been heard to say 'Oh, I will try that site again at home'. On occasion they type in something innocent such as 'games' and get an image none of us would want them to see. Schools will usually teach about the risks and hope the children remember, but they do need your help at home, where they often feel the restrictions and rules are different.

> "IT IS SIMPLY NOT HELPFUL TO BAN THE LOOKING UP OF ANYTHING OR EVERYTHING."

As often as possible, and at least annually, schools revisit the safety issues. They reiterate to the children that personal information should be kept private, and that it would be foolish to trust someone on any site that they cannot see. But still the dangers might seem remote to your child. I strongly recommend watching the BBC Newsround film created for families called '*Internet safety: Newsround Caught in the Web*' which is available on YouTube. This film will help you, as well as your children, to understand more about the social complexities of the technological world they live in.

Cyberbullying is referred to at school, and children are encouraged to understand that writing an unkind email or texting a negative message is not only wrong, but also an activity that is potentially criminal in the wider world (where it will not be tolerated). Most children understand, but the medium is so available and immediate, that it can be tempting after a minor spat with friends (for any of us) to put frustrations or retaliation into writing and hit 'send'. All of this needs to be talked through regularly and calmly with your child so that the actions of a moment, so hastily committed, don't create further conflicts or unhappiness. Do not imagine that your child would not do this; many do, and then regret their actions later when faced with the evidence and unintended consequences.

In summary, I believe that the Internet is a fantastic tool for everyone. Used with appropriate safeguards (eg safe surfing controls for children, adequate supervision, and training in how to find the right sort of material targeted at the right age), the Internet is brilliant. But, as ever, education is everything. Remember that not all inappropriate material can be caught by the filters – you can imagine the range of content you might see for the search term 'schoolgirl'! Keep reminding your child about safety, take nothing for granted, check up on them regularly, look at the search history and talk to them about what they are doing and what they are seeing, especially if you think it might be something unsuitable or risky. In short, help your child to develop better Internet behaviours that will be useful to them for many years. ■

ELIZABETH SAYS...

In addition to installing good parental controls on your child's electronic devices:
- Talk to your child regularly about their online activity.
- Tell them that you will be checking the sites they visit. And make sure you do that.
- As a parenting expert, I would recommend not to let your child have a TV, laptop, computer or smartphone in their bedroom overnight.
Insist that all electronics are kept downstairs, and mobiles (when they get one) should always be left charging downstairs at night. Many children watch things way later than their parents are aware, and see and hear things that frighten them, or draw them into activities you'd rather they weren't involved in. Please just exercise extreme caution; if necessary switch off wi-fi overnight.
- Have a list on the wall of what your child should do if ever they receive a message that upsets them. Your list might contain the following steps:
  1. Tell an adult. (As an adult you can empathise, keep your child calm and guide them through steps 2–5.)
  2. Save the evidence. (Put details on the list to explain to your child exactly how to do that.)
  3. Do not respond to the message.
  4. Log out.
  5. Report, block or stop the bully.

Chapter 24

What do test results mean?

24. What do test results mean?

In our lives today we are all subject to review and audit.

It has become so much part of our culture that what we used to think of as our daily work has become something under endless scrutiny. Rather than allowing for inspiration, creativity, rehearsal, formation thinking, practising and self-improvement, we seem to be obsessed with attainment test results, and have forgotten that learning is a process and not simply a one-off packaged 'result'.

Therefore, unfortunately, much of what we do becomes an instant measure of our self-worth. My own mother, in her mid-seventies and undertaking a Diploma with the Royal Society of Botanical Artists, was very upset when her 8.4 grade average dropped to 7.9 due to a 'badly' coloured leaf. 'The tutor liked the leaf shape,' she told me, 'but the depth of colour was not right in the leaf veins'. When I pointed out that 7.9 was 79% and probably an A grade, she was surprised. Nonetheless she was ready to go on to do battle with herself in the next assignment – despite not having practised or had a chance to get the leaf right – because she thought she had to go on to the next thing, and try to get that right in one bash too.

For me, education should not be like this; I believe it is a long and thoughtful process. Yes, educationalists have talked for a long time about building blocks that are the basis for learning, but that must not be understood to be each piece of knowledge being a brick in a wall in its own right. Most of the knowledge, skill and discerned understanding comes in a web or network of interconnected ideas. Like a newly cut tree, it takes time to season. Given that education in school takes place over at least 13 years, there is some time for a well-educated child to benefit from a gradual unfolding of the world of knowledge. It is well proven that early or rapid success is not the best precursor to lifelong achievement – look at Einstein, Mo Farrah or even Winston Churchill!

At my prep school, we have embarked on a holistic programme of giving the girls an opportunity each week to work independently on a task, under the sort of conditions she would face in a test, but with the work that she is doing in class. We believe this has a number of purposes:

- The first is **formative**, where we can see what the child can do unaided, where she needs support or scaffolding, where she can think for herself, where she can practise the little aspects of setting out that she has been shown, such as where to put titles and date if not instructed. ▶

24. What do test results mean?

- The second is **ipsitive** where the teacher sees how the child has done over time, and is able to make a pattern of her progress, comparing not just results, but also how she copes with the experience. The teacher can then create a bespoke plan to help. This is not a comparison with others, but a proper examination of the development of the child over time, by concentrating on her progress in relation to her ability and her journey.

- The third is **metacognitive**, where a child comes to understand for herself how she learns best, what helps her when she is learning, and what she needs to remember. It is the often unnoticed part of the process, where children become aware of their own ability, their own strengths and the things they can do for and by themselves that make things go right when they do them, and wrong when they don't. Each child soon gets the hang of how this feels, and is encouraged to look through the work to see what she could have done herself, to do better this time or next time.

These types of tests are always designed to be **formative**. They are not a close-of-play event such as GCSE or A Level, nor are they used in the way an entrance test or formal exam might be. They are not used as a measure of success (although success is valued) alongside good progress. They are not a test to check up what content or knowledge was learnt before moving on. They are used purely to allow the teacher to plan what the child needs to experience, learn or re-examine next. To see the learning skills in action and to check that the basic skills are still up to date, sharp, and age appropriate. It is important to be clear that the purpose of these tests is to help the child to move forward and to be able to plan what to do next in their learning journey.

End-of-term or end-of-year tests however are **summative**: they are a summary of progress or ability of those things covered in the test (and not actually of anything else). Many parents anxiously imagine that these test results are a label or a diagnosis, and that a badly done test should be repeated to prove something. However, that is not necessary at all. Wasting time on re-testing will not create improvement; that can only be provided by planning for the next learning experiences and good teaching. Be wary of assuming a test score is a badge of approval or the reverse – it only shows what your child can do with the particular item in the test on that particular day! Test scores, even standardised ones, will tend to fluctuate. It is important to find out from the teacher what that means, and not to be suspicious about minor discrepancies of 5% gained or lost, which is entirely normal between different tests. No school would use the same test twice, and one question in a

30-minute paper for a seven-year-old can be worth up to 12 marks. So there is bound to be some difference in scores over time unless your child always consistently scores 100% or 0% because she is either a genius or absent on the day.

My belief is that excellent teaching and learning must include space for children to rehearse, to come to an understanding about their work, to begin and then to become skilled at managing on their own. If these opportunities are not presented young, and repeated regularly, then real learning, real depth of knowledge, effective skills, creativity, self-esteem, confidence, resilience and inspiration will not develop. Tests certainly have their place, at the end of term or year, between phases and as rites of passage. They are a useful measure for the outside world, or for parents, of what has been achieved in a reasonable space of time. But, in between times, I believe children should be allowed to learn from having a go, free from the fear of their own results. ■

> "MANY PARENTS ANXIOUSLY IMAGINE THAT THESE TEST RESULTS ARE A LABEL OR A DIAGNOSIS, AND THAT A BADLY DONE TEST SHOULD BE REPEATED TO PROVE SOMETHING. HOWEVER, THAT IS NOT NECESSARY AT ALL. WASTING TIME ON RE-TESTING WILL NOT CREATE IMPROVEMENT; THAT CAN ONLY BE PROVIDED BY PLANNING FOR THE NEXT LEARNING EXPERIENCES."

Chapter 25

What should I do if grades are lower than expected?

25. What should I do if grades are lower than expected?

In my work as a Head Teacher I often encounter parents who are nonplussed that their child's teacher does not see the standard of work at school they can see at home or with a private tutor.

Sometimes they are concerned that assessment, test results or term grades are much lower than they had come to expect given the standard of classwork, despite the fact that their child has seemed to be getting on well during the weeks leading up to a test. Recently, I encountered this with some old friends, who were absolutely panic-stricken by their child's below-average results in maths, reported to them at both parents' evenings this year and now expected on the reports that follow a bad test result.

Teachers are expected to communicate factual information to parents, in order to clarify what children can do in the classroom unaided. They do use value judgements to choose what to teach, and to differentiate work according to what they have seen. They will always use formative assessment to make those decisions and choices; that is, assessment of what the child is doing and learning as they go, all the time, in every lesson. However, when they report results to parents they are expected to be more summative, to give concrete examples of what the child can do by herself or in team activities, but without the teacher's constant intervention. What a child can do independently is rarely the same as what she can achieve with a willing hand beside her, pointing out errors, managing the speed and accuracy of work, and encouraging focus.

In a lesson, teachers will be on hand to challenge, support and cajole. In a test situation this constant supervision is withdrawn and, naturally, the child will increasingly have to show that she can cope alone. Often, therefore, the grades can seem lower than expected, particularly for younger children, and the challenge for all teachers is to create a match between children's natural ability and their independent test results. It is not an easy feat for your child to learn how to manage in tests, as it means developing independence, resilience and concentration. All of these skills can be damaged or delayed by the ▶

25. What should I do if grades are lower than expected?

knee-jerk solutions generally applied in a crisis, such as providing a tutor or helping your child more with homework and classwork. I do like to remind parents that the moment their child needs to peak, to show her best test results, is usually GCSE. Although other tests can be important, they are generally signposts on the way showing a snapshot of progress (on the day). rather than final, and often not just indicative of things such as quality of teaching or proper expectations.

This week I was talking to my lovely friends, seeking my advice regarding their daughter Sara (not her real name), who were wondering (with palpable anxiety) whether they should make a complaint to their school (thankfully not my school and so not to me). They explained that their daughter could not do at school the maths she could easily do at home during homework. Mum explained that she really knows what her daughter can do because she sits with her every day without fail while homework is being completed. She explained that her daughter even did extra at weekends and in the holidays, and that Sara's maths was excellent. Much to their consternation, the teacher apparently disagreed.

I asked Mum to talk me through what happens at home, and then to outline what the school says. Firstly, she told me, she and Sara sit together quietly at the dining room table for homework, usually after a snack and a drink and catch up on the day. Mum always checks the homework diary so that she can see that Sara is doing the correct page, and turns to it for her if she has not

> "TEACHERS ARE EXPECTED TO COMMUNICATE FACTUAL INFORMATION TO PARENTS, IN ORDER TO CLARIFY WHAT CHILDREN CAN DO IN THE CLASSROOM UNAIDED. THEY DO USE VALUE JUDGEMENTS TO CHOOSE WHAT TO TEACH."

found it easily or started in the wrong place. From the maths book, Mum points to the question her daughter has to do, and makes her read it aloud. If Sara reads it correctly she is praised. If she reads it incorrectly Mum fills in the missing words. Sara will then tell Mum what type of sum she thinks it is. If she is wrong, Mum assured me she doesn't ever tell her what to do. Instead, she says 'no, have another go'. Then, mum tells me, her daughter works out what to do again and then if she has chosen the right method, mum will confirm, and she does the number work effectively by herself. If she gets it wrong, mum assures me she doesn't help or give the answers, she just tells her daughter to have another go. Her daughter always gets full marks for homework, and Mum was adamant that she had not helped her to get them right.

According to the school, however, Sara is below average in maths, has difficulty in class even trying to find the right page in lessons, and waits to be invited to start work rather than getting on by herself. She tends to check with the teacher whether she is on the right page even after instructions, because she isn't confident that she is doing the right thing, and she needs constant praise and reassurance. She rarely scores more than half marks by herself and constantly asks the teacher for help, often before she has made an attempt of her own. She does not see her own mistakes and is not good at self-checking. She is easily distracted by her classmates and spends a lot of time pointing to errors in their work, or commenting on their behaviour. She cries when she does badly and says she hates maths. Her teacher thinks that Sara is not reaching her potential and has said so. Mum and Dad cannot understand how things have gone wrong, and are convinced that the problem must therefore be the teacher, who cannot see how talented their daughter is. They are just about to go to see the Head to ask for a better teacher next year.

Sara is very like many of the children I have taught over the years. She is a wonderful, chatty, and bright girl. She is extremely eager to please. She has natural ability, but spends a lot of time trying to gauge her success by checking with the teacher. In my opinion she doesn't have a problem with maths at all, she has issues and growing fears about learning independently. I believe she is being held back by the mixed messages she has received between home and school. Unfortunately, Sara's difficulties are now being reinforced at school because she has come to rely on the sort of individual support she is used to getting at home. She has come to believe that the teacher should give her constant help. In class she cannot get on without ▶

25. What should I do if grades are lower than expected?

adult intervention, she looks for constant praise or reassurance and she fears failure. This is unsurprising given the level of panic her parents are showing about her results, and the extra attention being lavished to support her. Attending to what everyone else is doing in class rather than getting on with their own work often happens more if the child is distractible (even under normal classroom conditions, which is about concentration and needs specific support). It can also happen because failing to find approval from the teacher will mean seeking it from her peers, or else by pointing out the weaknesses in her classmates she can thereby highlight her own good behaviour to the teacher. None of these behaviours are much help to learning. Fortunately, these habits are easy to break if everyone understands that learning behaviour and steady improvement through managing the learning styles and environments are more important than the test results and the strictness of the teacher.

I have suggested to these friends of mine that, before they go into school, they try a new approach to maths homework (to all homework), focusing on independence. Settling down quietly is great. I suggested they tell Sara to go and start, and then pop in to check she is working and has found the right page. That can have a reward. To master that would be a fantastic first step. The key to reward is to praise when what you have seen warrants it, not to add empty or hopeful praise, which is a really mixed message. The next step is to withdraw the constant reassurance, say that they will be pleased to look when she has completed half, or three quarters. They should praise or reward at that stage. Mistakes made can of course be discussed, but do it immediately after the work is all completed, not as she goes. Homework isn't generally about teaching a new skill; it is about rehearsing one that has been taught before, and a little more practice can iron out the problems. If practice does not help, and if Sara has got it wrong consistently and doesn't understand, then it is important that her teacher knows. Covering up by asking to guess again or giving the answer will simply mask a gap in her learning. That gap will not be filled before it is encountered again and will reappear as a mistake. Unfortunately, formerly used methods are not always how we teach maths now, so it is also best to refer back to school if the methods are different from what you learnt at school.

Sara's parents were, I think, rather disappointed in my response and went away muttering about finding a tutor.

What do you think? ■

Chapter 26

How should I read a school report?

26. How should I read a school report?

In the summer term parents begin to tell me they are becoming anxious about what might be contained within the school report.

I thought, therefore, it would be useful to outline what the school creates these reports for.

Firstly, reports are a summary of progress throughout the year. Prep schools and teachers are encouraged by professional bodies, such as IAPS, to give this information as factually as possible. The written report is a completed round-up of what has been done (not what needs to be discussed – that should take place at other times in the year). That is why so many school reports include tick boxes. Secondly, they may (and most do) include a short passage written by the teachers to help to clarify any points that may not be absolutely clear in the facts given, such as the efforts your child has made, and any circumstances or learning behaviours worth commenting on. In some, as in ours, there is a chart outlining learning behaviour, because it is far more relevant to know how well your child listens in class or how well they can follow instructions, than what she can remember later or can currently achieve in tests. Learning behaviour is the area that I consider to be the most essential. Truly great teaching can only go so far in raising attainment of pupils who cannot listen, settle, work together (or alone), or use their own common sense (eg, to write the date and turn the page as they are expected to do every day).

Most schools will now include targets on their reports, and these are usually chosen in line with a weakness or an area that needs to be developed, and can be worked on at home too. Most targets have an element of learning behaviour in them that spills over into home life, such as insecurity and subsequent over-checking, or not being expected to organise her own things. Constructive criticism is important for improvement. While it is entirely natural to feel defensive or over-protective, it is better to think about how the target can be realistically met. Teachers try to be helpful to you and your child. So if they think that your child needs to take more responsibility for her work, or to try harder, then they say so to enable you to help make this happen. If you feel this needs the teacher's support, or you are not sure what is meant in the report, then follow it up with the new teacher in September. Do wait, though, for the settling-in period to be over (three or four weeks) so that the new teacher has started to build a good personal relationship with your child first.

Test results will be included in many reports too. These should always be read in conjunction with the rest of the report, because they cannot stand or fall on their own. You should also remember that tests tend to be a measure of your child working independently, in a silent room, without help deciphering the questions or encouraging the answers. Therefore, children who need this regular support or reassurance will struggle. The good news is that with familiarisation this tends to improve, and practice does help. Do beware that too much practice under forced conditions can also create pressure and anxiety, both of which are the enemies of success. It is also true to say that with prep-age children, a good day or a bad day can make all the difference. So exam results should only be used to help create a pattern over years, not in the short term, and it is helpful to take a longer-term view before having a panic about a few marks either way. It is worth remembering that no two tests will ever be entirely the same too, even if they are standardised, and that is why there is a reasonable margin of a few points up or down that is not considered significant.

Reports are written by teachers, checked across year groups, results and scores moderated and verified, then forwarded to the senior leadership team for checking, reading and signing. This takes the average teacher most of the summer term, including the half-term break, and then many evenings until the end of term, because they cannot be written in the normal course of their school and teaching duties. These written records are precious. They give as accurate as possible a snapshot of your child as can be written by a group of professionals working together over many hours of careful consideration. Sometimes they will include information or grades that make you uncomfortable because they are worryingly low or out of context, but the school does have a duty to share this information with you, even if it seems frightening.

If you feel the report does not entirely describe the child you know and love, that may be a good sign, because it means they have an independent persona from the child-parent one you see at home, which is just what they will need to develop in order to become fully and successfully themselves. ■

Chapter 27

How do I manage a parents' evening?

27. How do I manage a parents' evening?

Parents' evening is something of an endurance test for teachers and parents alike.

Both may be nervous about the conversation, under time pressure, and are in an environment and situation that may harbour bad memories for the adults. Parents are acutely aware that the evening is about their precious and beloved child, and an investment for the future, both of the child's well-being, and also in financial terms in fees for independent schooling. For the teacher, this child is one of many, and she has a responsibility in these five minutes to communicate the bad as well as the good, and make suggestions to support the child's learning.

The teacher will have aspirations for the child, backed up by classroom evidence and experience of dealing with children. She will have plans, class results and independent work at her disposal to create a picture of the child as a learner. The parent will have expectations, backed up by naturally biased support for their child, and a sense of entitlement, especially if they are paying fees for their child to succeed. Parents set their expectations by asking other parents, comparing with siblings and benchmarking test results, as well as reading regularly in the media about failing schools, missed chances and poor-quality teachers. They may expect results in line with payment, and see education as an expensive outcome and not a process. It is entirely usual for parents to believe that their child is a latent genius. After all, if parents don't stick up for their offspring, who will?

On the arranged evening all arrive for the most peculiar form of 'speed dating' imaginable. There are a few simple things that can make the evening easier for you as a parent:
- Check the logistics in advance.
- Make sure you arrive in time and can park.
- Register for your slot on time.
- Know who you are seeing by checking with your child about set and subject teachers.
- Think about the questions you might need to address.

A good opening question is 'how does homework done by my child reflect her classwork?'. Asking this will enable you to benchmark very quickly whether your understanding of your child's ability, based on what you see, is accurate. Bear in mind that it may not be. I have experienced ▶

27. How do I manage a parents' evening?

many children who can do wonderful homework at home supported one-to-one by a diligent parent, but that does not mirror the performance or even the true capability of their child in a classroom setting or a 30-minute test without support. Parents who 'overhelp' can be upset by the general progress in class; they have a false impression of what the attainment is about. If you are a parent who has supported homework very faithfully this is a good time to ask whether it is helping, and to reset the balance.

Sometimes it is entirely the other way around; a child who is tired and slapdash at home may be precise and effective in the classroom. However, parents have come ready to do battle because what they see on a daily basis is of poorer quality. A frank discussion about independent work is important, as is a grasp of what is really happening in class and why. The chapter on what the school expects from homework may provide some further guidance (chapter 21). A good parents' evening discussion, therefore, covers what you understand of their work at home and at school.

The second good question is about the child's natural ability to learn. Can your child:

- settle to work without fuss?
- organise her own belongings?
- listen and act upon instructions?
- read and interpret questions without support?
- use prior knowledge to know what to do?
- fulfil presentation tasks without being reminded (date, title, underlining etc.)?
- use strategies to unpack problems?
- know how to find targeted help fast?
- work quietly and independently for a period of time?
- check own work for errors and omissions?
- avoid copying?
- work collaboratively when necessary?
- cope with a test situation for 30-60 minutes (age-appropriate)?

If you cover no further questions than ones about learning behaviour, you will have enriched your understanding of why your child is progressing and what needs to be worked on. That is far more useful than which times-table needs work. Without good learning behaviour there can be no really high attainment, since the whole British education system is geared towards independent examination success. This requires confident question answering in a pressured time frame when they are 16 years old. In the preparatory phase of school it is important to establish good learning habits and foundation as well as to stretch the child and challenge them in all areas of the curriculum, in order that they have the mental energy and resilience to do well under their own steam.

If you have time during your meeting with the teacher, you may need to ask what the teacher has planned in order to support your child if she is struggling. Listen carefully; finding genuine ways to support learning are not easy. The risk may be that you do the work yourself at homework time to give an appearance of improvement, or you may put your child under pressure to perform without really helping them to develop strategies to improve. You should expect an update at the next meeting in a term, not at regular emergency meetings in the short-term (which are likely to show frustratingly unsatisfying incremental improvement no matter how worried or how determined you are). Measuring progress is not at all the same as creating and nurturing it.

All of these questions are designed around what you may be able to do to help your child. Should you back off from homework or check that it is really being done? Should you talk to the child about consistent effort? Should you encourage her to speed up to complete the work, or to slow down for accuracy and quality? Do you simply need to carry on as you are but adjust your expectations? Will something as simple as extra reading aloud help? If so, how can you fit that in? Is there something more fundamental you need to explore, and do you need to meet with other professionals such as a Learning Support Coordinator?

On the day, be as calm as you can. I often meet upset parents at parents' evening who simply want so much to hear that their child is top of the class, is performing well above average, the kindest child ever. Yet the teacher has the brief to help the child to improve by being clear and analytical about any problems and by being honest. View what you have been told in the way you would a visit to the doctor. First, the ▶

> "MEASURING PROGRESS IS NOT AT ALL THE SAME AS CREATING AND NURTURING IT."

27. How do I manage a parents' evening?

description told to you and by you makes sure that all are clear on the context. Next, advice is given and then a prescription for what really needs to be administered. A meeting at parents' evening follows the same idea, and the 'advice' and 'prescription' offered is essentially what you are paying for in order that your child is prepared for senior education (which is the purpose of a good preparatory school). During the meeting, the teacher is helping you by opening a window on your child when she is away from you, and presenting the opportunities to improve it. Be mindful that you are not paying for the teacher to do all the work – ultimately that needs to be done by your child, and there is no education in the world that can do it for them. Many children who underperform do so because the obstacles in their path through the whole of their lives are moved or mitigated by loving parents who accidentally disable the child's work ethic. Children have to know that the results are down to them and that the effort has some worth. Bribery may help but always reward the effort, as that is the thing you are trying to achieve, not the attainment (which is only a desirable by-product).

Not all teachers perform well at parents' evening. Some become anxious about the number of encounters they need to have, and become flippant or overly negative. This may be frustrating for you, but try to remember that the key to the success of the year is the bond they have with your child and the clarity with which they can see what needs to be done and taught through the year. I have investigated many complaints after a parents' evening because the parents did not feel confident in the parents' evening manner of the teacher. In fact, an awkward experience of the teacher at parents' evening generally has little bearing on what happens in class. I have known many good teachers fall under suspicion by a group of parents because they were not good at the small talk of a five-minute encounter.

In summary, arrive on time, stick to the set time limit (or make a supplementary appointment for another day), and listen as clearly as you can to the messages you are given about learning. The time you spend with the teacher is in no way as critical as the time she spends teaching your child. Extra meetings, constant checking of emails or requested individual updates on your child's progress may in fact be the straw that breaks the teachers ability to do properly what she should be doing best. Bear in mind that other parents may also be expecting extra meetings etc. which will add to the teacher's daily burden. ∎

Chapter 28
Why specifically teach life skills to children?

28. Why specifically teach life skills to children?

Teaching life skills to children is one of the key points of family life!

Every child benefits not only from 'nuts and bolts' skills such as learning to dress, using cutlery and organising belongings. Your child also benefits from fundamental interpersonal skills that will enable them to get on with others, to develop a sense of place in the world and a sense of proportion, in order to handle conflicts and to be resilient and robust in the face of unexpected (or even expected) challenges.

Schools obviously help with these life skills, because children are likely to face other children and complexities at school, away from parental guidance. It is important for them to have these skills supported, modelled and scaffolded as they develop in judgement and confidence. However, there are some skills that need to be explicitly addressed in order to develop children who are equipped to manage how to become incredible people in society. These skills may be academic, or they may be skills of judgement and discernment – either way they need to be identified, taught and practised.

One of my own 'hobby horses' is the teaching of basic first aid, which allows children to develop skills to act in a crisis. I believe this enables them to consider others with compassion, to have a sense of their responsibility towards others, to feel confidence by having usable knowledge, while they are learning about the essential organs of the body and obtaining a good understanding of good health and how their body works. The St John Ambulance runs a first aid course with 'young carers'. In my school this has been followed by all Year 6 pupils, culminating with certification and teams being put forward to the national competition.

Swimming is another essential life skill, not only for saving lives, but allowing for the pleasure of free movement underwater. It is an activity of lifelong benefit to those who become less fit over time for a host of reasons.

> "ONE OF MY OWN 'HOBBY HORSES' IS THE TEACHING OF BASIC FIRST AID."

One of the other, often overlooked, life skills is the ability to view your own self objectively, and without too much seriousness. From this comes the ability to apologise meaningfully and to offer and accept forgiveness with light-heartedness.

It may be worth having your own conversations with your child: ask them what they would do in a crisis? How would they call an ambulance? What would they do if they got lost? Do they know their own address and phone number? Could they pack their own overnight bag? These are just a few examples that might help to frame a discussion and keep them safe.

If you had to seek out a friend in a crisis of your own, a physical or an emotional one, what capital would you look for in terms of skills? Who could you turn to? How can you equip your child to be the person who can help? Real education, both at home and at school, needs to address these questions very carefully and to try to put in place some of the education required. Nobody will be able to do this for your child better than you can! ■

ELIZABETH SAYS...

When your child reaches the age of 18, it's important they know how to do everything you currently do for them. Your job as a parent is to make yourself redundant! And equip your child with all the life skills they need as an adult. So what will your child need to be competent in by the time they leave home? Swimming, first aid, as well as cooking, cleaning, shopping, laundry, ironing, mending, car maintenance, simple DIY, time management, managing their own money, etc.

Your role as a parent is to gradually help your child become confident doing all of these. And to teach and train them in the skills they'll need for independent living. If you don't, you'll be letting your child down and causing them a lot of anxiety and stress as they have to fend for themselves when they leave home. If you don't even expect your child to clear up after themselves you will be setting them up to be unpopular with future flatmates!

Every child should be doing jobs at ▶

28. Why specifically teach life skills to children?

ELIZABETH SAYS...

home because they're part of a family. And you can help your child learn what to do – and how to do a good job – by using the skills that a coach uses:

- Always stay calm, friendly and positive.
- Be clear about what you expect.
- Make the task fun.
- Break it down into small steps.
- Show them how to do something, do it together several times and let them practise each step.
- Watch them do it with minimal interference.
- Let them do it on their own.
- And then plan how they'll keep up the new skill.

It's also important to think of what characteristics you want your child to have as an adult, to work out how you will instil those values and qualities. The ability to cope in a crisis, and also the ability to be resilient, flexible, independent, compassionate, inquisitive, self-confident, reliable, organised, level-headed, emotionally mature, able to say 'no', trustworthy, honest, loyal, able to make good choices, etc. etc.

Your children need to see the qualities in the example you set. And they need to have an opportunity to experience what it is like. For instance, a child only learns how good it feels to be compassionate when they do things for others. And the best way to help them develop those qualities is to make an effort to notice and comment whenever they display behaviour and characteristics that you admire. When you mention their lovely qualities frequently enough, your child will have no doubt that they have that characteristic. And it will become part of their personality.

Chapter 29

What is the point of a Forest School or outdoor learning?

29. What is the point of a Forest School or outdoor learning?

It has been my privilege to have a little escape some days, to go outside with 3- and 4-year-old pupils to our 'Forest School'. This initiative, guided by the Forest Explorers Leader, allows our nursery pupils time in the natural environment learning not only new skills and concepts, but also developing their relationship with the world.

It is really important to use guided experiences to allow us to grow as whole people.

The little children I see tend to be happy, fully engaged, interested, inquisitive and bubbling with enthusiasm. They commandeer me to paint mud onto the trees with them, and show me the bugs they gather up, gently, into cups to examine. I am always surprised at their sophistication, gathering tiny fragments from around them to make fairy houses, and at their ability to explain what they are doing. I feel that pull from my own happy childhood, where I learned to be creative through a freedom to explore. These children are lucky indeed.

Most children spend a great deal of their educational lives indoors, only being allowed out to 'play'. This is appropriate if we believe that learning can only take place under certain conditions, if we think that a teacher has to push knowledge into a child in a sterile environment. However, we now understand far more about the growth of children's brains, and are beginning to understand that intelligence develops through activity, making connections, creative inspiration and rehearsal.

Creativity is never nurtured best in confined conditions, and inspiration rarely strikes if prescribed outcomes are valued above great ideas. If they are to have real meaning, connections certainly cannot be made for children instead of by them, and it is only possible to build on what is already understood. That is not to say that class-based learning is outdated, it still plays the major part, and much can be taught and learnt by conventional means, but there is more. Practical activities such as camping, forest skills, Duke of Edinburgh awards and environmental studies can extend a child's potential by 'encouraging and inspiring individuals through positive outdoor experiences', as the Forest Explorers and outdoor learning do.

In the future I sincerely hope that school leaders will come to accept that creativity is vital to the formation of human beings and to the future of society, and that it is generated not by the training of fixed outcomes but by open-ended experiences. None of us can be sure what the future will hold, nor what will happen to the shape of examinations in the next 20 years, nor to the world of work or even to society in general. However, those children who have developed resilience, interest, inspiration and independence, outside, in the beauty and complexity of creation, will have the advantage over the rest of us.

Now put down this book for a few minutes and go outside for a walk! ■

> "CREATIVITY IS NEVER NURTURED BEST IN CONFINED CONDITIONS, AND INSPIRATION RARELY STRIKES IF PRESCRIBED OUTCOMES ARE VALUED ABOVE GREAT IDEAS. IF THEY ARE TO HAVE REAL MEANING, CONNECTIONS CERTAINLY CANNOT BE MADE FOR CHILDREN INSTEAD OF BY THEM."

Chapter 30

Why and how should I support learning a musical instrument?

30. Why and how should I support learning a musical instrument?

In the summer term in my school, a wonderful little crop of afternoon soirées and lunchtime concerts is harvested from amongst the instrumentalists and singers who have been working hard all year with their individual teachers and at home practising to develop their musical skills.

It is wonderful to see these pupils flourishing and gaining confidence as they perform solos to their parents and peers. Children as young as Year 1 right up to Year 6 stand up in public and really show what they are made of. As they take their bow at the end of their piece, flushed and proud to receive their applause, all those hard hours and minutes of practising seem worthwhile.

Much has been made in the press of the so-called 'Mozart effect' – the effect of music on intelligence and on core subject skills such as literacy and numeracy when children learn an instrument or play in an ensemble.

It appears to be the case, supported by a number of studies, that:
- There is a correlation between music education and linguistic, mathematical and special awareness.
- Children studying music develop better memory capability.
- USA data from the National Longitudinal Study of 1988 showed more A and A* grades in pupils studying music.
- Musicians develop better flexible-thinking skills.

I am often approached by parents who are worried that taking their child out of English or Maths for their instrumental lesson will have a detrimental effect on their progress. Unless they are doing several instruments I can confidently reassure them that there is the balancing effect of learning an instrument which supports their learning skills and often improves them. Learning an instrument also improves all sorts of other skills and abilities. As children learning an instrument practise courage, resilience and patience, they learn delayed gratification and the value of daily study in small amounts. Their brains become involved in pattern making and matching, they develop abstract language skills in learning to read ▶

30. Why and how should I support learning a musical instrument?

music notation, and they practise fine and gross motor skills with their bodies. Most importantly of all, they learn to listen, not just to hear and process but to finely discern and tune in to fine-grained detail. Delightfully, many of them develop a joyful and beneficial relationship with their individual teacher and their instrument, which can last a lifetime.

So how do you decide on an instrument for your child? The piano is often a first instrument of choice for many parents, and is a brilliant instrument for children to learn as it helps to get to grips with music theory. Although the piano seems an obvious choice, however, it is not always the best one to start with. Some children struggle with reading two lines of music at once. Children with learning difficulties may benefit considerably from this different form of learning but often find two-line or two-handed instruments difficult. These children would benefit instead from perhaps a brass instrument or at least one with a solo written line rather than chords. Many young children cannot sit still for the required length of time and need an instrument that allows physical movement such as the violin. Temperament can also play a part – a quiet child may prefer the flute to the saxophone, and a child with a lot of energy may do better with the drums than with the recorder. Physical development is important to consider, too. For instance, wind instruments are tricky to manage when children do not have all their front teeth, as are larger instruments

> "LEARNING AN INSTRUMENT IMPROVES ALL SORTS OF SKILLS AND ABILITIES. AS CHILDREN LEARNING AN INSTRUMENT PRACTISE COURAGE, RESILIENCE AND PATIENCE, THEY LEARN DELAYED GRATIFICATION AND THE VALUE OF DAILY STUDY IN SMALL AMOUNTS."

when they may not be big enough to get their arms around a double bass or have the strength to have a heavy saxophone around their neck. Books are available to help you choose the best instrument, for example *The Right Instrument for Your Child* by Arah Ben-Tovim and Douglas Boyd (widely available in bookshops).

Most important of all is your child's preference. If they hate the sound of the saxophone, they will not commit to learning it. If they really want to learn the trumpet, they may not take kindly to the piano, and the promise 'learn the instrument I want you to play and when you pass Grade 1 you can do the one you have chosen' will very likely put them off both! Take your children to concerts and have them listen to a range of music styles, including classical, on the radio and see what excites them. Allow them to try out instruments in music shops or arrange a trial lesson on an instrument they have been interested in. The great Hungarian musician Zoltán Kodály said that 'children learn best that which they already know'. If they have been nagging you for two years to learn the harp, take a deep breath and hire one for a month. If you can't pull them away from it, start saving. You may have a harpist in the making.

There are other reasons for children to learn orchestral, jazz or rock instruments other than the piano, and that is the benefit of being able to play them in an ensemble, an activity which is only really available to advanced pianists. Ensemble playing is a highly social and sociable activity, which gets children working together collaboratively rather than competitively. A child can join an ensemble from the very first term that she begins the instrument. One person in an ensemble is only a tiny part of a whole picture, which only the whole ensemble can produce. Therefore, concentration, listening skills, forbearance with other children working at more or less advanced levels, timing, co-operation and an understanding of gradual progression are all benefits of involvement in an orchestra, choir or band. Musically it benefits the child in every possible way, giving them a strong sense of pulse, pitch, dynamics, structure, articulation, tempo, musical style and performance convention, and it also makes sense of their instrument in context.

Lastly, the buzz of performing in concert with many other musicians is something that can only really be understood once tried – a memorable, exhilarating and uplifting experience. ■

Time to re-read my chapter on perseverance (chapter 12)!

30. Why and how should I support learning a musical instrument?

ELIZABETH SAYS...

To encourage your child to persevere when learning an instrument, always notice the good things your child does when they practice. So many parents focus on the negatives, and the little things their children do wrong. But when you focus on the small improvements, the effort, the time spent getting a bit right, your child will be way more motivated to continue than they will if you point out everything they do wrong. Criticism is never motivating.

Also, set up a regular routine when your child knows they will do their music practice. When children know what time of the day is set aside to play their instrument it makes it much easier to do it regularly. Even 10 minutes a day can make a big difference. And 20 or 30 minutes a day will help your child progress quickly. If you can, try to leave a little time for fun at the end of a practice session, so your child can play the sort of music they love. It will keep up their motivation and help them to stay inspired.

Chapter 31
Why are celebration days (or feast days) important?

31. Why are celebration days (or feast days) important?

Most schools will have a day or two a year when normal lessons are suspended and an event takes place to mark a celebration or a feast day.

It is time for us to remind ourselves about the importance of these days, because in these busy times, when performance and attainment are uppermost in people's minds we often fear anything that cannot be measured as productive.

I believe that excellent education is a holistic affair. Children need to become rounded, moral, thinking and spiritual beings in order to be fulfilled in life and to contribute to society. These dispositions do not happen by accident and, although their own families are the first best educators, it is the experiences shared in common with their peers and their role models that really help them to develop. Experiences provided by schools help to shape and form an individual far more than the taught concepts. Living life and learning to manage it (with all the complexity of social interaction) and to understand what contributes to happiness and self-satisfaction, is far more likely to make a positive difference to success in life than an extra hour of maths and English. Balance is all-important – all work and no play makes Angela not only a dull girl, but one uncomfortable in her own skin, prone to anxiety, isolated, fixated on arbitrary success criteria and made vulnerable in the relationships with friends who are also competitors.

My school happily juggles a feast day to allow for most of the usual lessons to be fitted in. It makes space in the timetable for the whole school to come together for a service of celebration and thanksgiving, and for shared lunch where all of the age groups mix to make new friends, with older and younger classes mixing for play. Aside from the social aspects, the older children are role models for the younger ones. Their tenderness with the youngsters is touching to see, and a valuable part of learning to be upright, caring citizens.

The feast day for me also focuses attention on a shared celebration that touches this whole community. Unlike any other event, it does not reward the success of the few, it does not rely on competition, and it is not more applicable to some than others. A feast day simply offers itself as a shared celebration in common with the whole community, much as a birthday or Christmas celebration might in the family home. School spirit, something that translates itself throughout life into family spirit, community spirit, or even a willing or tireless work ethic, begins here, and cannot be created by lessons alone. Character is not the result of audited academic success. Being part of a community and being able to celebrate that 'belonging' is an essential part of personal happiness.

Other days that differ from the norm (for example, house competitions, rehearsals, concerts, assemblies, music ensembles, sports activities), give children opportunities to contribute to the community in a way that does not simply benefit them alone or lead to temporary personal success. I firmly believe that understanding the contribution that one can make to the whole is an essential discipline. Work in the twenty-first century is more than likely to involve collaboration, presentation, self-discipline, ability to listen, and discernment about one's place in the group and judgement about who to imitate and follow. All of these are learned more effectively through activities and experiences beyond the classroom. These events are a wonderful training for pupils who cannot be happily involved beyond the limelight, who are not prepared to watch and join in on cue, who don't know that there are strengths and rewards in being an anonymous part of a celebrating community, those who do not turn up to events after hours if their parents are not going to be in the audience, because without these experiences they may feel that is there is no reward and they are not motivated. For people who only look for extrinsic reward, life can be a deeply frustrating, empty and puzzling hard grind. ■

> "BEING PART OF A COMMUNITY AND BEING ABLE TO CELEBRATE THAT 'BELONGING' IS AN ESSENTIAL PART OF PERSONAL HAPPINESS."

Chapter 32

What can we do in the holidays?

32. What can we do in the holidays?

I spent much of my holidays as a child free to roam about in the garden, or tucked up in a cosy corner reading, but modern children seem to need far more entertaining than we did in the pre-digital era.

Here are some recommendations for what you can do to keep your child's brains ticking over while you all enjoy yourselves during the holiday season.

For real family time, why not turn your thoughts to history and geography? There are many great places for family visits, such as Hampton Court Palace, museums in London and most other cities (free admission to those), aquariums and art galleries. Websites will inform you of special exhibitions and of discount events, and travelling on the train often gives you two-for-one offers on the admission price – pick up the leaflets in the station to see what is available at low cost.

To make the experience particularly 'educational', don't focus on the event, instead over-involve your child in the planning. Train schedules, car parks, ticket prices, choice of visit, maps of venues and making a timetable for the day can all be worked out together. Children love to be trusted to organise events and will be proud to show you their skills. Learning experiences work best when they are enjoyable. Counting cash and sorting change on a shopping trip is the point of learning mathematics – it is what number work is for – so gather a bag of coins to use on the day (in my family we lovingly call this the 'purse of gold'!).

Allowing children to choose and make decisions also helps them to develop an essential skill. Buying them books is not quite the experience that being allowed to browse and choose them is. Don't forget the public library either, a great cheap and fruitful outing. Direct your children to the non-fiction sections of the library; children love history and will be fascinated by how others lived. I remember spending hours learning about the ancient Egyptians, just for fun, during one Christmas – my poor mother had to take me back to the library every two days to swap the books as I swallowed them whole!

Maps are also a great source of discussion. ▶

32. What can we do in the holidays?

◀ Plan a walk using a map of the local area, or see if you have a local heritage trail. During the walk, keep talking as you go – children understand more through discussion than they will take in for themselves. There are good apps to help – I use an app that has all the paths and some other features marked when I walk on my local Common – and there is great joy to be found in an unfolded Ordnance Survey map. Even a walk in the park (walking allows for far more observation than a car journey) or around the neighbourhood can be filled with discussions about what can be seen. Can you and your children name and recognise five types of trees or breeds of dog? Which houses do they like as they pass them? A walk is especially lovely after tea at Christmas time when it is dark and lights are twinkling, and has the added bonus of being a technology-free time to talk to your children.

If you have lots of children and the possibility of childcare, try making an individual plan for a special and different day out for each child – children like few things more than a day of a parent's undivided attention. My own mother took me to see the Tutankhamun exhibition on my own because of my Egyptian obsession, and I have never forgotten the pleasure of that exhibition or the delight of a day out with her by myself. She recently admitted to me that she remembered every minute of that day, it was one of her most treasured memories too. ■

> "IF YOU HAVE LOTS OF CHILDREN AND THE POSSIBILITY OF CHILDCARE, TRY MAKING AN INDIVIDUAL PLAN FOR A SPECIAL AND DIFFERENT DAY OUT FOR EACH CHILD – CHILDREN LIKE FEW THINGS MORE THAN A DAY OF THEIR PARENT'S UNDIVIDED ATTENTION."